The Applied Economics of Weight and Obesity

T0262962

This volume consists of a broad selection of studies on the applied economics of weight and obesity. The chapters cover a wide spectrum of topics, and employ a variety of applied techniques across a range of countries. Some of the issues explored include: the relationship between childhood obesity and food insecurity; adolescent weight gain and social networks; obesity and happiness; the relationship between fast food and obesity; tobacco control; race and gender differences; and consumer health.

This book is a compilation of articles originally published in the journals *Applied Economics* and *Applied Economics Letters*.

Mark P. Taylor is Dean of Warwick Business School, University of Warwick, UK, and is a leading international authority in open economy macroeconomics and international finance. Although interested in broad research subjects, he focuses particularly on empirical work on exchange rates. Amongst his many published works are studies on the presence of nonlinearity in real and nominal exchange rate movements, on the long-run behaviour of real exchange rates, on the nature and effectiveness of official foreign exchange market intervention and on the micro-structural effects of European Central Bank interest rate announcements.

The Applied Economics of Weight and Obesity

Edited by
Mark P. Taylor

 Routledge
Taylor & Francis Group

LONDON AND NEW YORK

First published 2013 by Routledge

2 Park Square, Milton Park, Abingdon, Oxfordshire OX14 4RN
711 Third Avenue, New York, NY 10017

Routledge is an imprint of the Taylor & Francis Group, an informa business

First issued in paperback 2018

British Library Cataloguing in Publication Data
A catalogue record for this book is available from the British Library

ISBN 13: 978-0-415-83321-9 (hbk)
ISBN 13: 978-1-138-37780-6 (pbk)

Typeset in Times New Roman
by Taylor & Francis Books

Publisher's Note
The publisher would like to make readers aware that the chapters in this book may be referred to as articles as they are identical to the articles published in the journal issue. The publisher accepts responsibility for any inconsistencies that may have arisen in the course of preparing this volume for print.

Contents

CONTENTS

Citation Information

The chapters in this book were originally published in *Applied Economics* or *Applied Economics Letters*. When citing this material, please use the original issue information and page numbering for each article, as follows:

Chapter 1
Adolescent weight gain and social networks: is there a contagion effect?
Mir M. Ali, Aliaksandr Amialchuk, Song Gao and Frank Heiland
Applied Economics, volume 44, issue 23 (2012) pp. 2969–2983

Chapter 2
Obesity and happiness
Marina-Selini Katsaiti
Applied Economics, volume 44, issue 31 (2012) pp. 4101–4114

Chapter 3
*The relationship between childhood obesity and food insecurity:
a nonparametric analysis*
Oluyemisi Kuku, Steven Garasky and Craig Gundersen
Applied Economics, volume 44, issue 21 (2012) pp. 2667–2677

Chapter 4
*Socio-economic characteristics and obesity in underdeveloped economies:
does income really matter?*
Awudu Abdulai
Applied Economics, volume 42, issue 2 (2010) pp. 157–169

Chapter 5
Dollars and pounds: the impact of family income on childhood weight
Y. F. Chia
Applied Economics, volume 45, issue 14 (2013) pp. 1931–1941

Chapter 6
Race and gender differences in the cognitive effects of childhood overweight
Susan L. Averett and David C. Stifel
Applied Economics Letters, volume 17, issue 17 (2010) pp. 1673–1679

Chapter 7
*The relationship between smoking, quitting smoking and obesity in Australia:
a seemingly unrelated probit approach*
N. Au, K. Hauck and B. Hollingsworth
Applied Economics, volume 45, issue 16 (2013) pp. 2191–2199

The applied economics of weight and obesity: introduction and overview

Mark P. Taylor

This volume consists of fourteen studies on the applied economics of weight and obesity. The studies cover a wide range of topics, and employ a variety of applied techniques across a range of countries.

In their study of adolescent weight gain and social networks, Mir M. Ali, Aliaksandr Amialchuk, Song Gao and Frank Heiland look at whether there is a contagion effect. In previous studies on the spread of obesity in social networks there has been a focus on the contemporaneous effect of peer weight outcomes on individuals. In their study, Ali *et al.*, investigate the longer term effects, within adolescence and from adolescence into early adulthood, of peers on individual weight outcomes. Using data from the first three waves of the National Longitudinal Study of Adolescent Health, and accounting for correlated effects using a number of empirical strategies including school-level fixed effects and accounting for neighbourhood preferences, they show that the body mass index (BMI) and overweight status in a person's friendship network influence their BMI and likelihood of being overweight. Their evidence suggests that there is some persistence of the effects of past peer weight experiences on individual weight outcomes during adolescence and into early adulthood. Their findings are consistent with adolescence being an important formative period of individuals' preference for ideal physique and body weight aspirations. The authors conclude that policy makers should be particularly concerned with interventions during childhood and adolescence, in order to slow the spread of obesity by promoting a healthy body image and positive health behaviours.

In the next chapter in the collection, Marina-Selini Katsaiti examines the relationship between obesity and happiness, providing insight on the relationship between individual obesity and happiness levels. Results indicate that in all three countries, Germany, UK and Australia, obesity has a negative effect on the subjective well-being of individuals. These results also have important implications for the effect of other socio-demographic, economic and individual characteristics on well-being.

Childhood obesity and food insecurity are major public health concerns in the United States and other developed countries. Research on the relationship between the two has provided mixed results across a variety of data sets and empirical methods. Common throughout this research, however, is the use of parametric frameworks for empirical analyses. Oluyemisi Kuku, Steven Garasky and Craig Gundersen, in their contribution, move beyond parametric methods by examining the relationship between childhood obesity and food insecurity among low-income children, using both parametric and nonparametric regression techniques. In particular, they examine data from the United States Child Development Supplement of the Panel Study of Income Dynamics, a nationally representative data set from the US consistent with recent work. Their parametric analyses indicate that there is no statistically significant relationship between childhood obesity and food insecurity. In contrast, their nonparametric results indicate that the probability of being obese varies markedly with the level of food insecurity being experienced by the child. Moreover, they suggest that this relationship differs across relevant subgroups including those defined by gender, race and ethnicity, and income.

Available evidence suggests that overweight and obesity prevalence is increasing worldwide at an alarming rate in both developed and developing countries. In a study which focuses on the determinants of being overweight in mothers and children, using a unique dataset collected in urban Accra, in Ghana, Awudu Abdulai finds that mothers' education, employment status and ethnicity significantly exert influence on the generation of body weight. In particular, those who attained secondary and tertiary education had lower body mass indices and were much less likely to be overweight or obese, lending support to the notion that more educated women normally have better health knowledge and are more likely to consume healthy foods and also engage in physical exercises that help to control weight gain. Abdulai also reports that a mother's education was found to exert a negative and significant impact on the weight status of children. Furthermore, household expenditure is found to exert a positive and significant impact on the probability of a mother being overweight or obese, but no significant impact on the probability of a child being overweight.

Y. F. Chia examines the impact of family income on childhood weight status for children in the United States using matched mother-child data from the National Longitudinal Survey of Youth (NLSY 79). Chia estimates instrumental variable (IV) models, family fixed effects (FE) models and family fixed effects IV (FEIV) models in order to control for causality. Chia suggests that although the prevalence of childhood obesity is higher in low-income families in the sample, family income might be acting primarily as a proxy for other unobserved characteristics that determine the child's weight status rather having a major direct causative role in determining the child's weight status.

In a study looking at race and gender differences in the cognitive effects of childhood obesity, Susan L. Averett and David C. Stifel show that the increase in the prevalence of overweight children (ages 6–13) in the United States over the past two decades is likely to result in adverse public health consequences. Using data covering children from a national survey (NLSY79) they investigate an additional consequence of childhood overweight, namely its effect on relative cognitive development. To control for unobserved heterogeneity, they estimate individual (child) fixed effects models and instrumental variables models. Although recent research suggests that there is a negligible effect of childhood overweight on cognitive ability, the results demonstrate that the effects are uncovered when examining the relationship separately by race. In particular, they find that overweight white boys have mathematics and reading scores approximately a standard deviation lower than the mean. Overweight white girls have lower mathematics scores while overweight black boys and girls have lower reading scores. Their results suggest that, in addition to well documented health consequences, overweight children may also be at risk in terms of experiencing adverse educational outcomes which could lead to lower future earning potential.

Given that smoking and obesity are known to be two leading causes of preventable death, further understanding of the relationship between these two risk factors can assist in reducing avoidable morbidity and mortality. In the next study, Nicole Au, Katharina Hauck and Bruce Hollingsworth investigate the empirical association between obesity and the propensity to smoke and to quit smoking, using a seemingly unrelated (SUR) probit approach that takes into consideration the potential for reverse causality and unobserved heterogeneity. Using Australian health survey data, they demonstrate the usefulness of the SUR probit approach in generating information on the relationship between unobserved factors influencing both smoking behaviour and obesity, and in providing estimates of the conditional probabilities of each risk factor. The results suggest the two risk factors are not independent. The presence, size and direction of correlation between the unobserved factors are found to vary by smoking behaviour and by gender. Estimates of conditional probabilities demonstrate smokers have a lower probability of obesity, particularly among females, and ex-smokers have a higher probability of obesity, particularly among males. These findings suggest that health policies targeted at one risk factor may have unintended implications for the other.

Craig A. Gallet's contribution begins by noting that, although several studies of highly developed countries find tobacco control efforts impact obesity rates, whether or not such results extend to less developed countries is unclear. Accordingly, Gallet re-examines this issue by using data from countries that lie across the development spectrum. Similar to the existing literature, the evidence suggests higher cigarette prices increase the percentage of the population that is overweight or obese. However, other tobacco control efforts appear to have less influence. Gallet also reports that a number of other factors, including health care expenditure, urban concentration, and undernourishment, are also found to influence population weight.

Rodolfo M. Nayga, Jr., examines the impact of socio-economic and demographic factors on the likelihood that an individual is aware of the link between being overweight and heart disease. His results indicate that non-whites, lower educated individuals, and those with lower income are less likely to be aware of the link between being overweight and heart disease. Considering the extent of the obesity problem in the United States, these results should be used as a guide in the design of food policy and health education campaigns about obesity and heart disease.

Obesity and overweight are central issues in the public health debate in most developed countries. Joan Costa-Font and Joan Gil examine some of the socio-economic determinants of obesity and overweight that are still relatively unexplored. They present an empirical examination of the possible influence of social interactions on contemporaneous obesity and (over)underweight. They use a joint estimation model for obesity and self-image applied to a sample for Spain taken from the European Union household panel for 1998. Their results suggest that obesity might be in part a social phenomenon connected to individuals' social life.

Laxmi Paudel, Murali Adhikari, Jack Houston and Krishna P. Paudel look at consumer health preferences and assess the impacts of low carbohydrate information on the market demand for fruits in the United States, using almost ideal demand system (AIDS), Rotterdam, and double-log models in their study. Their results indicate significant positive impacts of low carbohydrate information on the market demand of grapes and lemons. However, a significant negative effect exists on the market demand for apples and bananas.

In the next article, Rigoberto A. Lopez and Kristen L. Fantuzzi examine consumer choices of Carbonated Soft Drinks (CSDs) and their implications for obesity policy. Demand in relation to product and consumer heterogeneity is estimated via a random coefficients logit model applied to quarterly scanner data for 26 brands in 20 US cities, involving 40 000 consumers. The authors find that counterfactual experiments show that caloric taxes could be effective in decreasing caloric CSD consumption though having little impact on obesity incidence.

In the penultimate paper, Mario Mazzocchi and W. Bruce Traill report that theoretical models suggest that decisions about diet, weight and health status are endogenous within a utility maximization framework. In their article, they model these behavioural relationships in a fixed-effect panel setting using a simultaneous equation system, with a view to determining whether economic variables can explain the trends in calorie consumption, obesity and health in Organization for Economic Cooperation and Development (OECD) countries and the large differences among the countries. Their empirical model shows that progress in medical treatment and health expenditure mitigates mortality from diet-related diseases, despite rising obesity rates.

Finally, Michael L. Marlow and Alden F. Shiers discuss the public debate regarding the role of government in lowering obesity, by looking at the relationship between fast food and obesity. They focus on the hypothesized link between obesity and fast food employment by examining data on all US states over 2001–2009 and controlling for other factors that may influence obesity prevalence. Their conclusion indicates no support for the view that fast food is a significant causal factor behind the substantial weight gain exhibited by the US population.

Adolescent weight gain and social networks: is there a contagion effect?

Mir M. Ali[a,b], Aliaksandr Amialchuk[a], Song Gao[c] and Frank Heiland[d]

[a]*Department of Economics, University of Toledo, Toledo, OH 43606, USA*
[b]*Office of Regulations, Policy and Social Science, Food and Drug Administration, College Park, MD 20740, USA*
[c]*School of Public Finance and Public Policy, Central University of Finance and Economics, Beijing, 100011 China*
[d]*CUNY Institute for Demographic Research, School of Public Affairs, Baruch College, The City University of New York, New York, NY 10010, USA*

Previous studies on the spread of obesity in social networks have focused on the contemporaneous effect of peer weight outcomes on individuals. This article is the first to investigate the longer term effects, within adolescence and from adolescence into early adulthood, of peers on individual weight outcomes. Using data from the first three waves of the National Longitudinal Study of Adolescent Health (Add Health), and accounting for correlated effects using a number of empirical strategies including school-level fixed effects and accounting for neighbourhood preferences, we show that Body Mass Index (BMI) and overweight status in a person's friendship network influence their BMI and likelihood of being overweight. The evidence suggests that there is some persistence of the effects of past peer weight experiences on individual weight outcomes during adolescence and into early adulthood. The findings are consistent with adolescence being an important formative period of individuals' preference for ideal physique and own body weight aspirations. We conclude that policy makers should be particularly concerned with interventions during childhood and adolescence, in order to slow the spread of obesity by promoting a healthy body image and positive health behaviours.

I. Introduction

According to estimates from the National Health and Nutrition Examination Surveys, approximately one in three adults in the US (32.1%) were classified as obese in 1999–2004, suggesting that obesity rates have more than doubled in less than four decades (e.g. Flegal *et al.*, 1998; Ogden *et al.*, 2006). The rise in body weight among American children and adolescents since the 1970s is even more dramatic. The prevalence of overweight has more than doubled in children (age 6–11) and more than tripled in adolescents (age 12–19) since 1976–1980 (Hedley et al., 2004). In 2003–2004, 37.2% of children aged 6–11, and 34.3% of adolescents aged 12–19 were at risk of being overweight or were classified as overweight (Ogden et al., 2006). Given the well-documented adverse health impact of excessive body fat (e.g. Must et al., 1999), addressing the rise in obesity to epidemic proportions is one of the most pressing public health issues today.

Since the increase in obesity has occurred in genetically stable populations, the weight gains can only be attributed to behavioural factors related to increases in calorie intake or decreases in physical activity. Swinburn et al. (2009) estimate that American children consumed 350 calories more per day on average in the period 1999 to 2000 than they did in the 1970s and argue that the increase in energy intake alone is sufficient to explain the greater proportion of overweight children and adolescents today. The change in calorie consumption patterns has been linked to the greater availability of inexpensive (convenient and calorie-dense) prepared foods (Philipson and Posner, 1999; Lakdawalla and Philipson, 2002). Consistent with this explanation, the share of calories from fast food and calorie-dense snacks among children has been on the rise (Jahns et al., 2001; Guthrie et al., 2002). The increases in calorie consumption among US adolescents do not appear to have been accompanied by greater energy expenditure. Surveys of adolescents, starting in the 1990s, show either no change in physical exercise levels or a decline, and stable levels of involvement in sedentary activities (Pratt et al., 1999; Gordon-Larsen et al., 2000; Eisenmann, 2003; Dollman et al., 2005; Adams, 2006; Nelson et al., 2006).

An emerging literature emphasizes the role of social forces in explaining the rapid increase in obesity. Burke and Heiland (2007) argue that social interactions on body weight function as a multiplier on the effects of changing fundamentals (lower total food costs) on individuals' weight. They estimate that rising reference weights might have magnified the impact of the decline in the full price of calories since 1977 on the weight of adult females in the US by 24%. Étilé (2007) documents a positive association between body shape norms and individuals' ideal Body Mass Index (BMI) among French women.

Burke et al. (2010) show that perceptions of overweight became more lenient in the US between 1988 and 2004, a period during which the population grew significantly heavier. Johnson et al. (2009) provide similar evidence from UK data for the period 1999 to 2007. These findings agree with the notion that individuals judge their weight in relation to others around us rather than according to fixed standards. Christakis and Fowler (2007) investigate the person-to-person spread of obesity in social networks using data from the Framingham Heart Study (1971–2003). Consistent with the presence of social multiplier effects, they find that the likelihood of becoming obese increases (57% for close friends) if a friend became obese during the same period. Estimates consistent with a positive contemporaneous effect of peer weight outcomes on individual weight outcomes have been reported in several subsequent papers using different measures of weight status, peer groups and data and study samples (Fowler and Christakis, 2008; Renna et al., 2008; Trogdon et al., 2008; Halliday and Kwak, 2009).

Previous studies have paid little attention to the dynamics between peer outcomes and individuals' weight gain as they have focused primarily on the contemporaneous effect of peer weight. Consequently, the role of peer weight influences in the determination of longer term individual weight outcomes is unclear. If individuals' attitudes towards body image and weight-related behaviours are socially determined, then weight outcomes of a past peer group are expected to have a lasting impact on individuals. This should be especially true for social influences during adolescence, a period characterized by milestone physical, psychological and social developments and adjustments in response to the observed body weight norms and ideals (Turner, 1996; Kinsbourne, 2002). Consistent with the idea that individuals' weight preferences may originate from experiences during adolescence, Ali et al. (2011) and Maximova et al. (2008) find that young people's perceptions of weight and being overweight depend on the weight of their parents and friends.[1] In addition, since excess energy is not stored at 100% efficiency and it takes time for the body weight to accumulate (Hill et al., 2003), it seems relevant to examine the effect of lagged peer weight on individual's weight rather than the contemporaneous effect of peer weight.

This article provides the first systematic analysis of the longer term social interaction effects of weight.

---

[1] There are other reasons to consider the longer term effects of peer weight. As first suggested by Manski (1993), social forces may work with a lag. It may take time for individuals to realize and respond to changes in the weight status of their peer group.

Using a sample of adolescents who transit into adulthood, we investigate the effect of peer group weight outcomes on subsequent individual weight outcomes. We employ peer measures drawn from individuals' nominated friends as well as from grade-level school peers. Estimating models of adolescent overweight status (the term used to define childhood obesity), BMI, and of 'being at risk of being overweight', we find evidence consistent with a persistent effect of peer weight outcomes on individual weight status.

The remainder of the article is organized as follows. Section II contains a discussion of the challenges of estimating peer effects and outlines our approach in the context of the existing literature. Section III describes our data and variables of interest. Section IV describes our econometric model and estimation strategy. Section V presents the main findings of our analysis and Section VI concludes.

II. Estimating the Effect of Peers on Individual Weight Outcomes

Background

The objective of this study is to quantify the reaction of individual weight outcomes to peer weight outcomes. The challenges in identifying the causal link between a behaviour or outcome of a (reference) group and the behaviour or outcome of an individual are well-documented and are known as the 'reflection problem' after Manski (1993, 2000). In the present context, two of the main concerns are that individual weight outcomes are correlated with measures of group weight (i) because individual weight outcomes respond to exogenous characteristics of the group ('exogenous' or 'contextual' peer effects) or (ii) because of third factors influencing both individual and peer weights ('correlated effects'). Following previous papers in this literature, we assume that peers affect individuals' weights only through their own weight (see e.g. Trogdon et al., 2008). (We provide evidence supporting the absence of contextual effects below.) There are reasons to expect that correlated effects play an important role in the present context and we will briefly discuss these in turn.

Correlated effects can result from institutional and environmental factors that influence the weight of the individual and his or her peers. These common influences may include a local built environment that fosters a sedentary lifestyle, low-food prices, high concentration of fast-food restaurants, etc. If such common background influences are not accounted for, the effect of peers on the individual could be overstated because of spurious (positive) correlation between the weight outcome of the individual and his or her peers.

Similarly, the individual and his or her peers may experience comparable weight outcomes as a result of commonalities in individual attributes affecting weight, such as distaste for exercising, food preferences or desired physical appearance. This is particularly likely when the peer group is selected by the individual, as in the case of friendship networks since friends tend to match (positively) assortatively (see e.g. McPherson et al., 2001). If these attributes are not measured, estimates of peer effects may be biased because of selection on unobservable.

Identification of the (causal) effect of peer weight is further complicated by a potential simultaneity problem. In the presence of social interactions on weight, by definition, the changes in the weight outcomes of the individual will feed back into the weight outcomes of his or her reference group (bi-directionality). If the interactions on weight act with little or no delay then the estimates will likely overstate the true peer weight effect.

Existing estimates

Quantitative assessments of the role of social networks in individuals' decision making are not new in the literature (Hoxby, 2000; Gaviria and Raphael, 2001; Clark and Loheac, 2007; Ali and Dwyer, 2009, 2010), but the possibility of a person-to-person spread of obesity had been unexplored before Christakis and Fowler (2007). In a sample of individuals aged 21 and above, they examine the relationship between individual weight gain and their friends, neighbours and family members' rate of weight gain. They find that the likelihood that a person becomes obese over a period of time increases appreciably (57% for close friends) if he or she had a friend who became obese during that period. This correlation is largest among individuals ('ego' and 'alter') who are mutual friends and essentially absent if the 'alter' considers the 'ego' a friend but not *vice versa* or if the 'alter' is a neighbour. The authors argue that this variation in the magnitude of the association by directionality and type of the network is suggestive of a causal effect of obesity among close friends.

Subsequent articles have further examined the link between peer and individual weight outcomes using alternative definitions of what may constitute a person's peer group, complementary statistical approaches and additional data from the National

Longitudinal Study of Adolescent Health (Add Health). Cohen-Cole and Fletcher (2008) estimate models similar to Christakis and Fowler (2007), specifying BMI as a function of individuals' lagged BMI along with their peers (best same-sex friend) contemporaneous and lagged BMI. They find that the link between friends' BMI and own BMI becomes statistically insignificant when controlling for environmental factors using school-specific time trends and caution that the associations suggested by similar models in Christakis and Fowler (2007) may not be evidence of a causal relationship. In a follow-up analysis of the Framingham and the Add Health data, Fowler and Christakis (2008) report evidence consistent with their earlier findings, even after accounting for individual fixed effects, but they do not discuss the robustness of the estimates to region or school-specific time trends.

Related studies have estimated the effects of average peer weight outcomes on individual weight, constructing measures of peer group outcomes based on information on the nominated friends as well as the grade-level peers (Renna et al., 2008; Trogdon et al., 2008; Halliday and Kwak, 2009). Using samples from the Add Health and controlling for individual characteristics and common environmental factors (school fixed effects) to account for correlated effects, these papers provide evidence of a positive link between average peer weight and individual weight. The models estimated in these papers also assume contemporaneous peer influences, but, unlike Christakis and Fowler (2007), Fowler and Christakis (2008) and Cohen-Cole and Fletcher (2008), attempts are made to address the potential simultaneity concern that results from the bi-directional nature of peer influence. When instrumenting for peer group weight outcomes using information on the peers' parents, they find that the estimated peer effects become insignificant in some specifications.

Present study

Previous studies on the spread of obesity in social networks have focused on the contemporaneous effect of peer weight outcomes on individual weight outcomes. This article investigates the longer term effects, within adolescence and from adolescence into early adulthood, of peer weight outcomes on individual weight outcomes. Using all three waves of Add Health data, we test whether past peer group weight outcomes have lasting effects on the adolescents' weight status. We estimate models explaining

adolescent overweight status (the term used to define childhood obesity), BMI, as well as 'being at risk of being overweight'; the latter is an important intermediate state that has received little attention to date.

In addition to constructing proximal measures of peers based on the nominated closest friends as in Fowler and Christakis (2008), Trogdon et al. (2008) and Renna et al. (2008), we also construct peer measures from data on individuals who are in the same school and grade level as the respondents. Grade-level peers are likely to be a relevant reference group for adolescents and measures of grade level outcomes have the advantage that they are less likely to suffer from endogenous peer selection since, conditional on the school, the grade level assignment is based on age. On the other hand, using broad measures of peers may dilute the relevant social network and could attenuate the peer effect.

We use a number of empirical strategies to reduce potential biases in our estimates. Since we focus on the longer term effects, using past peer weight status, simultaneity (bi-directionality) concern is less of a concern.[2] To account for common confounders and peer selection ('correlated effects'), we control for school fixed effects, a rich set of individual characteristics and data on parental location preferences. When school fixed effects are accounted for the grade-level peer measures are plausibly exogenous (Clark and Loheac, 2007; Trogdon et al., 2008). Following Gaviria and Raphael (2001), Clark and Loheac (2007) and Trogdon et al. (2008), we also exploit information on whether families are recent movers and whether the neighbourhood was chosen because of the school district. Conditioning on neighbourhood preferences of the parents of the respondent is an attempt to reduce bias from endogenous peer selection. Lastly, we conduct a series of falsification exercises by regressing individual weight outcomes on *subsequent* peer weight outcomes to further examine whether the observed patterns could be spurious.

III. Data

We utilize panel data from the Add Health. Add Health consists of data on adolescents in 132 schools nationwide between grades 7 and 12. The in-school portion of the first wave of the survey (1994) contains

---

[2] The idea is that 'while my behavior may depend on what my peers did in the past, their past behavior cannot depend on what I currently do' (Clark and Loheac, 2007, p. 767).

a cross-section of data on about 90 000 adolescents. A subset of the initial sample (20 745 respondents) was also interviewed in their homes (in-home portion of the data) with follow-up surveys in 1996 and in 2002, when most respondents had made a transition to adulthood. The primary data for our analysis come from all three waves (1994, 1996 and 2002) of the in-home survey portion of Add Health. A key feature of the data set is that it contains information on individuals' nomination of their closest friends at two points in time, the first and second wave. Since these friends are also part of the survey we are able to observe their characteristics, including information on their parents, and follow them over a period of time. We note that Add Health did not ask the respondents to nominate friends in the third wave.

Weight status variables

The dependent variables of interest are BMI, constructed using self-reported (for wave 1) and measured (for waves 2 and 3) height and weight and indicators for being overweight and at-risk of being overweight.[3] The Centers for Disease Control and Prevention (CDC) growth charts for 2000 were used to categorize adolescents as overweight and at-risk of being overweight, which are based on the adolescents BMI relative to the national distribution and are age and gender specific. Adolescents who are between the 85th and the 94th percentile are categorized as 'at-risk of being overweight' and those who are at or above the 95th percentile are classified as 'overweight'. We construct the binary variables 'at risk of being overweight' and 'being overweight' accordingly.

Peer measure variables

We use various measures of peer group weight based on two definitions of social networks, the nominated friends and peers in the same school and grade as the individuals. For the nominated friends, we create variables pertaining to the percentage of friends who are overweight, percentage of friends who are at risk of being overweight and the average BMI of the nominated friends.[4] The school-level peer measures are the percentage of students in the same grade and school as the respondent who are overweight, who are at risk of being overweight and their mean BMI.

Other determinants of weight gain

In addition to various indicators of peer weight and demographic variables (age, gender, race and education), we also control for other factors expected to independently affect individual's weight. Such determinants include smoking status, hours of television watched per week, exercise and sports habit,[5] number of siblings, birth weight, whether the individual was first born, whether the individual was breast fed, family structure, parents working status, family income and parents' obesity status. Accounting for these factors should help reduce potential bias from correlated effects.

Smoking is expected to be negatively related to body weight (Chou et al., 2004; Fang et al., 2009). While the reasons are not fully understood yet, smoking (cessation) has been found to affect metabolism and appetite (e.g. Moffatt and Owens, 1991). Hours of television viewing are likely positively related to weight whereas exercise and sports are likely negatively correlated. Birth weight, being first born, number of siblings and parents' obesity status may proxy for a person's health endowments and thus contribute to weight outcomes. Family structure, parents' work status and family income are economic variables that, in addition to age, education and sex are likely to affect lifestyle and hence contribute towards the adolescent's weight. Having both parents who work full time outside the home or living in a single parent household might have an impact on the pattern of food consumption. Time intensive healthy home produced meals could be substituted for calorically denser prepared foods, take-out, or restaurant meals in a household where the opportunity cost of being at home is higher Anderson et al. (2003).

We note that some of these measures may proxy for structural determinants of obesity. As such they may serve as channels through which social forces affect the individual's weight status and hence may be part of the peer effect. For example, people may smoke or exercise more to lose weight in order to conform to a lower weight standard set by their peers. In the analysis below, we include measures of these variables at the baseline interview (in wave 1). This way, they do not reflect changes in behaviour in response to peer weight outcomes, but rather proxy for individual's tastes and endowments.

---

[3] Using the second wave of the Add Health data Goodman et al. (2000) find that the correlation between BMI based on self-reported height and weight and BMI based on measured height and weight to be 0.92. Thus, reporting errors are unlikely to be substantial.

[4] The average numbers of nominated friends used to construct weight status in wave 1 and wave 2 for those who nominated at least one friend are 2.28 and 2.07, respectively.

[5] Exercise and sports are binary variables constructed using questions asking how many times the adolescent exercised or played sport last week on a 0–5 scale.

IV. Econometric Model

We modify the standard linear equation describing the relationship between peer and individual behaviour (see e.g. Pollak, 1976; Manski, 1993) in several ways. As discussed in Section II, we want to examine the possible lagged peer influences on individual outcomes. Specifically, in addition to standard models relating weight status of individuals to the contemporaneous peer weight outcomes, we estimate the effect of average reference group weight status in 1996 and in 1994 on individuals' weight status in 2002 and 1996, respectively.

We note that the use of lagged reference group weight may facilitate the identification of causal peer effect. Intuitively, adolescent's weight outcome may depend on how his or her peers fared in the past, but peer past outcome cannot depend on what the adolescent currently does. As discussed in Clark and Loheac (2007), who employ 1-year lagged peer measures in their study of peer effects in risky behaviour (consumption of tobacco, alcohol and marijuana) in a sample of adolescents from the Add Health, the use of lagged peer measures requires that the degree of autocorrelation in the individual's and the peers' measures is not too high. They present year-over-year correlation coefficients and argue that the '[risky] consumption behaviour during adolescence was likely to be out of steady state, as individuals grow up and change their preferences and surroundings'. We adopt the same empirical strategy, additionally also accounting for adolescent's initial weight status. This implies that the regression coefficient on the lagged peer measure can be interpreted as the effect of peer weight status on the *change* in adolescent's weight status over 2, 6 and 8 years (from 1994 to 1996, and from 1996 and 1994 to 2002).

We introduce school-level fixed effects in all models to reduce the potential bias from correlated effects. School fixed effects capture unobserved characteristics that are common to all adolescents enrolled in the same school as well as any school-specific factors influencing the weight status of all students in a school. It is likely that schools differ in socio-economic and demographic composition of their student body, in the food supply conditions (the availability of fast food restaurants, vending machines, meal plans, local food prices, etc.) and the opportunities to expand energy (built environment, exercise and sports activities, facilities, etc.).

More formally, we estimate several specifications of the following model:

$$y_{ist} = \alpha + \beta_1 \bar{y}_{jst-1} + \beta_2 y_{ist-1} + \beta_3 x_{is0} + \gamma_s + \varepsilon_{ist} \quad i \neq j \tag{1}$$

which, for purpose of interpretation, can also be expressed as

$$\Delta y_{ist} = \alpha + \beta_1 \bar{y}_{jst-1} + \beta_2' y_{ist-1} + \beta_3 x_{is0} + \gamma_s + \varepsilon_{ist} \quad i \neq j \tag{2}$$

where $\Delta y_{ist} = y_{ist} - y_{ist-1}$ and $\beta_2' = \beta_2 - 1$

In Equation 2, Δy_{ist} refers to adolescent's gain in BMI or change in weight status between 1994, 1996 and 2002, $\bar{y}_{jst-1}$ refers to the average weight status within peer group in 1994 or 1996, x_{is0} refers to the vector of adolescent's individual and family characteristics measured at the baseline (1994), y_{ist-1} is adolescent's own BMI or weight status in 1994 or 1996 and γ_s is a vector of school fixed effects. This model investigates whether past peer weight status (2, 6 and 8 years ago) predicts individual weight status independent of past (initial) own weight status. Since the spacing between Add Health waves is different, each model is estimated using only two of the three waves (1994, 1996 and 2002).

V. Results

Table 1 (Panels A–C) presents summary statistics for weight status measures in waves 1–3 (1994, 1996 and 2002), peer weight status measures in waves 1 and 2 (1994 and 1996) and baseline individual and family characteristics in wave 1 (1994). BMI does not change substantially between 1994 and 1996 (22.6 and 23.1). However, BMI in 2002 is substantially greater (26.5). The prevalence of overweight also rises substantially as the adolescents transit into adulthood, increasing from 11% in 1994 to 13% in 1996 to 23% in 2002. The percentage of adolescents at risk of being overweight follows similar pattern: a rise from about 25% in 1994–1996 to 50% in 2002. Peer weight status measures in 1994 and 1996 are presented in Table 1 (Panel B). Table 1 (Panel C) presents descriptive statistics for individual and family characteristics. We have almost complete report within valid ranges for these variables in 1994 by adolescents and their families, except for pretax family income, birth weight and parental choice of school. We impute missing values on these variables with their sample means for the analysis.[6]

---

[6] Adding dummy variables for missing values and in the regressions produced very similar results.

Table 1. Summary statistics

Variable	N	Mean	SD	Minimum	Maximum
Panel A: Weight status measures					
BMI, 94	19 811	22.56	4.47	11.21	63.5
BMI, 96	14 517	23.06	5.03	12.54	61.03
BMI, 02	14 362	26.55	6.18	13.46	63.84
BMI pct., 94	19 744	59.42	28.5	0	99.98
BMI pct., 96	14 342	58.58	29.85	0	99.97
At risk, 94	19 811	0.25	0.43	0	1
At risk, 96	14 518	0.26	0.44	0	1
At risk, 02	14 362	0.5	0.5	0	1
Overweight, 94	19 811	0.11	0.31	0	1
Overweight, 96	14 518	0.12	0.33	0	1
Overweight, 02	14 362	0.23	0.42	0	1
Panel B: Peer measures					
Friends BMI, 94	6451	22.33	3.63	11.21	48.42
Friends BMI, 96	3842	22.73	4.08	12.69	51.69
Friends BMI pct., 94	6447	58.53	24.32	0	99.76
Friends BMI pct., 96	3828	57.09	25.35	0	99.91
Share of friends overweight, 94	6451	0.09	0.25	0	1
Share of friends overweight, 96	3842	0.1	0.26	0	1
Share of friends at risk, 94	6451	0.22	0.36	0	1
Share of friends at risk, 96	3842	0.22	0.36	0	1
Same grade BMI, 94	19 811	22.56	1.31	13.56	32.54
Same grade BMI, 96	14 518	23.06	1.55	15.66	36.81
Same grade BMI pct., 94	19 811	59.41	7.02	0.02	98.69
Same grade BMI pct., 96	14 516	58.56	8.94	0.34	99.45
Same grade overweight, 94	19 811	0.11	0.07	0	1
Same grade overweight, 96	14 518	0.12	0.09	0	1
Same grade at risk, 94	19 811	0.25	0.1	0	1
Same grade at risk, 96	14 518	0.26	0.12	0	1

Variable	Mean	SD	Minimum	Maximum
Panel C: Personal and family characteristics				
Black	0.22	0.41	0	1
Hispanic	0.17	0.36	0	1
Mother's education	2.06	0.65	1	3
Father's education	2.09	0.58	1	3
Grade	9.7	1.58	7	12
Age	15.18	1.68	11	20
Male dummy	0.5	0.49	0	1
Smokes	0.26	0.43	0	1
Watches TV regularly	0.79	0.4	0	1
Exercising	0.84	0.36	0	1
Sports	0.43	0.48	0	1
Parents work fulltime	0.29	0.45	0	1
Mother obese	0.15	0.35	0	1
Father obese	0.08	0.26	0	1
Pretax family income	46.16	44	0	999
Lives with 2 parents	0.5	0.49	0	1
First born	0.49	0.49	0	1
Number of siblings	2.42	1.69	0	15
Birth weight	6.82	1.22	3	12
Breast fed	0.53	0.48	0	1
Years old when moved	8.73	5.64	0	19
Parents chose school	0.48	0.45	0	1
N	20 701			

Source: Add Health, authors' calculations.

Notes: Missing observations on personal and family characteristics were imputed with sample means before tabulating descriptive statistics.

'BMI pct' refers to BMI percentile. BMI percentiles were not calculated in 2002, as most individuals were above age 20, which is the last age at which BMI percentiles are calculated using CDC methodology.

Table 2. The influence of close friends weight status in 1994 on the individuals own weight in 1994

	BMI (OLS)		Overweight (Probit ME)		At risk (Probit ME)	
Friends BMI, 94	0.178***	(0.038)				
Share of friends overweight, 94			0.066***	(0.013)		
Share of friends at risk, 94					0.129***	(0.025)
Black (d)	0.584***	(0.211)	0.017	(0.014)	0.016	(0.018)
Hispanic (d)	0.377*	(0.220)	0.005	(0.014)	0.017	(0.018)
Mother's education	−0.079	(0.107)	−0.002	(0.005)	−0.015	(0.010)
Father's education	−0.318***	(0.084)	−0.014***	(0.005)	−0.032***	(0.011)
Grade	0.203**	(0.096)	0.003	(0.005)	0.006	(0.010)
Age	0.175	(0.113)	−0.005	(0.005)	−0.014	(0.011)
Male dummy (d)	0.596***	(0.095)	0.032***	(0.005)	0.062***	(0.011)
Smokes (d)	0.264	(0.234)	0.010	(0.011)	0.020	(0.015)
Watches TV regularly (d)	0.087	(0.120)	0.010*	(0.005)	0.012	(0.013)
Exercising (d)	0.107	(0.133)	−0.005	(0.008)	−0.001	(0.013)
Sports (d)	−0.081	(0.116)	−0.012*	(0.007)	0.011	(0.011)
Parents work fulltime (d)	−0.158	(0.109)	−0.008	(0.007)	−0.021*	(0.013)
Mother obese (d)	1.779***	(0.220)	0.076***	(0.013)	0.128***	(0.022)
Father obese (d)	1.584***	(0.327)	0.062***	(0.018)	0.117***	(0.024)
Pretax family income	−0.001*	(0.001)	−0.000	(0.000)	−0.000*	(0.000)
Lives with two parents (d)	−0.007	(0.109)	−0.003	(0.006)	0.000	(0.009)
First born (d)	0.476***	(0.092)	0.017***	(0.006)	0.037***	(0.012)
Number of siblings	0.028	(0.040)	0.002	(0.002)	−0.001	(0.004)
Birth weight	0.201***	(0.039)	0.006**	(0.002)	0.016***	(0.004)
Breast fed	−0.139	(0.113)	−0.004	(0.006)	−0.008	(0.011)
Years old when moved	−0.024***	(0.009)	−0.002***	(0.000)	−0.002**	(0.001)
Parents chose school	0.108	(0.109)	0.004	(0.007)	0.010	(0.010)
Observations	6451		6451		6451	
R^2	0.160					
AIC	36 496.199		3969.491		6557.402	

Source: Add Health, authors' calculations.
Notes: OLS- Ordinary Least Squares; AIC - Akaike Information Criterion; ME for marginal effects; (d) for discrete change of dummy variable from 0 to 1. Robust, clustered at school level SEs are given in parentheses. All regressions include controls for individual characteristics measured in 1994 along with school fixed effects.
*$p < 0.1$, **$p < 0.05$, ***$p < 0.01$.

The sample size differs between waves due to the loss to follow-up in later waves since wave 1; however, we did not find these differences to result in systematic differences in the observable characteristics.

We first provide estimates of the contemporaneous effects from regressions of individual weight status in 1994 on the contemporaneous peer weight measures (Tables 2 and 3).[7] Estimates in Table 2 suggest that close friends' weight status has a statistically significant effect on BMI, on risk of being overweight and on overweight. However, the effect is larger in magnitude for being at risk of overweight than on overweight. In Table 3, we also find significant effects of same school grade peers on adolescent's weight status, with greater magnitudes than for close friends. School fixed effects are included in all models to control for the influence of common school environment.

Turning briefly to individual control variables we find that coming from a minority race/ethnic group increases the chances of having higher weight and greater educational attainment of father reduces the chances of being overweight. Males have higher BMI values and are more likely to be overweight or to be at risk of overweight compared to females. Interestingly, none of the behavioural variables (smoking, exercising, watching TV and sports) show significant effects on BMI or on being overweight in the regressions with close friends measures (Table 2). On the other hand, watching TV and playing sports have the expected sign and are statistically significant in the regressions with grade-level peer measures (Table 3). Controlling for family-level factors and individual-level developmental and genetic characteristics shows the expected results: if the mother or the father is obese, if the birth weight is higher and if the

[7] The corresponding estimates for 1996 are given in Table A1.

Table 3. The influence of same school grade-level friends' weight status in 1994 on the individuals own weight status in 1994

	BMI (OLS)		Overweight (Probit ME)		At risk (Probit ME)	
Same grade BMI, 94	0.945***	(0.012)				
Same grade overweight, 94			0.757***	(0.022)		
Same grade at risk, 94					1.046***	(0.018)
Black (d)	0.941***	(0.148)	0.029***	(0.011)	0.065***	(0.017)
Hispanic (d)	0.666***	(0.122)	0.019**	(0.009)	0.054***	(0.012)
Mother's education	−0.100*	(0.058)	−0.005	(0.004)	−0.012**	(0.005)
Father's education	−0.271***	(0.052)	−0.014***	(0.004)	−0.030***	(0.006)
Grade	−0.217***	(0.042)	−0.002	(0.003)	0.002	(0.005)
Age	0.280***	(0.046)	0.003	(0.003)	−0.000	(0.005)
Male dummy (d)	0.359***	(0.093)	0.036***	(0.005)	0.046***	(0.008)
Smokes (d)	0.083	(0.130)	0.001	(0.008)	0.002	(0.010)
Watches TV regularly (d)	0.152**	(0.070)	0.013***	(0.005)	0.020***	(0.007)
Exercising (d)	0.152*	(0.091)	0.002	(0.005)	0.010	(0.009)
Sports (d)	−0.136**	(0.063)	−0.014***	(0.005)	−0.012*	(0.007)
Parents work fulltime (d)	−0.218***	(0.056)	−0.011**	(0.005)	−0.025***	(0.006)
Mother obese (d)	1.897***	(0.116)	0.094***	(0.008)	0.151***	(0.011)
Father obese (d)	1.534***	(0.160)	0.077***	(0.011)	0.105***	(0.013)
Pretax family income	−0.000	(0.001)	−0.000	(0.000)	−0.000	(0.000)
Lives with two parents (d)	−0.067	(0.075)	−0.003	(0.004)	0.002	(0.007)
First born (d)	0.240***	(0.077)	0.006	(0.005)	0.022***	(0.007)
Number of siblings	−0.025	(0.023)	−0.000	(0.002)	−0.003	(0.002)
Birth weight	0.198***	(0.023)	0.006***	(0.001)	0.016***	(0.002)
Breast fed	−0.132*	(0.069)	−0.004	(0.005)	−0.009	(0.007)
Years old when moved	−0.016***	(0.006)	−0.001***	(0.000)	−0.001*	(0.001)
Parents chose school	0.022	(0.076)	0.003	(0.005)	−0.004	(0.007)
Observations	19 811		19 811		19 811	
R^2	0.143					
AIC	112 522.168		12 126.375		20 343.692	

Source: Add Health, authors' calculations.
Notes: ME for marginal effects; (d) for discrete change of dummy variable from 0 to 1. Robust, clustered at school level SEs are given in parentheses. All regressions include controls for individual characteristics measured in 1994 along with school fixed effects.
*$p < 0.1$, **$p < 0.05$, ***$p < 0.01$.

adolescent is first born, he or she has a significantly higher weight.[8]

Tables 4 and 5 present the results of our main specification of the influence of peer weight status in 1994 and 1996 on the individuals' weight gain by 2002, using close friends measures in Table 4 and same school grade measures in Table 5. Only the estimates on peer measures are reported.

The estimates are consistent with persistence of the peer influence on weight among friends. Table 4 shows that the lagged peer BMI and overweight status of peers significantly affect adolescents' BMI and the probability of becoming overweight or at risk of overweight in early adulthood. The estimated effect sizes imply that a 10% increase in close friends'

BMI, the probability of overweight, and the probability of becoming at risk of overweight are associated with 0.3–0.7% increase in adolescent's own corresponding measures of body weight by the time when he or she is a young adult. The effect of average BMI of close friends on adolescent's BMI is only significant at the 10% level. These results suggest that the influence of past peer body weight on the adolescent's weight gain by early adulthood is greatest among people at the (upper) tail of the BMI distribution (those who are overweight and at risk of overweight).

Comparison of the estimates using close friends in 1994 and 1996 (Panels A and B) suggests similarly strong effects on individual weight by 2002.[9] As shown in Panel C, peer weight status in 1994

[8] In alternative models, we used BMI percentiles instead of linear BMI measure, since the latter may not be as informative for children as it is for adults. Table A2 suggests that if percentiles are used instead of BMI, the magnitudes of the effects change only slightly. Since BMI percentiles are only available for waves 1 and 2, we conducted our analysis with linear BMI measure.
[9] We note that most adolescents experience some change in the composition of their friendship network between 1994 and 1996. Approximately 85% of individuals changed their friend nominations in some way between 1994 and 1996. Therefore, these estimates reflect both the change in weight and the change in composition of the peer group. In a separate set of estimates, we restrict nominated friends to only those who appeared in both 1994 and 1996 nominations. Restricting the composition of friends to be the same does not change our results significantly (results not shown).

Table 4. The influence of close friends' weight status in 1994 and 1996 on the individual's own weight gain by 2002 and 1996

	BMI (OLS)		Overweight (Probit ME)		At risk (Probit ME)	
Panel A: Adolescent's weight status in 2002, peer weight status in 1994						
Friends BMI, 94	0.029*	(0.017)				
Share of friends overweight, 94			0.060**	(0.024)		
Share of friends at risk, 94					0.047*	(0.026)
Observations	4718		4718		4718	
R^2	0.599					
AIC	26 306.883		3908.345		5081.794	
Panel B: Adolescent's weight status in 2002, peer weight status in 1996						
Friends BMI, 96	0.033*	(0.018)				
Share of friends overweight, 96			0.059**	(0.026)		
Share of friends at risk, 96					0.068***	(0.026)
Observations	2971		2971		2971	
R^2	0.680					
AIC	15 874.770		2131.218		2979.758	
Panel C: Adolescent's weight status in 1996, peer weight status in 1994						
Friends BMI, 94	0.019	(0.013)				
Share of friends overweight, 94			0.031***	(0.009)		
Share of friends at risk, 94					0.040***	(0.015)
Observations	4782		4782		4782	
R^2	0.783					
AIC	21 652.941		1892.908		2851.665	

Source: Add Health, authors' calculations.
Notes: ME for marginal effects. Robust, clustered at school level SEs are given in parentheses. All regressions include controls for individual characteristics measured in 1994 along with school fixed effects. All models control for individual's own BMI or weight status in 1994 or 1996.
*$p < 0.1$, **$p < 0.05$, ***$p < 0.01$.

Table 5. The influence of same school grade-level friends' weight status in 1994 and 1996 on individual's own weight gain by 2002 and 1996

	BMI (OLS)		Overweight (Probit ME)		At risk (Probit ME)	
Panel A: Adolescent's weight status in 2002, peer weight status in 1994						
Same grade BMI, 94	0.022	(0.045)				
Same grade overweight, 94			−0.016	(0.065)		
Same grade at risk, 94					0.034	(0.070)
Observations	13 743		13 743		13 743	
R^2	0.577					
AIC	77 009.707		11 546.138		15 297.237	
Panel B: Adolescent's weight status in 2002, peer weight status in 1996						
Same grade BMI, 96	0.021	(0.042)				
Same grade overweight, 96			0.040	(0.061)		
Same grade at risk, 96					−0.014	(0.065)
Observations	10 391		10 391		10 391	
R^2	0.646					
AIC	56 277.457		7880.243		10 979.321	
Panel C: Adolescent's weight status in 1996, peer weight status in 1994						
Same grade BMI, 94	−0.029	(0.034)				
Same grade overweight, 94			0.064	(0.043)		
Same grade at risk, 94					0.062	(0.050)
Observations	13 823		13 823		13 823	
R^2	0.765					
AIC	63 580.133		5617.908		8707.630	

Source: Add Health, authors' calculations.
Notes: ME for marginal effects. Robust, clustered at school level SEs are given in parentheses. All regressions include controls for individual characteristics measured in 1994 along with school fixed effects. All models control for individual's own BMI or weight status in 1994 or 1996.

exerts significant pressure on adolescents' weights by 1996, however, these effects are smaller than the effects on weight outcomes in 2002, which the latter reflecting the longer term impact of the peer weight (from high school to young adulthood, see Panels A and B). Overall, the results are consistent with some degree of persistence in the impact of peer weight on individual weight outcomes during adolescence. The fact that we find peer effects on individual weight gain by 2002 to be similar in magnitude for 1994 and 1996 peers corroborates the claim that the peer weight has a lasting impact on individual weight.[10]

The estimates in Table 5, where peer group is defined as the same grade in school, suggest no effect of peers' weight status on adolescent's weight gain. This is in stark contrast to the estimated influences of nominated friends as shown in Table 4. Taken at face value this suggests that school level peer weights exert no systematic long-term influence on individuals, which is consistent with the idea that grade-level peers are not as important a reference group as close friends.

We note that the social interaction effects are estimated conditional on a wide range of individual and family-level control variables. Omitting many of these variables could result in biases in the peer effects estimates. To account for endogeneity of school choice, we control for age at which adolescent moved to the current location, and whether adolescent's parents chose the neighbourhood for the school. However, they are not significant predictors of adolescent weight gain after accounting for other characteristics (results not shown). Second, all of the models control for school fixed effects, and the estimated individual weight changes are driven only by the differences in the past weight status of peers from the same school. The school fixed effects play an important role: they are always jointly statistically significant and in regressions without school fixed effects the estimated peer effects are much larger (results not shown). Thus, estimates without school fixed effects would have been biased due to omitting correlated effects operating at the school level. Third, we also estimate models including peer group averages of parental characteristics (family income, education level, etc.) to test for contextual effects (results not shown). Their coefficients were individually and jointly insignificant, providing evidence against the hypothesis that the peer effects are driven by contextual effects.

We also conducted extensive falsification tests. In one analysis, we regressed individual weight status in 1994 on peer weight status in 1996. The idea is that if current peers are found to affect individual weight outcomes in the past, then the effects in Tables 4 and 5, Panel C may be spurious. Tables A3 and A4 show the results of regressing adolescent's 1994 weight status on 1996 peer weight status. Own weight status of the adolescent in 1996 is included as a control in the specifications in Table A4, but excluded in Table A3. All of the effects are significant in Table A3 and almost all of the effects are statistically insignificant in Table A4. This comparison points to the importance of controlling for individual's initial weight status and reinforces our earlier concern that estimates from simple cross-sectional regressions of individual weight status on peer weight status, such as the ones shown here in Tables 2 and 3, are likely to be spurious.

We also estimated models that controlled for both nominated friends and school grade peer measures in the same specification. Estimates on school grade peer measures remained insignificant in these regressions (results not shown). Also, concerned about having different samples for the regressions with nominated friends and with school grade peers, we restricted the estimation sample used for school grade peers to be the same as the sample used for nominated friends. Estimates of school grade peer effects remained insignificant after this restriction (results not shown). In another set of estimates (results not shown), we explored the possibility that the effect of peers may vary by the age of adolescents. However, the estimate on the interaction between high-school dummy (equal to 1 if in 10–12th grade in 1994) and peer weight was not statistically significant.

VI. Conclusion

Previous studies on the spread of obesity in social networks have focused on the contemporaneous effect of peer weight outcomes on individual weight outcomes (Christakis and Fowler, 2007; Cohen-Cole and Fletcher, 2008; Fowler and Christakis, 2008; Renna *et al.*, 2008; Trogdon *et al.*, 2008; Halliday and Kwak, 2009). To our knowledge, this article is the first to investigate the longer term effects, within adolescences and from adolescence into early

---

[10] We also estimated models that control jointly for lagged and contemporaneous peer weight outcomes. For BMI and the risk of being overweight in 1996, we found that the lagged peer group measures (1994 friends) exerted a significantly stronger effect than the contemporaneous (1996) friends.

adulthood, of peer weight outcomes on individual weight outcomes. Using all three waves of Add Health data, and accounting for correlated effects using a number of empirical strategies including school-level fixed effects and controlling for neighbourhood preferences, we show that friends' BMI and overweight status lead to changes in individual BMI and risk of being overweight among adolescents. The results also indicate that the influence of peers during adolescence may persist both within adolescence and into young adulthood. Some degree of persistence of the impact of the influence of peer weight outcomes in adolescence is plausible given that adolescence is the formative period of preferences for ideal physique and individual body weight aspirations (Maximova et al. 2008; Ali et al., 2011). We find similar effects of 1994 and 1996 friend weight outcomes on individual weight gain by 2002, which corroborates the lasting influence of past peer weight status on individual weight.

The observed relationship between peer weight and individual weight gain suggests that obesity can spread in social networks and helps to explain the rapid rise in obesity among adolescents in the US. While we cannot directly compare our estimates of the effects of lagged peer weight to the estimates from other studies, our coefficients tend to be smaller in magnitude (3–10 times) than the corresponding estimates on the contemporaneous peer group measures. We find that individuals are more influenced by their close network of friends compared with the grade-level peers. This is consistent with Christakis and Fowler (2007) who find that peer effects diminish as the degree of separation from the person increases.

Our findings also suggest that the peer effects are greater for individuals with higher initial BMI value, specifically, those who are classified as 'at risk of being overweight' or as 'overweight'. Trogdon et al. (2008) note a similar pattern in quantile regressions looking at the effect of mean peer BMI in different parts of the adolescents' BMI distribution. This is also consistent with evidence from the energy expenditure literature which suggests that resting metabolism is concave in weight, such that the same increase in calorie intake leads to a greater weight gain in an initially heaver person (Burke and Heiland, 2007).

The presence of peer influence suggests that it may be possible to slow the spread of obesity by promoting a healthy body image and positive (group) health behaviours. As noted by Christakis and Fowler (2007), public health interventions might be more cost effective than previously estimated, since health promoting behaviour in one person may spread to others. In light of our evidence of the long-term influences of peer weight outcomes during adolescence, policy makers should be particularly concerned with facilitating change in weight-related behaviours among children and adolescents.

Acknowledgements

The views expressed here are those of the authors and do not necessarily reflect the views of the Food and Drug Administration. This research uses data from Add Health, a program project designed by J. Richard Udry, Peter S. Bearman and Kathleen Mullan Harris, and funded by a grant P01-HD31921 from the National Institute of Child Health and Human Development, with cooperative funding from 17 other agencies. Special acknowledgment is due to Ronald R. Rindfuss and Barbara Entwisle for assistance in the original design. Persons interested in obtaining data files from Add Health should contact Add Health, Carolina Population Center, 123 W. Franklin Street, Chapel Hill, NC 27516-2524 (addhealth@unc.edu).

References

Adams, J. (2006) Trends in physical activity and inactivity amongst US 14–18 year olds by gender, school grade and race, 1993–2003: evidence from the Youth Risk Behavior Survey, BMC Public Health, **6**, 57.

Ali, M. M., Amialchuk, A. and Renna, F. (2011) Social network and weight misperceptions among adolescents, Southern Economics Journal, forthcoming.

Ali, M. M. and Dwyer, D. S. (2009) Estimating peer effects in adolescent smoking behavior: a longitudinal analysis, Journal of Adolescent Health, **45**, 402–8.

Ali, M. M. and Dwyer, D. S. (2010) Social network effects in alcohol consumption among adolescent, Addictive Behaviors, **35**, 337–41.

Anderson, P. M., Butcher, K. F. and Levine, Ph. B. (2003) Maternal employment and overweight children, Journal of Health Economics, **22**, 477–504.

Burke, M. and Heiland, F. (2007) Social dynamics of obesity, Economic Inquiry, **45**, 571–91.

Burke, M., Heiland, F. and Nadler, C. (2010) From 'overweight' to 'about right': evidence of a generational shift in body weight norms, Obesity, **18**, 1226–34.

Chou, S.-Y., Grossman, M. and Saffer, H. (2004) An economic analysis of adult obesity: results from the behavioral risk factor surveillance system, Journal of Health Economics, **23**, 565–87.

Christakis, N. A. and Fowler, J. H. (2007) The spread of obesity in a large social network over 32 years, The New England Journal of Medicine, **357**, 370–9.

Clark, A. E. and Loheac, Y. (2007) 'It wasn't me, it was them!' Social influence in risky behavior by adolescents, *Journal of Health Economics*, **26**, 763–84.

Cohen-Cole, E. and Fletcher, J. M. (2008) Is obesity contagious? Social networks versus environmental factors in the obesity epidemic, *Journal of Health Economics*, **27**, 1382–7.

Dollman, J., Norton, K. and Norton, L. (2005) Evidence for secular trends in children's physical activity behaviour, *British Journal of Sports Medicine*, **39**, 892–7.

Eisenmann, J. C. (2003) Secular trends in variables associated with the metabolic syndrome of North American children and adolescents: a review and synthesis, *American Journal of Human Biology*, **15**, 786–94.

Étilé, F. (2007) Social norms, ideal body weight and food attitudes, *Health Economics*, **16**, 945–66.

Fang, H., Ali, M. M. and Rizzo, J. A. (2009) Does smoking affect body weight and obesity in China?, *Economics and Human Biology*, **7**, 334–50.

Flegal, K. M., Carroll, M. D., Kuczmarski, R. J. and Johnson, C. L. (1998) Overweight and obesity in the United States: prevalence and trends, 1960–1994, *International Journal of Obesity*, **22**, 39–47.

Fowler, J. H. and Christakis, N. A. (2008) Estimating peer effects on health in social networks, *Journal of Health Economics*, **27**, 1400–5.

Gaviria, A. and Raphael, S. (2001) School-based peer effects and juvenile behavior, *Review of Economics and Statistics*, **83**, 257–68.

Goodman, E., Hinden, B. R. and Khandelwal, S. (2000) Accuracy of teen and parental reports of obesity and body mass index, *Pediatrics*, **106**, 52–8.

Gordon-Larsen, P., McMurray, R. G. and Popkin, B. M. (2000) Determinants of adolescent physical activity and inactivity patterns, *Pediatrics*, **105**, e83.

Guthrie, J. F., Lin, B.-H. and Frazao, E. (2002) Role of food prepared away from home in the American diet, 1977–78 versus 1994–96: changes and consequences, *Journal of Nutrition Education and Behavior*, **34**, 140–50.

Halliday, T. J. and Kwak, S. (2009) Weight gains in adolescents and their peers, *Economics and Human Biology*, **7**, 181–90.

Hedley, A. A., Ogden, C. L., Johnson, C. L., Carroll, M. D. and Flegal, K. M. (2004) Prevalence of overweight and obesity among US children, adolescents, and adults, 1999–2002, *Journal of the American Medical Association*, **291**, 2847–50.

Hill, J. O., Wyatt, H. R., Reed, G. W. and Peters, J. C. (2003) Obesity and the environment: where do we go from here?, *Science*, **299**, 853.

Hoxby, C. (2000) Peer effects in the classroom: learning from gender and race variation, NBER Working Paper No. 7867, Cambridge.

Jahns, L., Siega-Riz, A. M. and Popkin, B. M. (2001) The increasing prevalence of snacking among US children from 1977 to 1996, *Journal of Pediatrics*, **138**, 493–8.

Johnson, F., Cooke, L., Croker, H. and Wardle, J. (2009) Changing perceptions of weight in Great Britain: comparison of two population surveys, *British Medical Journal*, **337**, a494.

Kinsbourne, M. (2002) The brain and body awareness, in *Body Image: A Handbook of Theory, Research and Clinical Practice* (Eds) T. F. Cash and T. Pruzinsky, Guildford Press, New York, pp. 22–37.

Lakdawalla, D. and Philipson, T. J. (2002) The growth of obesity and technological change: a theoretical and empirical examination, NBER Working Paper No. 8946, Cambridge.

Manski, C. F. (1993) Identification of endogenous social effects: the reflection problem, *Review of Economic Studies*, **60**, 531–42.

Manski, C. F. (2000) Economic analysis of social interactions, *Journal of Economic Perspectives*, **14**, 115–36.

Maximova, K., McGrath, J. J., Barnett, T., O'Loughlin, J., Paradis, G. and Lambert, M. (2008) Do you see what I see? Weight status misperception and exposure to obesity among children and adolescents, *International Journal of Obesity*, **32**, 1008–15.

McPherson, M., Smith-Lovin, L. and Cook, J. M. (2001) Birds of a feather: homophily in social networks, *Annual Review of Sociology*, **27**, 415–44.

Moffatt, R. J. and Owens, S. G. (1991) Cessation from cigarette smoking: changes in body weight, body composition, resting metabolism, and energy consumption, *Metabolism*, **40**, 465–70.

Must, A., Spadano, J., Coakley, E. H., Field, A. E., Colditz, G. and Dietz, W. H. (1999) The disease burden associated with overweight and obesity, *Journal of the American Medical Association*, **282**, 1523–9.

Nelson, M. C., Neumark-Sztainer, D., Hannan, P. J., Sirard, J. R. and Story, M. (2006) Longitudinal and secular trends in physical activity and sedentary behavior during adolescence, *Pediatrics*, **118**, e1627–34.

Ogden, C. L., Carroll, M. D., Curtin, L. R., McDowell, M. A., Tabak, C. J. and Flegal, K. M. (2006) Prevalence of overweight and obesity in the United States, 1999–2004, *Journal of American Medical Association*, **295**, 1549–55.

Philipson, T. J. and Posner, R. A. (1999) The long-run growth in obesity as a function of technological change, NBER Working Paper No. 7423, Cambridge.

Pollak, R. A. (1976) Interdependent preferences, *American Economic Review*, **66**, 309–20.

Pratt, M., Macera, C. A. and Blanton, C. (1999) Levels of physical activity and inactivity in children and adults in the United States: current evidence and research issues, *Medicine and Science and Sports and Exercise*, **31**, S526–33.

Renna, F., Grafova, I. B. and Thakur, N. (2008) Effect of friends on adolescent weight, *Economics and Human Biology*, **6**, 377–87.

Swinburn, B., Sacks, G. and Ravussin, E. (2009) Increased food energy supply is more than sufficient to explain the US epidemic of obesity, *American Journal of Clinical Nutrition*, **90**, 1453–6.

Trogdon, J. G., Nonnemaker, J. and Pais, J. (2008) Peer effects in adolescent overweight, *Journal of Health Economics*, **27**, 1388–99.

Turner, B. S. (1996) *The Body and Society*, Sage, London.

Appendix

Table A1. The influence of peer weight status in 1996 on the individual own weight status in 1996

	BMI (OLS)		Overweight (Probit ME)		At risk (Probit ME)	
Panel A: Close friends peer measures						
Friends BMI, 96	0.186***	(0.049)				
Share of friends overweight, 96			0.069***	(0.014)		
Share of friends at risk, 96					0.112***	(0.019)
Observations	3757		3757		3757	
R^2	0.160					
AIC	22 282.507		2535.749		3852.918	
Panel B: Same school grade peer measures						
Same grade BMI, 96	0.891***	(0.018)				
Same grade overweight, 96			0.735***	(0.026)		
Same grade at risk, 96					1.009***	(0.020)
Observations	13 823		13 823		13 823	
R^2	0.148					
AIC	81 402.789		8823.146		14 142.964	

Source: Add Health, authors' calculations.
Notes: ME for marginal effects. Robust, clustered at school level SEs are given in parentheses. All regressions include controls for individual characteristics measured in 1994 along with school fixed effects.
***$p < 0.01$.

Table A2. The influence of peer BMI percentile on the individual's own BMI percentile

	BMI percentile (OLS)		BMI percentile (OLS)	
Panel A: Year 1994 measures				
Friends BMI pct., 94	0.148***	(0.024)		
Same grade BMI pct., 94			0.969***	(0.009)
Observations	6438		19 744	
R^2	0.108		0.105	
AIC	60 599.583		186 174.839	
Panel B: Year 1996 measures				
Friends BMI pct., 96	0.142***	(0.035)		
Same grade BMI pct., 96			0.931***	(0.013)
Observations	3716		13 665	
R^2	0.133		0.128	
AIC	35 311.386		129 725.539	

Source: Add Health, authors' calculations.
Notes: ME for marginal effects. Robust, clustered at school level SEs are given in parentheses. All regressions include controls for individual characteristics measured in 1994 along with school fixed effects.
***$p < 0.01$.

Table A3. The influence of 1996 peer weight on the individual's 1994 weight, not controlling for 1996 individual's weight (falsification exercise 1)

	BMI (OLS)		Overweight (Probit ME)		At risk (Probit ME)	
Panel A: Close friends peer measures						
Friends BMI, 96	0.153***	(0.037)				
Share of friends overweight, 96			0.045***	(0.011)		
Share of friends at risk, 96					0.115***	(0.022)
Observations	3757		3757		3757	
R^2	0.176					
AIC	21 344.596		2295.746		3778.990	
Panel B: Same school grade peer measures						
Same grade BMI, 96	0.709***	(0.025)				
Same grade overweight, 96			0.429***	(0.026)		
Same grade at risk, 96					0.672***	(0.037)
Observations	13 823		13 823		13 823	
R^2	0.151					
AIC	78 215.517		8371.029		14 129.410	

Source: Add Health, authors' calculations.
Notes: ME for marginal effects. Robust, clustered at school level SEs are given in parentheses. All regressions include controls for individual characteristics measured in 1994 along with school fixed effects.
***$p < 0.01$.

Table A4. The influence of 1996 peer weight on the individual's 1994 weight, controlling for 1996 individual's weight (falsification exercise 2)

	BMI (OLS)		Overweight (Probit ME)		At risk (Probit ME)	
Panel A: Close friends peer measures						
Friends BMI, 96	0.009	(0.010)				
Share of friends overweight, 96			0.004	(0.005)		
Share of friends at risk, 96					0.045**	(0.018)
Observations	3757		3757		3757	
R^2	0.809					
AIC	15 844.624		1245.306		2042.366	
Panel B: Same school grade peer measures						
Same grade BMI, 96	0.031*	(0.017)				
Same grade overweight, 96			0.005	(0.020)		
Same grade at risk, 96					0.050	(0.043)
Observations	13 823		13 823		13 823	
R^2	0.768					
AIC	60 277.436		4888.437		8401.861	

Source: Add Health, authors' calculations.
Notes: ME for marginal effects. Robust, clustered at school level SEs are given in parentheses. All regressions include controls for individual characteristics measured in 1994 along with school fixed effects.
*$p < 0.1$, **$p < 0.05$.

Obesity and happiness

Marina-Selini Katsaiti

*Department of Economics and Finance, Faculty of Business and Economics,
United Arab Emirates University, PO BOX 17555, Al Ain, UAE*

This article provides insight on the relationship between individual obesity
and happiness levels. Using the latest available panel data from Germany
German Socio-Economic Panel (GSOEP), UK British Household Panel
Survey (BHPS), and Australia Household, Income and Labour Dynamics
in Australia (HILDA), we examine whether there is statistical evidence on
the impact of overweight on subjective well-being. Instrumental Variable
(IV) analysis is utilized under the presence of endogeneity, stemming from
several explanatory variables. Results indicate that in all three countries
obesity has a negative effect on the subjective well-being of individuals.
The results also have important implications for the effect of other socio-
demographic, economic and individual characteristics on well-being.

I. Introduction

Happiness is one of life's fundamental goals. Whether
people pursue better jobs or higher income, try to
achieve better health or a stable family life, want to
win an Olympic medal or the Nobel prize, the
motivation behind their effort is normally happiness.
People may engage in risky behaviour, such as
smoking or racing, because they derive temporary
satisfaction from this. Similarly, people derive instant
pleasure from food consumption. As with numerous
habits and consumption patterns, the effect of food
consumption is usually immediate gratification, however in the long run, consumption of food in excess of
daily calorific needs leads to excessive weight gain,
which in turn can lower subjective well-being.

Happiness can be defined as the degree to which
people positively assess their life situation
(Veenhoven, 1996) and depends on a variety of
individual and social characteristics. These characteristics differ in how important they are to each
individual and are measured by ordinal ranking.
Happiness is often defined in terms of living a good
life, rather than a simple emotion.

Happiness is naturally the subject of psychological
and sociological research as well as medicine, and is
often associated with good health. Economics
research has connected happiness with the concept
of utility since the eighteenth century and the works
of Bentham and Jevons. This multidisciplinary
research has identified several determinants of happiness. The most important ones include demographics, socioeconomic traits, education and
health-related characteristics.

Empirical work in economics has shed light on
significant determinants of individual well being.
Age, gender, income, employment status, marital
status and education are among them. Body Mass
Index (BMI) has recently been added to the list of
factors that can explain life satisfaction levels. BMI
can influence happiness through deterioration in
health, lower self-esteem or lower social acceptance.
In addition, it may affect self confidence, personal
and social relationships and attitude. Though not

perfect, BMI is a well-established measure of obesity, employed by the Centers for Disease Control (CDC) and by the World Health Organization (WHO). Individuals with BMI (i) between 18 and 25 are indexed as normal weight, (ii) between 25 and 30 are categorized as overweight and (iii) over 30 are classified as obese.

Moods often affect consumption patterns and are associated with eating habits and disorders. In addition, it is intuitive that subjective well-being itself influences numerous other aspects of life, both in the short and long run. Examples of the factors arguably influenced by happiness levels are, among other things, education and income levels, marital status and employment. Thus, in the empirical estimation several explanatory variables are endogenous and do not obey the standard assumptions, since the causality could be running in both directions. This issue, not adequately addressed in the happiness literature, cannot be neglected as it may affect the robustness of the results, when the estimator is inconsistent. Stutzer (2007) is the only study that addresses this issue, however, acknowledging and treating for reverse causality only between happiness and BMI.

The purpose of this study is to examine the impact of BMI on individual well-being. It contributes to the literature in the following ways. First, it analyses the most recently available panel data from Germany, Australia and the UK. In addition, it is the first study to examine the Australian case. Last, it identifies the endogeneity issues arising from dual causality in the model and addresses them appropriately.

This article is structured as follows: Section II reviews the relevant literature. Section III describes the estimation methodology and the data, and Section IV presents and discusses the empirical results. Section V summarizes the primary findings and offers some final remarks.

II. The Literature

The medical literature provides diverse conclusions about the relationship between obesity and depression. Roberts *et al.* (2000) use data from Alameda County, California, to investigate whether the obese are at greater risk for depression. They conclude that, among other groups, the obese, females and those with two or more chronic health conditions are at higher risk for depression. In addition, they find that, when all individuals with depressive symptoms in the previous year are excluded, there is greater relative risk for future depression for the obese than for

the nonobese. This result holds in specifications that control for a number of variables affecting the risk of depression. Based on their results and on the results of other studies, they conclude 'that the obese may be at increased risk for depression'.

Reed (1985) uses data from the First National Health and Nutrition Examination Survey (NHANES I) and identifies young, more educated, obese females as a subgroup of worse mental health condition. Several studies find strong evidence of the relationship between overweight/obese individuals and depression in females (Noppa and Hällström, 1981; Reed, 1985; Palinkas *et al.*, 1996). Larsson *et al.* (2002) analyse the effect of overweight and obese on Health-Related Quality-of-Life (HRQL) in Sweden. Using data from a cross-sectional survey on 5633 men and women aged 14–64, their regression analysis finds the following: overweight and obesity in young men and women (16–34 years) leads to poor physical health, but not mental health. For middle-aged (35–64 years) individuals, obese men and women report health impairments, however only women report mental health problems.

The same result for females is supported by a study of adolescents aged 11–21 years. Needham and Crosnoe (2005) find evidence that relative weight is associated with depressive symptoms for girls but not for boys. Greeno *et al.* (1998) also confirm that females with the lack of perceived eating control and higher BMI are associated with lower life satisfaction levels. For men only the lack of perceived eating control explains lower happiness levels.

Stutzer (2007) investigates (i) the probability of being obese given certain socioeconomic and demographic characteristics and (ii) the effect of obesity on happiness taking into account self-reported self-control levels. His intuition stands on the hypothesis that only individuals who feel unable to control their food consumption should have lower happiness levels due to obesity. Using Swiss data, he finds that lower self-control is associated with lower happiness levels given the presence of obesity. Stutzer (2007) checks for reverse causality. He finds no evidence that eating due to stress leads to lower happiness levels of obese individuals with limited self control.

A similar study by Oswald and Powdthavee (2007) examines cross-sectional data from the UK and Germany, using regression analysis to identify the relationship between BMI and self-reported life satisfaction. For the British data they also explore the impact of BMI on psychological distress and on self-reported 'perception of own weight'. Under all univariate and multivariate specifications in both datasets, BMI has a negative and significant effect on subjective well-being. Moreover, for the British regressions they find that BMI increases psychological distress and is positively associated with the perception of own weight. Employment status, age, education, income, marital status and disability status stand out as significant determinants of individual happiness under most specifications. However, Oswald and Powdthavee (2007) do not correct for endogeneity.

III. Empirical Estimation

Data

The data for Germany come from the German Socio-Economic Panel (GSOEP), a representative longitudinal study of individuals and households. The aim of the GSOEP survey is to collect data on living conditions, together with demographic, economic, sociological, political and other individual and household characteristics. The data contains information about German citizens, foreigners and immigrants to Germany. Weight and height data are available only for the years 2002, 2004, 2006 and 2008. Most other variables included in our specifications are available for all years, with no breaks.

For UK, the data come from the British Household Panel Survey (BHPS). This survey includes households from England, Scotland, Wales and Northern Ireland. It surveys approximately 22 000 individuals yearly, and provides information on demographics, economic situation, household characteristics and individual health. The main information of interest here, the weight and height data, are available for 2005 and 2007. Once again most other variable information included in the analysis is available for all years.

For Australia the data source is the Household, Income and Labour Dynamics in Australia (HILDA) Survey. BMI information is available for years 2006, 2007 and 2009. HILDA provides similar or equivalent information with that of BHPS and GSOEP. In the Australian data the financial information variables are only available for 1 year, and this fact makes it not possible to contain this information in the panel regressions.

Descriptive statistics on German, British and Australian data are presented in Tables 1–3, respectively. Correlation matrices for the variables of interest are shown in Tables 4–6, respectively.

Besides BMI the following variables are included in the multivariate specifications: age, gender, years of education, income, employment status,[1] marital status, number of children, disability and household size. When data is available, some additional variables are also included in the analysis: political party membership, house ownership, saving habits, whether one has a second job, smoking habits, labour union membership, religion, region and nationality. BMI is used to control for individual obesity level. Happiness is measured using the self-reported life-satisfaction index. Here we have to acknowledge that individual happiness and self-reported life satisfaction may not be perfect substitutes and in fact, as the literature has concluded, the two are distinct. However, due to the fact that life satisfaction levels are reported, and there is no clear existing alternative variable that could be used as a proxy for happiness, we feel confident that for the purposes of this study the use of life satisfaction measure can offer a good approximation of individual happiness and well-being levels.

In the German and the Australian data the happiness indicators are measured using an 11-point index from 0 'completely dissatisfied' to 10 'completely satisfied'. The question is: 'How satisfied are you with your life, all things considered?'. For British data, the satisfaction index is measured on a 0–7 scale.

Subjective survey data, like that used in this study, could be prone to several systematic or nonsystematic biases (Kahneman et al., 1999). However as Frey and Stutzer (2005) report, 'the relevance of reporting errors depends on the intended usage of the data'. Thus, when the purpose is not to measure or to compare levels in an absolute sense, the bias does not seem to be relevant. So, for the purpose of identifying parameters that influence happiness, these measures are valid.

Methodology

Although availability of data is often not an issue, existing studies do not exploit all the available information, neglecting the strength of panel analysis. This study utilizes panel methodology in order to exhaust the possible sources of information and enhance the explanatory power of the model. Differences across individuals are expected to have some influence on the dependent variable, and thus a

---

[1] For BHPS, the employment status contains information on whether individuals are employed or unemployed. For GSOEP and HILDA data, the information is on whether individuals are employed or not employed. This requires attention in the interpretation of the results, as for Germany and Australia the results do not refer to the impact of unemployment on life satisfaction.

Table 1. Descriptive statistics for German data

Variable		Mean	SD	Min.	Max.	Obs.
German Data – GSOEP – Years: 2002, 2004, 2006, 2008						
Age	Overall	46.053	18.242	15	100	$N = 180714$
	Between		18.923	15	99	$n = 33272$
	Within		2.016	41.553	50.553	T-bar $= 5.43141$
Household size	Overall	3.023	1.370	1	13	$N = 215766$
	Between		1.306	1	13	$n = 39311$
	Within		0.448	−6.23	9.82	T-bar $= 5.48869$
No children	Overall	0.820	1.088	0	9	$N = 215766$
	Between		1.042	0	7.875	$n = 39311$
	Within		0.357	−4.805	4.820	T-bar $= 5.48869$
Education	Overall	12.068	2.676	7	18	$N = 157209$
	Between		2.654	7	18	$n = 28833$
	Within		0.331	6.924766	17.21048	T-bar $= 5.4524$
Life satisfaction	Overall	6.964	1.785	0	10	$N = 165630$
	Between		1.491	0	10	$n = 30615$
	Within		1.101	−1.61	14.11	T-bar $= 5.41009$
Height	Overall	1.713	0.093	0.82	2.1	$N = 83227$
	Between		0.092	1.31	2.09	$n = 28545$
	Within		0.016	0.96	2.11	T-bar $= 2.91564$
Weight	Overall	75.433	15.514	32	230	$N = 82681$
	Between		15.039	35	200	$n = 28452$
	Within		3.962	7.43	156.18	T-bar $= 2.90598$
BMI	Overall	25.619	4.589	11.63	197.23	$N = 82644$
	Between		4.338	12.86	73.46	$n = 28449$
	Within		1.556	−20.66	152.64	T-bar $= 2.90499$
ln Income	Overall	10.384	0.641	0	15.62	$N = 215763$
	Between		0.591	0	13.83	$n = 39310$
	Within		0.304	0.80	15.82	T-bar $= 5.48876$
Female	Overall	0.510	0.500	0	1	$N = 215766$
	Between		0.500	0	1	$n = 39311$
	Within		0.000	0.510	0.510	T-bar $= 5.48869$
Widowed	Overall	0.050	0.219	0	1	$N = 215766$
	Between		0.209	0	1	$n = 39311$
	Within		0.063	−0.825	0.925	T-bar $= 5.48869$
Divorced	Overall	0.054	0.226	0	1	$N = 215766$
	Between		0.206	0	1	$n = 39311$
	Within		0.087	−0.821	0.929	T-bar $= 5.48869$
Separated	Overall	0.013	0.115	0	1	$N = 215766$
	Between		0.088	0	1	$n = 39311$
	Within		0.080	−0.862	0.888	T-bar $= 5.48869$
Unemployed	Overall	0.367	0.482	0	1	$N = 215766$
	Between		0.426	0	1	$n = 39311$
	Within		0.247	−0.508	1.242	T-bar $= 5.48869$
Disabled	Overall	0.088	0.283	0	1	$N = 208742$
	Between		0.249	0	1	$n = 39030$
	Within		0.120	−0.787	0.963	T-bar $= 5.34824$
Political party member	Overall	0.448	0.497	0	1	$N = 166048$
	Between		0.413	0	1	$n = 30638$
	Within		0.297	−0.427	1.323	T-bar $= 5.41967$
Has a second job	Overall	0.027	0.162	0	1	$N = 166048$
	Between		0.118	0.000	1	$n = 30638$
	Within		0.120	−0.848	0.902	T-bar $= 5.41967$
German	Overall	0.926	0.261	0	1	$N = 166048$
	Between		0.263	0.000	1	$n = 30638$
	Within		0.045	0.0513	1.8013	T-bar $= 5.41967$

Random Effects (RE) model is used. RE here allow to control for time invariant variables, i.e. gender, disability status, etc. In order to test whether our model of choice, that is RE versus Fixed Effects (FE), is the appropriate one, we run a Hausman Test. The results indicate that RE should be used.

The choice of explanatory variables used in the regression analysis follows on (i) our

THE APPLIED ECONOMICS OF WEIGHT AND OBESITY

Table 2. Descriptive statistics for British data

Variable		Mean	SD	Min.	Max.	Obs.
British data – BHPS – Years: 2005 and 2007						
Age	Overall	45.958	18.649	15	99	$N = 63\,036$
	Between		19.267	15	99	$n = 18\,961$
	Within		1.073	41.46	50.46	T-bar $= 3.32451$
Household size	Overall	2.870	1.405	1	14	$N = 63\,038$
	Between		1.382	1	13.5	$n = 18\,961$
	Within		0.402	−3.880	8.870	T-bar $= 3.32461$
No children	Overall	0.499	0.914	0	7	$N = 46\,800$
	Between		0.884	0	7	$n = 17\,675$
	Within		0.182	−1.834	3.166	T-bar $= 2.64781$
Education	Overall	11.329	5.052	2	20	$N = 28\,575$
	Between		4.999	2	20	$n = 15\,968$
	Within		0.568	2.329	20.329	T-bar $= 1.78952$
Height	Overall	1.646	0.112	0.55	2.275	$N = 28\,522$
	Between		0.103	0.85	2.125	$n = 16\,088$
	Within		0.046	1.05	2.25	T-bar $= 1.77287$
Weight	Overall	76.051	15.802	12.7	184.15	$N = 23\,499$
	Between		15.969	12.7	184.15	$n = 14\,768$
	Within		2.576	37.05	115.05	T-bar $= 1.59121$
BMI	Overall	27.925	5.913	5.161	227.769	$N = 23\,249$
	Between		5.526	6.040	125.133	$n = 14\,652$
	Within		2.316	−74.710	130.560	T-bar $= 1.58675$
Life satisfaction	Overall	5.228	1.280	1	7	$N = 58\,402$
	Between		1.104	1	7	$n = 18\,066$
	Within		0.709	0.727852	9.727852	T-bar $= 3.2327$
Female	Overall	0.535	0.499	0	1	$N = 63\,038$
	Between		0.495	0	1	$n = 18\,961$
	Within		0.066	−0.215	1.035	T-bar $= 3.32461$
Widowed	Overall	0.076	0.265	0	1	$N = 63\,038$
	Between		0.254	0	1	$n = 18\,961$
	Within		0.061	−0.674	0.826	T-bar $= 3.32461$
Divorced	Overall	0.080	0.271	0	1	$N = 63\,038$
	Between		0.254	0	1	$n = 18\,961$
	Within		0.083	−0.670	0.830	T-bar $= 3.32461$
Separated	Overall	0.021	0.142	0	1	$N = 63\,038$
	Between		0.121	0	1	$n = 18\,961$
	Within		0.076	−0.729	0.771	T-bar $= 3.32461$
Unemployed	Overall	0.032	0.176	0	1	$N = 63\,038$
	Between		0.150	0	1	$n = 18\,961$
	Within		0.120	−0.718	0.782	T-bar $= 3.32461$
Disabled	Overall	0.078	0.269	0	1	$N = 63\,038$
	Between		0.217	0	1	$n = 18\,961$
	Within		0.169	−0.672	0.828	T-bar $= 3.32461$
ln Income	Overall	8.883	2.031	0	13.99	$N = 59\,036$
	Between		2.070	0	12.23	$n = 17\,902$
	Within		1.009	1.212	15.728	T-bar $= 3.29773$
Has a second job	Overall	0.058	0.234	0	1	$N = 63\,038$
	Between		0.188	0	1	$n = 18\,961$
	Within		0.147	−0.692	0.808	T-bar $= 3.32461$
Political party	Overall	0.264	0.441	0	1	$N = 63\,038$
	Between		0.315	0	1	$n = 18\,961$
	Within		0.309	−0.486	1.014	T-bar $= 3.32461$
Smoker	Overall	0.240	0.427	0	1	$N = 63\,038$
	Between		0.405	0	1	$n = 18\,961$
	Within		0.148	−0.510	0.990	T-bar $= 3.32461$
Labour union member	Overall	0.151	0.358	0	1	$N = 63\,038$
	Between		0.320	0	1	$n = 18\,961$
	Within		0.142	−0.599	0.901	T-bar $= 3.32461$
Saves	Overall	0.392	0.488	0	1	$N = 63\,038$
	Between		0.390	0	1	$n = 18\,961$
	Within		0.304	−0.358	1.142	T-bar $= 3.32461$
House owner	Overall	0.743	0.437	0	1	$N = 63\,038$
	Between		0.425	0	1	$n = 18\,961$
	Within		0.157	−0.007	1.493	T-bar $= 3.32461$

Table 3. **Descriptive statistics for Australian data**

Variable		Mean	SD	Min.	Max.	Obs.
Australlian – data HILDA – Years: 2006, 2007 and 2009						
Age	Overall	43.85421	18.59439	15	93	$N = 67\,729$
	Between		19.05329	15	93	$n = 17\,315$
	Within		1.320974	38.35421	49.35421	T-bar $= 3.91158$
Household size	Overall	3.207649	1.462235	1	14	$N = 82\,649$
	Between		1.363177	1	13.5	$n = 21\,265$
	Within		0.657998	−4.99235	10.20765	T-bar $= 3.88662$
No children	Overall	1.241713	1.394873	0	14	$N = 81\,787$
	Between		1.23369	0	9.6	$n = 20\,736$
	Within		0.747201	−5.95829	12.44171	T-bar $= 3.9442$
Education	Overall	11.58874	2.391224	0	18.5	$N = 63\,909$
	Between		2.023765	0	18.5	$n = 16\,348$
	Within		1.260333	3.088743	19.58874	T-bar $= 3.90929$
Height	Overall	1.704411	0.104764	0.82	2.29	$N = 28\,695$
	Between		0.10352	1.27	2.29	$n = 13\,759$
	Within		0.022699	1.204411	2.204411	T-bar $= 2.08554$
Weight	Overall	76.87511	17.98581	28	260	$N = 32\,870$
	Between		17.51675	28	236.6667	$n = 14\,216$
	Within		4.691137	7.541781	160.5418	T-bar $= 2.31218$
BMI	Overall	26.32283	5.573583	12.12121	163.5931	$N = 28\,248$
	Between		5.379719	13.06122	98.85366	$n = 13\,650$
	Within		1.74933	−38.4166	91.06226	T-bar $= 2.06945$
Income	Overall	65529.32	51454.74	1	611 361	$N = 81\,902$
	Between		42482.27	1	562 353	$n = 21\,209$
	Within		30003.61	−35 4404	474 042.1	T-bar $= 3.86166$
ln Income	Overall	10.30597	2.517529	0	13.32344	$N = 81\,902$
	Between		1.48586	0	13.23989	$n = 21\,209$
	Within		2.129551	0.327107	16.8477	T-bar $= 3.86166$
Female	Overall	0.514283	0.499799	0	1	$N = 86\,816$
	Between		0.499899	0	1	$n = 20\,710$
	Within		0	0.514283	0.514283	T-bar $= 4.19198$
Married	Overall	0.456497	0.498107	0	1	$N = 82\,649$
	Between		0.463687	0	1	$n = 21\,265$
	Within		0.174039	−0.3435	1.256497	T-bar $= 3.88662$
Single	Overall	0.191339	0.393358	0	1	$N = 82\,649$
	Between		0.362321	0	1	$n = 21\,265$
	Within		0.161919	−0.60866	0.991339	T-bar $= 3.88662$
Widowed	Overall	0.041936	0.200445	0	1	$N = 82\,649$
	Between		0.186951	0	1	$n = 21\,265$
	Within		0.055324	−0.75806	0.841936	T-bar $= 3.88662$
Divorced	Overall	0.052064	0.222157	0	1	$N = 82\,649$
	Between		0.195576	0	1	$n = 21\,265$
	Within		0.091528	−0.74794	0.852064	T-bar $= 3.88662$
Separated	Overall	0.022335	0.147773	0	1	$N = 82\,649$
	Between		0.122422	0	1	$n = 21\,265$
	Within		0.083549	−0.77766	0.822335	T-bar $= 3.88662$
Not employed	Overall	0.469455	0.499069	0	1	$N = 82\,649$
	Between		0.427514	0	1	$n = 21\,265$
	Within		0.283706	−0.33054	1.269455	T-bar $= 3.88662$
Disabled	Overall	0.152379	0.35939	0	1	$N = 82\,649$
	Between		0.293779	0	1	$n = 21\,265$
	Within		0.204189	−0.64762	0.952379	T-bar $= 3.88662$

intuition regarding the possible determinants of individual happiness given natural limitations in the data and (ii) the literature on this topic (Cornlisse-Vermatt *et al.*, 2006; Oswald and Powdthavee, 2007).

Surprisingly, existing literature, with the exception of Stutzer (2007), examining the relationship between happiness and obesity does not address the issue of endogeneity that could be resulting from reverse causality running from dependent and

Table 4. Correlation matrix for GSOEP variables

	Age	Household size	No children	Education	Life satisfaction	Height	Weight
Age	1						
Household size	−0.4380*	1					
No children	−0.3878*	0.7934*	1				
Education	−0.0892*	0.0089*	0.0355*	1			
Life satisfaction	−0.0631*	0.0670*	0.0460*	0.1370*	1		
Height	−0.2298*	0.0991*	0.0675*	0.1900*	0.0665*	1	
Weight	0.1055*	−0.0102*	−0.0170*	−0.0005	−0.0348*	0.5266*	1
BMI	0.2647*	−0.0748*	−0.0655*	−0.1230*	−0.0835*	−0.0181*	0.8298*
ln Income	−0.1515*	0.4198*	0.1791*	0.3403*	0.2179*	0.1650*	0.0253*
Female	0.0281*	−0.0387*	−0.0055*	−0.0805*	−0.0005	−0.6696*	−0.4832*
Widowed	0.3583*	−0.2648*	−0.1574*	−0.1325*	−0.0471*	−0.1921*	−0.0493*
Divorced	0.0672*	−0.1780*	−0.0936*	−0.0164*	−0.0812*	−0.0260*	−0.0108*
Separated	0.0084*	−0.0850*	−0.0322*	0.0119*	−0.0544*	0.0007	−0.0015
Not Employed	0.2638*	−0.1934*	−0.2561*	−0.2486*	−0.0665*	−0.2079*	−0.0893*
Disabled	0.2815*	−0.1875*	−0.1849*	−0.1025*	−0.1618*	−0.0564*	0.0708*
Political party member	0.1741*	−0.0756*	−0.0641*	0.1989*	0.1021*	0.0663*	0.0634*
Has a second job	−0.0567*	0.0150*	0.0112*	0.0455*	0.0145*	0.0300*	0.0037
German	0.0698*	−0.1210*	−0.1009*	0.1703*	0.0272*	0.0814*	0.0284*

	BMI	ln Income	Female	Widowed	Divorced	Separated	Not Employed
BMI	1						
ln Income	−0.0784*	1					
Female	−0.1447*	−0.0605*	1				
Widowed	0.0656*	−0.2051*	0.1264*	1			
Divorced	0.002	−0.1438*	0.0372*	−0.0551*	1		
Separated	−0.0031	−0.0732*	0.0045*	−0.0268*	−0.0279*	1	
Not employed	0.0332*	−0.2330*	0.0907*	0.2285*	−0.0284*	−0.0259*	1
Disabled	0.1182*	−0.1104*	−0.0277*	0.1092*	0.0371*	0.0093*	0.2117*
Political party member	0.0287*	0.1386*	−0.0789*	0.0228*	−0.0188*	−0.0038	−0.0082*
Has a second job	−0.0144*	0.0288*	−0.0061*	−0.0280*	0.0144*	0.0118*	−0.0799*
German	−0.0209*	0.0495*	0.0076*	0.0438*	0.0176*	−0.0039	−0.0077*

	Disabled	Political party member	Has second job	German
Disabled	1			
Political party member	0.0432*	1		
Has a second job	−0.0269*	0.0177*	1	
German	0.0234*	0.1299*	0.0048	1

Note: *Denotes significance at 5% level.

independent variables. Endogeneity could stem from multiple sources here since happiness influences and is being influenced by a series of factors. In addition to obesity, several other factors included in happiness regressions, i.e. employment status, marital status, income and which arguably have an impact on individual well-being, are at the same time influenced by it. As a consequence, dual causality might run in these types of specifications for more than one variable, in fact it could run for most regressors which are not exogenous by nature (such as age and gender).

In the presence of endogeneity we build the following model:

$$y_{it} = \alpha_i + X'_{it}\beta + u_{it} \qquad (1)$$

Here X is an $n \times K$ matrix of control variables (Frey and Stutzer, 2000; Cornlisse-Vermatt *et al.*, 2006; Blanchflower, 2008), some of which are endogenous and thus $EX'u \neq 0$.

Given the panel structure of our dataset, for all potentially endogenous variables, excluding BMI, we instrument using their first lag. The availability of data for all years, i.e. income, employment status,

Table 5. Correlation matrix for BHPS variables

	Age	Household size	No children	Education	Height	Weight	BMI
Age	1						
Household size	−0.4448	1					
No children	−0.248	0.5744*	1				
Education	0.3231*	−0.0854*	−0.1227*	1			
Height	−0.1569	0.0528*	0.014*	−0.1488*	1		
Weight	0.0183*	0.0129*	0.0327*	−0.0479*	0.4023*	1	
BMI	0.1256*	−0.0265*	0.0134*	0.0554*	−0.2978*	0.7281*	1
Life satisfaction	0.0709*	−0.0278*	−0.0447*	−0.0086	0.0108	−0.0394*	−0.0446*
Female	0.0233*	−0.0176*	0.0317*	0.0556*	−0.5426*	−0.4119*	−0.0701*
Widowed	0.4268*	−0.2946*	−0.1449*	0.2199*	−0.1382*	−0.0998*	−0.0086
Divorced	0.0678*	−0.1277*	−0.0178*	0.0167*	−0.0419*	0.0014	0.0307*
Separated	−0.0125*	−0.0453*	0.0397*	0.007	−0.0159*	0.0004	0.0082
Unemployed	−0.1169*	0.0454*	0.0018	0.0452*	0.0195*	−0.0057	−0.0167*
Disabled	0.1771*	−0.1089*	−0.0605*	0.1368*	−0.0253*	0.0464*	0.0675*
ln Income	0.1984*	−0.1433*	0.1413*	−0.1935*	0.0614*	0.1622*	0.1161*
Has a second job	−0.0976*	0.0561*	0.0105*	−0.1025*	0.0381*	0.0101	−0.0207*
Political party member	0.2346*	−0.1067*	−0.0833*	0.0618*	−0.0107	0.0396*	0.0456*
Smoker	−0.1386*	0.0362*	0.0523*	0.1264*	0.0087	−0.0706*	−0.0731*
Labour union member	−0.0919*	0.0354*	0.0746*	−0.2149*	0.0163*	0.0453*	0.0274*
Saves	−0.0187	−0.0451*	−0.0438*	−0.1716*	0.0215*	0.0038	−0.0117
House owner	0.0912*	0.0685*	−0.0017	−0.1913*	0.0507*	0.0353*	−0.0043

	Life satisfaction	Female	Widowed	Divorced	Separated	Unemployed	Disabled
Life Satisfaction	1						
Female	−0.0093	1					
Widowed	0.0166*	0.1236*	1				
Divorced	−0.0928	0.0563*	−0.0842*	1			
Separated	−0.0649	0.022*	−0.0416*	−0.0428*	1		
Unemployed	−0.0841	−0.0443*	−0.0449*	0.0115*	0.0236*	1	
Disabled	−0.1683*	0.0072	0.1001*	0.0615*	0.0094*	−0.0295*	1
Ln Income	−0.0124	−0.1207*	0.0325*	0.0686*	0.0412*	−0.1133*	0.0004
Has a second job	0.0031	0.0011	−0.0551*	0.0074	−0.0056	−0.0066	−0.0599*
Political party member	0.0267*	−0.0259*	0.0843*	−0.0090*	−0.0180*	−0.0407*	0.0048
Smoker	−0.1337*	−0.0039	−0.0524*	0.0929*	0.0666*	0.1158*	0.0613*
Labour union member	0.0094*	0.0224*	−0.0964*	0.0225*	0.0113*	−0.0738*	−0.0993*
Saves	0.0945*	0.002	−0.0240*	−0.0233*	−0.0254*	−0.0984*	−0.0706*
House owner	0.1262*	−0.0308*	−0.0389*	−0.0895*	−0.0641*	−0.1232*	−0.1269*

	ln Income	Has Second Job	Political party member	Smoker	Labour union member	Saves	House owner
ln Income	1						
Has a second job	−0.0424	1					
Political party member	0.0764*	−0.0135*	1				
Smoker	−0.0032	−0.0031	−0.0529*	1			
Labour union member	0.2040*	0.0339*	0.0152*	−0.0361*	1		
Saves	0.1505*	0.0405*	0.0402*	−0.1051*	0.1622*	1	
House owner	0.0952*	0.0391*	0.0788*	−0.1835*	0.1378*	0.1670*	1

Note: *Denotes significance at 5% level.

marital status, etc., makes the use of lags as Instrumental Variables (IVs) are the best option. Following the existing theory (Cameron and Trivedi, 2009) lags of endogenous variables can offer consistent estimators of the coefficients of interest when they serve as excluded instruments and are exogenous by nature.

For BMI the instrument of choice is individual height. BMI is correlated with the instrument by definition since height is used in the construction

Table 6. Correlation matrix for Australian variables

	Age	Household size	No children	Education	Life satisfaction	Height	Weight
Age	1						
Household size	−0.3244*	1					
No children	−0.1221*	0.7610*	1				
Education	−0.1421*	0.0273*	−0.0693*	1			
Life satisfaction	0.0623*	0.0237*	−0.0104*	−0.0453*	1		
Height	−0.1473*	0.0442*	0.0103	0.0827*	−0.01	1	
Weight	0.0698*	0.0039	0.0380*	−0.0063	−0.0350*	0.4728*	1
BMI	0.1675*	−0.0216*	0.0279*	−0.0483*	−0.0335*	−0.0731*	0.8314*
ln Income	−0.2022*	0.1604*	−0.0986*	0.2714*	0.0498*	0.0643*	0.0230*
Female	0.0284*	−0.0212*	0.0100*	−0.0281*	0.0250*	−0.6629*	−0.3986*
Single	−0.5084*	−0.0787*	−0.1751*	−0.0429*	−0.0353*	0.0890*	−0.1085*
Widowed	0.3776*	−0.2125*	−0.0878*	−0.1555*	0.0405*	−0.1449*	−0.0676*
Divorced	0.1353*	−0.1736*	−0.0575*	−0.0258*	−0.0804*	−0.0558*	0.003
Separated	0.0419*	0.0967*	−0.0164*	−0.0048	−0.0935*	−0.0093	0.0126*
Not employed	0.3009*	0.1431*	0.1070*	−0.1721*	0.0407*	−0.1327*	−0.0640*
Disabled	0.3188*	−0.1988*	−0.1197*	−0.1732*	−0.1582*	−0.0751*	0.0586*

	BMI	ln Income	Female	Single	Widowed	Divorced	Separated
BMI	1						
ln Income	0.0012	1					
Female	−0.0570*	−0.0489*	1				
Single	−0.1721*	−0.0488*	−0.0398*	1			
Widowed	0.0132*	−0.1686*	0.1284*	−0.1018*	1		
Divorced	0.0352*	−0.0761*	0.0507*	−0.1140*	−0.0490*	1	
Separated	0.0160*	−0.0333*	0.0126*	−0.0735*	−0.0316*	−0.0354*	1
Not employed	0.0157*	0.1530*	0.0305*	−0.1963*	0.1011*	−0.0672*	−0.0464*
Disabled	0.1097*	−0.2413*	0.0304*	−0.0346*	0.1901*	0.1083*	0.0393*

	Not employed	Disabled
Not employed	1	
Disabled	0.0719*	1

Note: *Denotes significance at 5% level.

of BMI. Hence the first IV assumption, $cov(Z, y_2) \neq 0$, where Z is the IV and y_2 is BMI, holds. The second critical assumption is that $EZ'u = 0$. In order to provide necessary and appropriate justification that the instrument of choice serves the second assumption too, we test whether it is uncorrelated with the error term u in the main equation. The correlation results show that the second critical assumption for consistent IV, that is $EZ'u = 0$, holds.

Recent literature analysing the relationship between height and happiness cannot be neglected at this point. The findings of Deaton and Arora (2009) reveal a positive relationship between height and happiness levels. However, after controlling for income this relationship is not statistically different from zero. The effect captured in this case is the one of height on wages, and thus indirectly on happiness, and not a direct effect of height on happiness. For this reason we argue that, both intuitively and statistically, height is exogenous to happiness and thus can be used to instrument for BMI in the main equation.

IV. Results

Results for Germany

All results for Germany are shown in Table 7. Below, we analyse only the IV results (*IVREG1* through *IVREG7*). Ordinary Least Square (OLS) results are presented in columns 1 and 2. The regression results for Germany point to a clear negative and statistically significant relationship between obesity and happiness. Under all specifications, *IVREG1* to *IVREG6* in Table 7, the coefficient on BMI is in the range (−0.0729, −0.0797), significant at the 1% level. Given the size of the coefficient and its robustness in the different specifications used, one can conclude that

Table 7. Regression results for Germany

Independent variable	OLS1	OLS2	IVREG1	IVREG2	IVREG3	IVREG4	IVREG5	IVREG6	IVREG7
Age	−0.0164 (−7.11)	−0.0149 (−5.62)	0.0068 (1.22)	0.0071 (1.41)	−0.0034 (−0.45)	−0.0086 (−1.15)	−0.0111 (−1.20)	−0.0102 (−1.30)	−0.0114 (−1.30)
Age^2	0.000 (2.03)	0.0001 (2.85)	−0.0001 (−2.46)	−0.0001 (−2.01)	0.00 (0.59)	0.0001 (1.22)	0.0001 (1.07)	0.0001 (1.11)	0.0001 (1.09)
Female	0.0077 (0.46)	−0.0335 (−1.83)	−0.1132 (−3.39)	−0.1309 (−5.21)	−0.0874 (−3.16)	−0.0915 (−2.93)	−0.0678 (−1.95)	−0.0688 (−2.35)	−0.0726 (−2.75)
BMI		−0.0141 (−6.58)	−0.0776 (−4.44)	−0.0797 (−5.29)	−0.0739 (−4.98)	−0.0733 (−4.07)	−0.0728 (−3.81)	−0.074 (−4.38)	−0.0619 (−4.12)
Disabled				−0.5352 (−13.2)	−0.5667 (−13.32)	−0.5889 (−15.9)	−0.6031 (−14.31)	−0.599 (−15.39)	−0.5985 (−15.55)
ln Income					0.3232 (7.69)	0.4557 (8.29)	0.4166 (7.13)	0.4127 (7.63)	0.4208 (7.89)
Education					0.0472 (9.58)	0.0353 (5.41)	0.0238 (4.28)	0.0249 (4.94)	0.0316 (6.36)
Separated					−0.1277 (−1.60)	−0.1886 (−1.94)	−0.2155 (−1.85)	−0.2127 (−1.66)	−0.2263 (−1.66)
Widowed					0.0965 (1.74)	0.02 (0.36)	0.017 (0.27)	0.0227 (0.36)	0.0582 (0.90)
Single					−0.1182 (−3.26)	−0.1423 (−3.94)	−0.1543 (−3.94)	−0.1503 (−4.07)	−0.1443 (−4.04)
Divorced					−0.2438 (−5.16)	−0.294 (−5.99)	−0.2993 (−6.04)	−0.2954 (−5.09)	−0.2603 (−4.57)
Not employed					0.0199 (0.57)	0.0534 (1.66)	0.0435 (1.05)	0.0441 (1.19)	0.0418 (0.97)
No children						0.0935 (5.30)	0.0852 (5.07)	0.084 (4.33)	0.0873 (4.25)
Household size						−0.1188 (−4.91)	−0.1052 (−4.60)	−0.1041 (−4.69)	−0.1067 (−4.79)
Second job							0.2368 (1.51)	0.2379 (1.79)	0.226 (1.52)
Politics							0.3678 (8.75)	0.3707 (8.89)	0.2973 (5.20)
German								−0.0641 (−1.43)	−0.1006 (−1.97)
Constant	7.63 (151.65)	7.83 (112.36)	8.96 (27.43)	8.99 (32.58)	5.06 (9.06)	4.25 (6.99)	4.66 (6.22)	4.76 (6.93)	4.49 (7.43)
Religion dummies	No	No	No	No	No	No	No	No	Yes
N	165 630	82 466	82 466	82 423	70 287	70 287	70 247	70 247	65 338
R^2									
Within	0.0103	0.0007	0.000	0.0001	0.0005	0.0008	0.0014	0.0013	0.0017
Between	0.0089	0.121	0.0121	0.0285	0.0778	0.0868	0.094	0.0929	0.121
Overall	0.0044	0.0075	0.0078	0.0194	0.0555	0.0624	0.0668	0.066	0.081
Wald χ^2	692.63	377.55	349.34	614.08	1339.96	1549.52	1866.61	2366.19	2455.42
p-value	0.000	0.000	0.000	0.000	0.000	0.000	0.000	0.000	0.000

Note: Robust *t*-statistics are given in parentheses.

higher levels of BMI are associated with lower levels of self-reported life satisfaction.

Regarding the rest of the explanatory variables, females report to be less 'satisfied' with life compared to men. All results on gender are statistically significant at the 5% or 1% levels. As expected, disability reduces life-satisfaction by approximately 0.5 units under all specifications. This result is statistically significant at the 1% level. Income is associated with higher levels of happiness. The coefficient on income suggests that individuals with 20% higher income report life-satisfaction levels one unit higher than others, *ceteris paribus*. Educational attainment is positively associated with individual well-being. The sign of the coefficient is consistently positive and significant at the 1% level across specifications.

The size varies in the range between 0.0238 and 0.0472. With respect to marital status, only being single or being divorced appears to be statistically different from 0. In agreement with intuition, as well as past research, the number of children increases life-satisfaction. One additional child in the family appears to be associated approximately with a 0.09 unit increase in the self-reported happiness levels. These results are significant at the 1% level across all specifications. Individuals who live in 'crowded' homes seem to suffer a loss in their well being, equivalent to almost 0.1 of a unit, for every additional person added to the household. Agents who report to be members of a political party, report self-satisfaction levels approximately 0.3 units higher than those who report the opposite.

Results for the UK

Regressions output for Britain are shown in Table 8. Columns *IVREG1* to *IVREG7* present the instrument variable regression results.

The coefficient on BMI has the expected sign. However, except for *IVREG1*, the results across specifications are not statistically significant. Life satisfaction is decreasing with age, at an increasing rate. The results on age are all significant. Disability status appears to decrease the life satisfaction by 1 whole unit, under all specifications, a result that is significant at less than 1% level. Surprisingly, the coefficient on income is negative. However, across specifications *IVREG3* to *IVREG6* this result is not statistically significant. The results regarding the relationship between education and happiness are not robust. For the most part, they are not statistically significant, leading to no-single firm conclusion. Being separated, widowed or divorced are all received as negative shocks to individual life satisfaction. Similar to the German results, being divorced or separated appears to have the most severe negative impact on personal well-being, among different marital statuses. All marital status results are statistically significant. Smoking appears to negatively affect the well-being. In particular, under specifications *IVREG5*, *IVREG6* and *IVREG7*, the coefficient ranges between –0.22 and –0.28, significant at the 1% level. Regarding financial information, our findings indicate that people who save and people who own their own home are happier, *ceteris paribus*.

Results for Australia

The Australian regression results are presented in Table 9. Here, like in the German data, the regression analysis reveals a negative and highly statistically significant relationship between BMI and self-reported life satisfaction. In particular, in the multivariate IV specifications *IVREG4* to *IVREG7* the coefficient on BMI is approximately –0.04 at the 1% level of significance. Older age decreases the well-being, at an increasing rate. Disability is found to lower life satisfaction slightly more than half a unit, on the 0–10 scale. These findings are highly statistically significant. As expected, income is associated with higher levels of individual happiness. Individuals with 10% higher income are expected to report higher levels of life satisfaction of approximately 0.3 units. Educational attainment has a negative and statistically significant coefficient. Individuals with more years of education are expected to report a 0.04 lower happiness levels for every extra year of education they have acquired. With respect to marital status, individuals who are single, separated, widowed or divorced are expected to report lower self satisfaction levels than married ones, *ceteris paribus*. Once again, the most severe effect appears to come from being separated, where the coefficient is close to –0.85 under all specifications. The number of children in the Australian regressions does not exhibit statistically significant results, unlike the German and the British regressions. On the contrary, the size of the household is negatively related with individual self-reported life satisfaction levels. In particular, an one member difference in the size of a household is expected to result in a 0.07 difference in the individual happiness levels. The results are significant at the 1% level.

V. Conclusions

This study investigates the impact of obesity on individual happiness using panel analysis for Germany, the UK and Australia. The contribution to the literature is three fold: first, to our knowledge, this is the first study to explore the panel dimension of the existing data in the investigation of the addressed research question. Second, this is the first study that examines the Australian data to identify the possible relationship between obesity and happiness. In addition, this study addresses the potential endogeneity problems that arise from most variables included in the specifications used, as a result of reverse causality. These endogeneity issues are tackled using the panel elements of the data which offer the necessary exogenous instruments. Last, but not least, we identify other significant determinants of life satisfaction and discuss them.

Table 8. Regression results for Britain

Independent variable	OLS1	OLS2	IVREG1	IVREG2	IVREG3	IVREG4	IVREG5	IVREG6	IVREG7
Age	−0.0225 (−10.11)	−0.0174 (6.32)	−0.0182 (−6.64)	−0.0107 (−4.00)	−0.0078 (−1.88)	−0.0067 (−1.54)	−0.0063 (−1.74)	−0.0111 (−2.92)	−0.0111 (−3.06)
Age^2	0.0002 (11.97)	0.0002 (8.45)	0.0002 (8.20)	0.0002 (5.85)	0.0001 (3.53)	0.0001 (2.84)	0.0001 (2.83)	0.0002 (4.08)	0.0002 (4.10)
Female	−0.032 (−1.98)	−0.041 (−2.09)	−0.0391 (−1.65)	−0.0384 (−1.75)	−0.0202 (−1.01)	−0.0162 (−0.76)	−0.0266 (−1.49)	−0.0201 (−0.78)	−0.0262 (−1.06)
BMI		−0.007 (−5.30)	−0.0055 (−1.96)	−0.004 (−1.36)	−0.0038 (−1.29)	−0.0036 (−1.41)	−0.0042 (−1.75)	−0.0026 (−0.82)	−0.0028 (−0.82)
Disabled				−1.055 (−18.09)	−1.0458 (−16.26)	−1.0533 (−18.46)	−1.0352 (−16.84)	−0.9978 (−16.32)	−1.0018 (−12.85)
ln Income					−0.0116 (−1.04)	−0.0083 (−0.72)	−0.0105 (−0.87)	−0.0179 (−1.43)	−0.0194 (−1.81)
Education					−0.0024 (−1.00)	−0.002 (−0.90)	0.0032 (1.16)	0.0078 (2.47)	0.0072 (2.97)
Separated					−0.3256 (−2.94)	−0.3261 (−2.82)	−0.2626 (−1.95)	−0.2998 (−2.47)	−0.3094 (−2.79)
Widowed					−0.2042 (−4.60)	−0.2025 (−3.20)	−0.1838 (−3.32)	−0.1944 (−3.89)	−0.1971 (−3.93)
Divorced					−0.37 (−7.75)	−0.377 (−8.21)	−0.33 (−6.48)	−0.282 (−6.43)	−0.264 (−5.92)
Unemployed					−0.833 (−3.76)	−0.842 (−3.44)	−1.109 (−4.28)	−0.469 (−2.20)	−0.459 (−1.96)
No children						−0.032 (−2.29)	−0.0348 (−2.65)	−0.0171 (−1.56)	−0.0203 (−1.85)
Household size						−0.003 (−0.31)			
Smoker							−0.28 (−9.03)	−0.232 (−7.73)	−0.218 (−6.55)
Union								−0.049 (−1.59)	−0.053 (−1.42)
Second job								−0.002 (−0.04)	−0.018 (−0.22)
Politics								0.004 (0.05)	0.001 (0.01)
Saves								0.322 (7.87)	0.315 (7.16)
Home owner								0.181 (6.13)	0.191 (6.15)
Constant	5.59 (110.90)	5.69 (83.28)	5.64 (69.46)	5.48 (60.14)	5.59 (43.94)	5.57 (43.54)	5.65 (45.04)	5.40 (33.79)	5.49 (44.87)
Religion dummies	No	No	No	No	No	No	No	No	Yes
N	43 504	22 390	22 390	22 390	20 550	20 550	20 550	20 550	20 154
R^2									
Within	0.000	0.0001	0.0001	0.0032	0.0047	0.0046	0.0042	0.0041	0.0041
Between	0.0119	0.0134	0.0131	0.0586	0.0785	0.0792	0.0843	0.0958	0.098
Overall	0.0105	0.0141	0.0139	0.0532	0.0703	0.0708	0.0741	0.0842	0.0863
Wald χ^2	209.80	205.07	126.39	491.24	470.69	616.49	1131.16	1320.17	1420.62
p-value	0.000	0.000	0.000	0.000	0.000	0.000	0.000	0.000	0.000

Note: Robust *t*-statistics are given in parentheses.

For Germany and Australia, BMI has a negative and statistically significant relationship with self-reported life satisfaction levels. For Britain, although the coefficient on BMI is negative in all specifications, the results are not statistically different from 0. The findings across specifications for all three countries point to some common conclusions. First, disability severely damages individual happiness more than any other individual characteristic. Second, being separated or divorced (compared to

Table 9. Regression results for Australia

Independent Variable	OLS1	OLS2	IVREG1	IVREG2	IVREG3	IVREG4	IVREG5	IVREG6	IVREG7
Age	−0.042	−0.044	−0.033	−0.034	−0.034	−0.037	−0.036	−0.036	−0.039
	(−13.26)	(−17.78)	(−7.82)	(−8.10)	(−5.85)	(−3.94)	(−4.31)	(−4.23)	(−5.52)
Age^2	0.0005	0.0005	0.0004	0.0005	0.0005	0.0005	0.005	0.0005	0.0005
	(15.54)	(19.5)	(11.01)	(11.55)	(8.41)	(5.37)	(6.11)	(5.99)	(6.98)
Female	0.044	0.058	0.036	0.036	0.063	0.062	0.061	0.060	0.069
	(1.87)	(2.91)	(1.64)	(1.59)	(2.49)	(2.45)	(1.89)	(2.64)	(2.55)
BMI		−0.005	−0.03	−0.0306	−0.0439	−0.0409	−0.0412	−0.0412	−0.037
		(−2.27)	(−2.74)	(−2.66)	(−3.04)	(−2.16)	(−2.53)	(−2.10)	(−2.21)
Disabled				−0.570	−0.524	−0.533	−0.531	−0.531	−0.534
				(−15.8)	(−12.46)	(−8.41)	(−11.19)	(−9.65)	(−8.59)
ln Income					0.232	0.326	0.311	0.311	0.349
					(3.52)	(2.13)	(2.76)	(3.28)	(2.53)
Education					−0.036	−0.041	−0.041	−0.040	0.034
					(−6.73)	(−4.76)	(−5.57)	(−6.33)	(−4.03)
Single					−0.241	−0.271	−0.283	−0.282	−0.260
					(−4.55)	(−5.13)	(−5.30)	(−5.54)	(−5.35)
Separated					−0.826	−0.875	−0.853	−0.853	−0.850
					(−4.99)	(−6.28)	(−5.47)	(−5.47)	(−5.03)
Widowed					−0.198	−0.241	−0.214	−0.214	−0.189
					(−2.46)	(−2.56)	(−2.38)	(−2.57)	(−2.14)
Divorced					−0.326	−0.372	−0.358	−0.358	−0.327
					(−3.95)	(−5.64)	(−4.78)	(−5.42)	(−4.26)
Not employed					0.132	0.2135	0.221	0.221	0.217
					(1.60)	(1.78)	(2.31)	(2.34)	(1.69)
No children						0.053			
						(0.97)			
Household size						−0.104	−0.068	−0.068	−0.074
						(−1.47)	(−2.35)	(−2.78)	(−2.16)
Constant	8.68	8.63	9.21	9.20	7.47	6.77	6.86	6.86	6.29
	(112.19)	(161.2)	(38.84)	(37.64)	(8.44)	(4.14)	(5.46)	(5.67)	(4.02)
Regional dummies	No	No	No	No	No	No	No	No	Yes
N	51 209	21 887	21 887	21 887	19 739	19 739	19 739	19 739	19 739
R^2									
Within	0.000	0.003	0.0013	0.0013	0.0045	0.0047	0.0048	0.0048	0.0047
Between	0.0283	0.0267	0.0583	0.0583	0.0708	0.0697	0.0695	0.0696	0.0777
Overall	0.0212	0.0253	0.0495	0.0495	0.0619	0.0614	0.0614	0.0614	0.0677
F		105.23		29.7873					
Wald χ^2	427.15	352.09	714.41	1053.32	882.29	839.96	1089.32	1104.06	1574.61
p-value	0.0000	0.0000	0.0000	0.0000	0.0000	0.0000	0.0000	0.0000	0.0000

Note: Robust *t*-statistics are given in parentheses.

being married) reduces well-being at a statistically significant level. Other results indicate that for Germany and Australia income is positively associated with happiness, as expected. For education, the results are mixed: for Australia the relationship is negative and significant, whereas for Germany the opposite holds. For Britain, house ownership and saving habits appear to be beneficial for individual happiness whereas smoking impairs well-being. Household size, measured as number of people living in a household, decreases life satisfaction at a statistically significant level, both in Germany and Britain. In Australia, females appear to be happier

whereas in Germany they are found to be less happy compared to males.

Disclaimer

This article uses unit record data from the HILDA Survey. The HILDA Project was initiated and is funded by the Australian Government Department of Families, Housing, Community Services and Indigenous Affairs (FaHCSIA) and is managed by the Melbourne Institute of Applied Economic and

Social Research (Melbourne Institute). The findings and views reported in this article, however, are those of the author and should not be attributed to either FaHCSIA or the Melbourne Institute.

The data used in this publication was made available to us by the GSOEP at the German Institute for Economic Research (DIW Berlin), Berlin.

Acknowledgements

A special thanks goes out to Dennis Heffley, Christian Zimmermann, Philip Shaw and Osiris Parcero as well as the anonymous referee for their valuable comments.

References

Blanchflower, D. G. (2008) International evidence on well-being, IZA Discussion Paper No. 3354, Institute for the Study of Labor (IZA).

Cameron, C. and Trivedi, P. (2009) *Microeconometrics Using Stata*, 1st edn, Stata Press, College Station, TX.

Cornlisse-Vermatt, J. R., Antonides, G., Ophem, J. V. and den Brink, H. M. V. (2006) Body mass index, perceived health, and happiness: their determinants and structural relationships, *Social Indicators Research*, **79**, 143–58.

Deaton, A. and Arora, R. (2009) Life at to top: the benefits of height, NBER Working Paper No. 15090. Available at http://ideas.repec.org/p/nbr/nberwo/15090.html (accessed 25 May 2011).

Frey, B. and Stutzer, A. (2000) Maximising happiness?, *German Economic Review*, **1**, 145–67.

Frey, B. and Stutzer, A. (2005) Happiness research: state and prospects, *Review of Social Economy*, **62**, 207–28.

Greeno, C., Jackson, C., Williams, E. and Fortmann, S. (1998) The effect of perceived control over eating on the life satisfaction of women and men: results from a community sample, *International Journal of Eating Disorders*, **24**, 415–19.

Kahneman, D., Diener, E. and Schwarz, N. (1999) *Well-being: The Foundations of Hedonic Psychology*, Russel Sage Foundation, New York.

Larsson, U., Karlsson, J. and Sullivan, M. (2002) Impact of overweight and obesity on health-related quality of life – a Swedish population study, *International Journal Obesity*, **26**, 417–24.

Needham, B. and Crosnoe, R. (2005) Overweight status and depressive symptoms during adolescence, *Journal of Adolescent Health*, **36**, 48–55.

Noppa, H. and Hällström, T. (1981) Weight gain in adulthood in relation to socioeconomic factors, mental illness, and personality traits: a prospective study of middle-aged women, *Journal of Psychosomatic Research*, **25**, 83–9.

Oswald, A. and Powdthavee, N. (2007) Obesity, unhappiness, and the challenge of affluence: theory and evidence, *Economic Journal*, **117**, F441–59.

Palinkas, L., Wingard, D. and Barrett-Connor, E. (1996) Depressive symptoms in overweight and obese older adults: a test of the 'jolly fat' hypothesis, *Journal of Psychosomatic Research*, **40**, 56–60.

Reed, D. (1985) The relationship between obesity and psychological general well-being in United States women, *Journal of Psychosomatic Research (Abstract)*, **46**, 3791.

Roberts, R., Kaplan, G., Shema, S. and Strawbridge, W. (2000) Are the obese at greater risk of depression?, *American Journal of Epidemiology*, **152**, 163–70.

Stutzer, A. (2007) Limited self-control, obesity and the loss of happiness, IZA Discussion Paper No. 2925, Institute for the Study of Labor (IZA).

Veenhoven, R. (1996) Happy life-expectancy, *Social Indicators Research*, **39**, 1–58.

The relationship between childhood obesity and food insecurity: a nonparametric analysis

Oluyemisi Kuku[a], Steven Garasky[a] and Craig Gundersen[b]

[a]*Department of Human Development and Family Studies, Iowa State University, 4380 Palmer Building, Room 2330, Ames, IA 50011, USA*
[b]*Department of Agricultural and Consumer Economics, University of Illinois, 324 Mumford Hall, 1301 West Gregory Dr, Urbana, IL 61801-3605, USA*

Childhood obesity and food insecurity are major public health concerns in the United States and other developed countries. Research on the relationship between the two has provided mixed results across a variety of data sets and empirical methods. Common throughout this research, however, is the use of parametric frameworks for empirical analyses. This study moves beyond parametric methods by examining the relationship between childhood obesity and food insecurity among low-income children with nonparametric regression techniques. We examine data from the Child Development Supplement (CDS) of the Panel Study of Income Dynamics (PSID), a nationally representative data set from the US. Consistent with recent work, our parametric analyses indicate that there is no statistically significant relationship between childhood obesity and food insecurity. In contrast, our nonparametric results indicate that the probability of being obese varies markedly with the level of food insecurity being experienced by the child. Moreover, this relationship differs across relevant subgroups including those defined by gender, race/ethnicity and income. Fully understanding the relationship between childhood obesity and food insecurity has significant policy implications.

I. Introduction

Childhood obesity is a major public health concern in most developed countries throughout the world (Koplan *et al.*, 2005). In the US, the problem is especially severe as recent estimates indicate that one-in-three (31.9%) US children are considered overweight or obese (Ogden *et al.*, 2008). In addition to energy imbalance and genetic factors, environmental factors such as the availability of food, social interactions and stress also cause a predisposition to obesity (Ebbeling *et al.*, 2002; Costa-Font and Gil, 2004; Krebs *et al.*, 2007; Gundersen *et al.*, 2008; Garasky *et al.*, 2009; Lohman *et al.*, 2009).

Another US public health concern is food insecurity. Over one-in-five (22.5%) children in the US lives in a food insecure household, where food insecurity is defined as the uncertainty of having, or the inability to acquire, enough food for all household members to sustain active, healthy living because of insufficient money or other resources (Nord *et al.*, 2009). As with obesity, food insecurity has been shown to lead to a plethora of medical problems for children (e.g. Cook *et al.*, 2004; Slack and Yoo, 2005; Daniels, 2006; Skalicky *et al.*, 2006; Whitaker *et al.*, 2006).

Research on the relationship between childhood obesity and food insecurity has provided mixed results.[1] Some studies have found a positive relationship (e.g. Jyoti *et al.*, 2005; Casey *et al.*, 2006; Dubois *et al.*, 2006), others have found no relationship (e.g. Martin and Ferris, 2007; Bhargava *et al.*, 2008; Gundersen *et al.*, 2008, 2009) and others have found a negative relationship (e.g. Matheson *et al.*, 2002; Jimenez-Cruz *et al.*, 2003; Rose and Bodor, 2006). These studies have used a variety of data sets and empirical methods, but common to each is the use of parametric frameworks to examine the relationship.

This study moves beyond parametric methods by examining the relationship between childhood obesity and food insecurity among low-income children with nonparametric regression techniques. These analyses use data from the Child Development Supplement (CDS) of the Panel Study of Income Dynamics (PSID), a nationally representative data set from the US. Our parametric results are consistent with the work noted above that found no relationship between childhood obesity and food insecurity. The relationship is insignificant for all children in the study sample and for subgroups based on gender, race/ethnicity and poverty status. In contrast, our nonparametric results tell a much different story. In particular, our results indicate that parametric methods overlook the marked changes that occur in the probability of being obese as food insecurity levels increase. Moreover, these changes vary across gender, race/ethnicity and poverty status.

II. Background

Childhood obesity has increased dramatically in the United States in recent decades (Ogden *et al.*, 2008). For example, obesity prevalence among children aged 6–11 increased from 4% between 1963 and 1974, to 15.3% by 1999 to 2000. The trend was very similar for children aged 12–19 with obesity prevalence increasing from 6.1% in the early 1970s, to 15.5% in 1999–2000. There are significant differences in obesity rates by race, ethnicity and gender as well. Between 2003 and 2006, about 10% of white children were considered obese, compared to 15% of black children and 15.5% of Hispanic children. During the same period, boys (12.2%) had higher rates of obesity than girls (10.5%).

Regarding current trends in food insecurity in the US, in 2008, children (22.5%) were more likely to be food insecure than adults (14.4%), while households with children reported being food insecure at nearly double the rate of households without children (21.0% versus 11.3%). In addition, households headed by a black non-Hispanic person (25.7%) or a Hispanic person (26.9%) reported higher rates of food insecurity relative to households headed by a white non-Hispanic person (10.7%). Children living in poverty had a substantially higher food insecurity rate (51.5%) compared to all children (22.5%) and children in households with income greater than 185% of the poverty line (9.8%) (Nord *et al.*, 2009).

Obesity and food insecurity have immediate and long-term health consequences for children. Childhood obesity has been associated with metabolic disorders such as insulin resistance, the metabolic syndrome, dyslipidemia (abnormal levels of fat in the blood), type 2 diabetes mellitus (e.g. Klein *et al.*, 2004; Daniels, 2006), insulin resistance syndrome (e.g. Ebbeling *et al.*, 2002; Srinivasan *et al.*, 2002), sleep apnea (e.g. Patel, 2005) and asthma (e.g. Figueroa-Munoz *et al.*, 2001). Food insecurity has been shown to lead to a range of medical problems for children as well, including frequent stomach aches and headaches (Alaimo *et al.*, 2001b), increased odds of being hospitalized (Cook *et al.*, 2004), greater propensities to have seen a psychologist (Alaimo *et al.*, 2001a) and higher levels of iron deficiency with anaemia (Skalicky *et al.*, 2006).

On the surface, one might imagine that childhood obesity and food insecurity would be inversely related insofar as reductions in food intake would be expected to lead to reductions in weight. Clearly, in the extreme, low food intake will lead to a decline in weight as is seen in developing countries. Dietz (1995), however, pondered a positive relationship after having observed the paradox of hunger and obesity coexisting in the same individual. Some have ascribed this paradox among children to a range of

---

[1] Despite studies in other countries about the effects of various factors on childhood obesity (e.g. Abdulai, 2010) and the relationship between obesity and other health outcomes (e.g. Bastida and Soydemir, 2009), the literature examining the connection between food insecurity and childhood obesity has almost always used data from the United States.

factors including overconsumption of cheaper, energy-dense foods (Drewnowski and Specter, 2004), overeating during times when food is more plentiful (Scheier, 2005), metabolic changes to ensure a more efficient use of energy (Alaimo et al., 2001a), different standards of what constitutes an adequate diet (Gundersen and Ribar, 2005), parents overprotecting their children by giving them more food than needed when food is available (McIntyre et al., 2003) and mothers being food insecure during pregnancy (Laraia et al., 2006). Overall, however, as noted above, evidence regarding the relationship between food insecurity and childhood obesity is mixed.

III. Methodology

Consistent across the literature examining the relationship between food insecurity and childhood obesity is the use of parametric frameworks (e.g. regression models). Parametric models require the function $f(\cdot)$ relating the response to the predictors to be specified in advance. These models are estimated to assess the parameters of the relationship (e.g. regression coefficients). In contrast, nonparametric regression techniques estimate the function $f(\cdot)$ directly, allowing the data to define the relationship between x and y (Fox, 2002; Hastie et al., 2009). Nonparametric models offer an important flexible alternative to parametric frameworks when parametric modelling assumptions may be invalid or data are limited (e.g. Mukhopadhyay and Marsh, 2006; Ozaki et al., 2008; Kim et al., 2009).

Additionally, all of the work discussed above employs a binary measure of food insecurity. Implicit with the use of a binary measure is an assumption that the effect of being food insecure is the same for all food insecure children (conditional on relevant covariates) and the effect of being food secure is the same for all food secure children. This assumption is unlikely to hold. In this article, we estimate nonparametric models using a continuous measure of food insecurity in an effort to shed new light on the relationship between food insecurity and childhood obesity.

Nonparametric regression

Most methods of nonparametric regression implicitly assume that $f(\cdot)$ is a smooth, continuous function (Fox, 2000). While many methods of nonparametric regression exist, we employ Locally Weighted Scatterplot Smoothing (LOWESS). LOWESS can be described as a series of overlapping locally weighted regressions (Di Matteo, 2003; Hastie et al., 2009). For any given i, we estimate a linear regression with a fraction of the data around i called the local neighbourhood. Local weighted regression estimation builds upon kernel estimation (locally weighted averaging) techniques which give greater weight to observations that are closer to a focal i and less weight to more remote observations (Statacorp, 2007; Hastie et al., 2009). The weights for each observation j in a local neighbourhood where $j = i_-, \ldots, i_+$ are defined as follows:

$$W_j = \left\{ 1 - \frac{|FI_j - FI_i|^3}{1001 \times \max(FI_{i+} - FI_i, FI_i - FI_{i-})} \right\}^3 \tag{1}$$

The size of the local neighbourhood is referred to as the *bandwidth*. The number of neighbouring observations used to estimate the locally weighted regression is based on the selected bandwidth such that observations $i_- = \max(1, i - k)$ to $i_+ = \min(i + k, N)$ around a focal i are used where

$$k = \frac{N \times bandwidth - 0.5}{2} \tag{2}$$

Choosing an optimal bandwidth requires balancing two statistical issues – bias and variability (Grogger, 2007; Hastie et al., 2009). The bias of the estimate is the difference between the conditional population mean of the estimate at a focal $i(\mu \mid f_i)$ and the estimator $E(\mu|f_i)$. Regarding variability, a narrow bandwidth results in relatively less data contributing to each estimation of the regression, producing potentially greater variability in results (Fox, 2000). A narrow bandwidth also increases the likelihood of an invalid observation for a focal i resulting from a lack of sufficient variability within the bandwidth to estimate the regression, particularly in cases in which measures are categorical. Thus, while a narrow bandwidth reduces bias, it leads to greater variability. The opposite occurs with a bandwidth that is too wide – the variability of the estimate is minimized, but bias is increased.

In this study, the general form of the relationship between the probability of a child being obese (OB) and his or her food insecurity status (FI) is expressed as

$$OB_i = f(FI_i) + \varepsilon_i \tag{3}$$

where i is a child, OB and FI are measured as described below and ε is an error term. Observations are ordered by FI values such that

$$FI_i \leq FI_{i+1} \quad \text{for } i = 1, \ldots, N - 1 \tag{4}$$

where N is the number of children in the sample. Observations with equal FI values are randomly ordered. For each observation i, a predicted value of OB (OB_i') is calculated with coefficients derived from a LOWESS estimation of (3) using observations from the local neighbourhood. Specifically,

$$OB_i' = a' + b'(FI_i) \qquad (5)$$

Balancing bias and variability in practical terms means choosing a bandwidth that minimizes the Mean Squared Error (MSE) of the estimator (Fox, 2000). The MSE of the estimator for a focal i can be defined as

$$MSE\left(O\hat{B}|FI_i\right) = E\left[\left(O\hat{B}|FI_i - \mu|FI_i\right)^2\right] \qquad (6)$$

where the right-hand side is the sum of the variance and squared bias (Fox, 2000). For this study, $MSE = \frac{1}{N}\sum_{i=1}^{N} e_i^2$; where $e_i = OB_i - O\hat{B}_i$.

Parametric regressions

We compare our nonparametric results with standard parametric models of the relationship between food insecurity status and child weight status that have been estimated in the literature. More specifically, we estimate the following two models:

$$P(OB_i = 1|BFI, \mathbf{X}) = \Phi(\alpha + \beta BFI_i + \lambda \mathbf{X}_i + \varepsilon_i) \qquad (7)$$

and

$$P(OB_i = 1|CFI, \mathbf{X}) = \Phi(\alpha + \beta CFI_i + \lambda \mathbf{X}_i + \varepsilon_i) \qquad (8)$$

where OB is as described above; Φ is the standard cumulative normal probability distribution; BFI is a binary measure of food insecurity (=1 if food insecure; 0 otherwise); CFI is a continuous measure of food insecurity (ranging from 0 to 18) and $\mathbf{X}$ is a vector of standard covariates.

Measuring child weight status and food insecurity

Establishing a child's weight status begins with height and weight measurements. From this information, one can calculate a Body Mass Index (BMI, kg/m^2). As height and weight for children naturally increase with age and differ by gender, BMI is mapped into a percentile using age- and sex-specific reference values from the US Center for Disease Control (CDC) growth charts for US children (Ogden *et al.*, 2002). The American Academy of Pediatrics considers a child to be obese if his or her BMI is above the 95th percentile for age and sex (Barlow, 2007).

Food insecurity status is derived from the methodology employed to calculate official food insecurity rates in the US. The United States Department of

Agriculture (USDA) uses a survey module (The Core Food Security Module, CFSM) that is a set of 18 questions for households with children (10 for households without children) (Nord *et al.*, 2009). In the CFSM, some of the conditions respondents are asked about include 'I worried whether our food would run out before we got money to buy more', (the least severe item), 'Did you or the other adults in your household ever cut the size of your meals or skip meals because there wasn't enough money for food', 'Were you ever hungry but did not eat because you couldn't afford enough food' and 'Did a child in the household ever not eat for a full day because you couldn't afford enough food' (the most severe item for households with children). The 18-question CFSM is found in Table A1 in the Appendix. Note that each of these questions is qualified by the proviso that the condition is due to financial constraints. Consistent with the USDA methodology for calculating official US food insecurity rates, we convert the response to each CFSM question into a negative or affirmative response (Bickel *et al.*, 2000; Nord *et al.*, 2009). Food insecurity status is assessed based on the number of affirmative responses (in bold in Table A1 in the Appendix) provided.

In this study, we use two measures of food insecurity. For our initial parametric analyses, we employ the same methodology used by the USDA to calculate official US food insecurity rates and define a binary measure of food insecurity such that a child is said to be in a food insecure household if the household responded affirmatively to three or more CFSM questions (Bickel *et al.*, 2000; Nord *et al.*, 2009). This is the standard measure of food insecurity used throughout the literature, including the studies cited above on the relationship between food insecurity and childhood obesity.

A key disadvantage to using any binary measure is lost information. Often, much of the variance in responses is removed as a result of grouping respondents into two broad categories. Considering the set of 18 questions in the CFSM as an example, a household responding affirmatively to, say, 3 questions is treated the same as a household responding affirmatively to, say, 9 questions. (They are both food insecure.) Regarding establishing the food insecurity status of a household, this identical treatment is in contrast to the underlying methodology that established the validity of the CFSM and demonstrated that the latter household is more food insecure (Hamilton *et al.*, 1997). We also employ a continuous measure of food insecurity in this article in response to this deficiency in using a binary measure of food insecurity. Our continuous measure is consistent with other studies of food insecurity (e.g. Gundersen *et al.*,

2003; Gundersen, 2008) and is defined as the sum of affirmative responses to the CFSM.

Data

A large nationally representative survey data set from the US is utilized for these analyses, the second round of the Child Development Supplement (CDS-II) of the PSID. The PSID, begun in 1968, is a longitudinal study of a sample of individuals and the family units in which they reside that is representative of the US population. In 1997, a refresher sample of post-1968 immigrant families and their adult children was introduced to keep the study representative of the US population. The CDS was introduced in 1997 and focuses on the human capital development of children age 0–12 in PSID families at that time (PSID, 2005). CDS-II was conducted in 2002. CDS-II measures of children's height and weight were obtained by trained personnel (e.g. nurses or field interviewers). The full set of CFSM questions was asked in the 2003 PSID and was matched to CDS-II data for these analyses.

Since food insecurity is rare among households above 200% of the poverty line (Nord *et al.*, 2009), the sample for the study was limited to households below this threshold ($n = 959$). To examine how the relationship between childhood obesity and food insecurity might vary across groups, we analyse the full study sample and a series of subsamples: males ($n = 488$), females ($n = 471$), non-Hispanic white children ($n = 223$), non-Hispanic black children ($n = 568$), Hispanic children who were neither white nor black ($n = 120$), children in households with incomes below the poverty line ($n = 411$) and children in households with incomes between 100% and 200% of the poverty line ($n = 548$). As discussed above, these subsamples vary widely in their propensities to experience food insecurity and to be obese. Moreover, these subsamples are those that have been widely studied in previous research on the relationship between food insecurity and obesity.

IV. Results

Descriptive information and parametric regression results

Table 1 presents descriptive information for the full sample and the demographic subgroups examined in

Table 1. Descriptive statistics (%)

Subgroup	All	Obese	Food insecure
All children	100.00	22.42	20.54
Male children	50.89	23.16	20.29
Female children	49.11	21.66	20.81
White children	23.25	17.94	20.18
Black children	59.23	22.71	19.01
Hispanic children	12.51	23.33	27.50
Less than 100% of the poverty line	42.86	21.65	27.01
Between 100% and 200% of the poverty line	57.14	22.99	15.69

Notes: Data taken from the second Child Development Supplement (CDS-II) of the PSID; $n = 959$. Obese defined as having a BMI greater than the age- and sex-specific reference values for the 95th percentile obtained from US CDC growth charts for the US (Ogden *et al.*, 2008). Food insecurity status is based on responses to the 18-question CFSM using USDA methodology (Nord *et al.*, 2009). A child is classified as living in a food insecure household if the household responds affirmatively to three or more questions.

this study. About one-in-five children were obese (22.42%) and a similar proportion was in a food insecure household (20.54%). Consistent with the review above, prevalences of obesity and food insecurity varied by gender, race/ethnicity and poverty level. Boys were more likely to be obese than girls, but their rates of food insecurity were similar.[2] Almost one-in-four Hispanic and black children were obese with rates substantially lower for white children. In contrast, food insecurity rates were similar for black and white children, but higher for Hispanic children. With respect to income groups, while children living in poverty had similar obesity rates to children between 100% and 200% of the poverty line, they were nearly twice as likely to be living in a food insecure household.

We present parametric regression results in Table 2. We regress whether a child is obese on (1) the binary measure of food insecurity status and (2) the continuous measure of food insecurity status discussed above. Both regressions reveal no statistically significant relationships between the two variables for the full sample, as well as for each of the subgroups. Additionally, in similar parametric regression specifications for which the continuous measure of food insecurity was modelled via a

---

[2] As described above, food insecurity is defined at the household level. It is generally not possible to distinguish the food insecurity status of individual children with the Core Food Security Module (CFSM). Nevertheless, for simplicity, we refer to a child as being food insecure or food secure.

Table 2. Parametric (probit) regressions of obesity on food insecurity

Subgroup	Binary measure of food insecurity	Continuous measure of food insecurity
All children	0.018	−0.013
	(0.111)	(0.016)
Male children	0.044	−0.019
	(0.154)	(0.022)
Female children	−0.010	−0.007
	(0.159)	(0.021)
White children	−0.118	−0.001
	(0.251)	(0.036)
Black children	−0.099	−0.037
	(0.151)	(0.021)
Hispanic children	0.427	0.051
	(0.273)	(0.045)
Less than 100% of the poverty line	0.040	−0.008
	(0.155)	(0.020)
Between 100% and 200% of the poverty line	0.010	−0.018
	(0.162)	(0.026)

Notes: Estimated coefficients are reported with SEs in parentheses. Constant terms were included in each regression, but are not reported for brevity. Data taken from the second Child Development Supplement (CDS-II) of the PSID; $N = 959$. Obese defined as having a BMI greater than the age- and sex-specific reference values for the 95th percentile obtained from US CDC growth charts for the US (Ogden *et al.*, 2008). Food insecurity status is based on responses to the 18-question CFSM using USDA methodology (Nord *et al.*, 2009). A child is classified as living in a food insecure household if the household responds affirmatively to three or more questions.

series of indicator (dummy) variables, no pattern in the relationship was evident (results not reported in Table 2).[3]

Nonparametric regression results

Balancing bias and variability requires identifying a bandwidth with a relatively low MSE that is based on a relatively high percentage of valid observations. A bandwidth of 0.5 was selected as it had the lowest MSE for bandwidths with over 60% valid observations. Our nonparametric regression results are presented in Figs 1–4.[4] In each figure, the probability of being obese is on the vertical axis, while the number of affirmative responses to the CFSM food insecurity questions is on the horizontal axis. Plausible values on the horizontal axis range from 0 to 18, although no household in the study sample responded affirmatively to all 18 CFSM questions.

While there was no evident relationship between obesity and food insecurity from the parametric regressions, the nonparametric regressions suggest that the relationship is complex, nonlinear and differs by demographic and economic subgroups. In Fig. 1, results are presented for the full study sample. The graph indicates that the probability of being obese is highest for food secure children. One also observes a slight decline in the probability of obesity as food insecurity becomes more extreme. This decline continues over the length of the food insecurity distribution.

Figure 2 presents the relationship by gender. A sharp contrast is seen in the relationship between obesity and food insecurity for male and female children. For boys, at lower levels of food insecurity, an increase in the number of affirmative CFSM responses is associated with a higher probability of obesity. At higher levels of food insecurity, however, an increase in the number of affirmative responses is associated with a lower probability of obesity. In contrast, for girls, there is no relationship over low levels of food insecurity, but higher probabilities of being obese are observed at the highest levels of food insecurity.

Results by race and ethnicity are presented in Fig. 3. For white children, there is a slight positive relationship between the probability of obesity and food insecurity. This positive relationship between obesity and food insecurity begins near the point of six affirmative CFSM responses and continues over the remainder of the food insecurity distribution. The relationship is negative for black children as the probability of obesity almost uniformly declines over the length of the food insecurity distribution. The relationship for Hispanic children is more complex. There is a positive relationship between the probability of being obese and food insecurity at relative low levels of food insecurity. However, the relationship shifts to being negative for children experiencing moderate levels of food insecurity (between three and six affirmative responses). At six affirmative responses, the relationship shifts again and becomes positive and continues to be positive throughout the remainder of the food insecurity distribution.

Finally, Fig. 4 presents the relationship between childhood obesity and food insecurity by poverty level. Once again, the results across groups are noticeably different. For children below the poverty line, the relationship between obesity and food insecurity is positive at low levels of food insecurity. The probability of being obese is negatively

---

[3] These results are available from the authors by request.

[4] Results from nonparametric regressions are typically presented graphically (Fox, 2000).

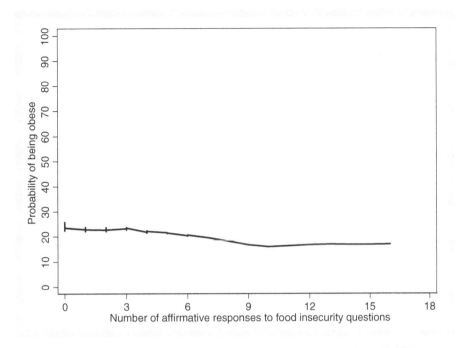

Fig. 1.   Nonparametric regressions of obesity and food insecurity, all children

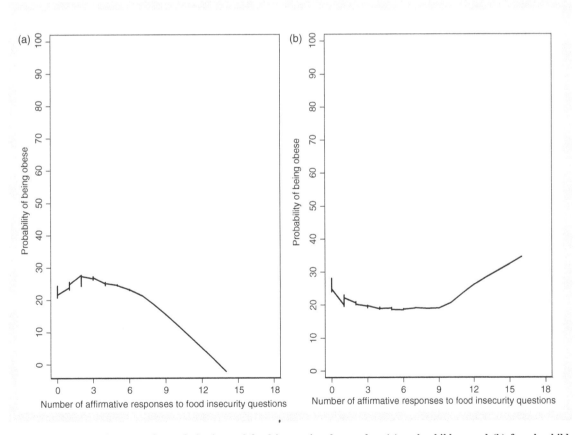

Fig. 2.   Nonparametric regressions of obesity and food insecurity, by gender: (a) male children and (b) female children

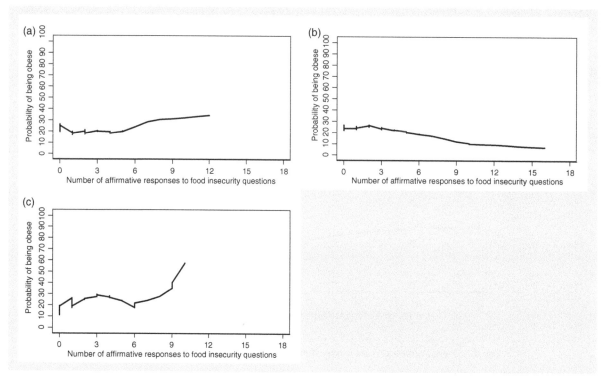

Fig. 3. **Nonparametric regressions of obesity and food insecurity, by race and ethnicity: (a) White children, (b) Black children and (c) Hispanic children**

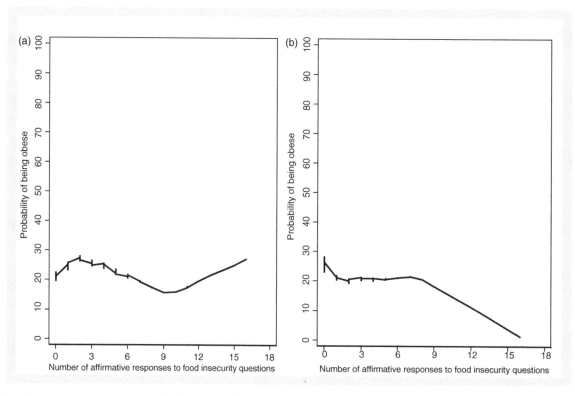

Fig. 4. **Nonparametric regressions of obesity and food insecurity, by poverty level: (a) children below the poverty line and (b) children between 100% and 200%**

associated with food insecurity over the range of about three to six affirmative CFSM responses, and then is positively associated thereafter. For children between 100% and 200% of the poverty line, the relationship is nearly a mirror image of that for children below the poverty line.

V. Conclusion

Previous research on the relationship between childhood obesity and food insecurity has reached mixed conclusions. What is common to all this work, though, is its reliance on parametric approaches to assess the association between these two variables. In this article, we depart from previous studies by specifying this relationship with nonparametric models. Consistent with recent work (e.g. Martin and Ferris, 2007; Bhargava et al., 2008; Gundersen et al., 2008, 2009), our parametric models find that food insecurity is not associated with childhood obesity. In contrast, our nonparametric results describe a more complicated relationship that varies by gender, race, ethnicity and poverty status.

Understanding the relationship between childhood obesity and food insecurity has significant policy implications. For example, the US Food Stamp Program (now called the Supplemental Nutrition Assistance Program – SNAP) is the largest food assistance and the largest near-cash entitlement program in the United States. The central goal of SNAP is to alleviate food insecurity and hunger in the United States (US Department of Agriculture, Food and Nutrition Service, 1999). Our parametric results indicate that there would be no spillovers from reductions in food insecurity to changes in obesity. Our nonparametric results, however, present a different story suggesting that the effects on childhood obesity of reducing food insecurity, especially for the most food insecure, may vary widely by demographic categories. While reducing food insecurity in and of itself leads to improvements in well-being, policymakers should be cognisant that the effects on obesity from reductions in food insecurity may vary. To aid policymakers in their efforts to improve child well-being, future research may wish to consider the relationship between food insecurity and childhood obesity using other data sets and examining other demographic categories not considered in this article. In addition, researchers are encouraged to pursue other nonparametric and parametric representations of the relationship between food insecurity and obesity; the results in this article may help in these constructions.

References

Abdulai, A. (2010) Socio-economic characteristics and obesity in underdeveloped economies: does income really matter?, *Applied Economics*, **42**, 157–69.

Alaimo, K., Olson, C. M. and Frongillo, E. A. (2001a) Food insufficiency and American school-aged children's cognitive, academic, and psychosocial development, *Pediatrics*, **108**, 44–53.

Alaimo, K., Olson, C., Frongillo, E. and Briefel, R. (2001b) Food insufficiency, family income, and health in US preschool and school-aged children, *American Journal of Public Health*, **91**, 781–6.

Barlow, S. (2007) Expert committee recommendations regarding the prevention, assessment, and treatment of child and adolescent overweight and obesity: summary report, *Pediatrics*, **120**, S164–92.

Bastida, E. and Soydemir, G. (2009) Obesity and employment as predictors of diabetes in Mexican Americans: findings from a longitudinal study, *Applied Economics*, **41**, 2533–40.

Bhargava, A., Jolliffe, D. and Howard, L. (2008) Socio-economic, behavioural and environmental factors predicted body weights and household food insecurity scores in the early childhood longitudinal study – kindergarten, *British Journal of Nutrition*, **100**, 438–44.

Bickel, G., Nord, M., Price, C., Hamilton, W. and Cook, J. (2000) *Guide to Measuring Household Food Security*, US Department of Agriculture, Washington, DC.

Casey, P., Simpson, P., Gossett, J., Bogle, M., Champagne, C., Connell, C., Harsha, D., McCabe-Sellers, B., Robbins, J., Stuff, J. and Weber, J. (2006) The association of child and household food insecurity with childhood overweight status, *Pediatrics*, **118**, e1406–13.

Cook, J., Frank, D., Berkowitz, C., Black, M., Casey, P., Cutts, D., Meyers, A., Zaldivar, A., Skalicky, A., Levenson, S., Heeren, T. and Nord, M. (2004) Food insecurity is associated with adverse health outcomes among human infants and toddlers, *Journal of Nutrition*, **134**, 1432–48.

Costa-Font, J. and Gil, J. (2004) Social interactions and the contemporaneous determinants of individuals' weight, *Applied Economics*, **36**, 2253–63.

Daniels, S. (2006) The consequences of childhood overweight and obesity, *The Future of Children*, **16**, 47–67.

Di Matteo, L. (2003) The income elasticity of health care spending: a comparison of parametric and nonparametric approaches, *The European Journal of health economics*, **4**, 20–9.

Dietz, W. (1995) Does hunger cause obesity?, *Pediatrics*, **95**, 766–7.

Drewnowski, A. and Specter, S. (2004) Poverty and obesity: the role of energy density and energy costs, *American Journal of Clinical Nutrition*, **79**, 6–16.

Dubois, L., Farmer, A., Girard, M. and Porcherie, M. (2006) Family food insufficiency is related to overweight among preschoolers, *Social Science and Medicine*, **6**, 1503–16.

Ebbeling, C., Pawlak, D. and Ludwig, D. (2002) Childhood obesity: public-health crisis, common sense cure, *Lancet*, **360**, 473–82.

Figueroa-Munoz, J., Chinn, S. and Rona, R. (2001) Association between obesity and asthma in 4–11 year old children in the UK, *Thorax*, **56**, 133–7.

Fox, J. (2000) *Nonparametric Simple Regression: Smoothing Scatterplots*, Sage University Papers Series on Quantitative Applications in the Social Sciences, 07-130, Sage, Thousand Oaks, CA.

Fox, J. (2002) *An R and S-Plus Companion to Applied Regression*, Sage, Thousand Oaks, CA.

Garasky, S., Stewart, S. D., Lohman, B. J., Gundersen, C. and Eisenmann, J. (2009) Family stressors and child obesity, *Social Science Research*, **38**, 755–66.

Grogger, J. (2007) Markov forecasting methods for welfare caseloads, *Children and Youth Services Review*, **29**, 900–11.

Gundersen, C. (2008) Measuring the extent, depth, and severity of food insecurity: an application to American Indians in the United States, *Journal of Population Economics*, **21**, 191–215.

Gundersen, C., Garasky, S. and Lohman, B. J. (2009) Food insecurity is not associated with childhood obesity as assessed using multiple measures of obesity, *Journal of Nutrition*, **139**, 1173–8.

Gundersen, C., Lohman, B. J., Garasky, S., Stewart, S. D. and Eisenmann, J. C. (2008) Food security, maternal stressors, and overweight among low-income US children: results from national health and nutrition examination survey (1999–2002), *Pediatrics*, **122**, e529–40.

Gundersen, C. and Ribar, D. (2005) Food insecurity and insufficiency at low levels of food expenditures, Working Paper No. 1594, Institute for the Study of Labor (IZA).

Gundersen, C., Weinreb, L., Wehler, C. and Hosmer, D. (2003) Homelessness and food insecurity, *Journal of Housing Economics*, **12**, 250–72.

Hamilton, W., Cook, J., Thompson, W., Buron, L., Frongillo, E., Olson, C. and Wehler, C. (1997) Household food security in the United States in 1995: technical report, Report prepared for the USDA Food and Nutrition Service (formerly Food and Consumer Service), Alexandria, VA.

Hastie, T., Tibshirani, R. and Friedman, J. (2009) *The Elements of Statistical Learning: Data Mining, Inference, and Prediction*, 2nd edn, Springer, New York.

Jimenez-Cruz, A., Bacardi-Gascon, M. and Spindler, A. (2003) Obesity and hunger among Mexican-Indian migrant children on the US–Mexico border, *International Journal of Obesity*, **27**, 740–7.

Jyoti, D. F., Frongillo, E. A. and Jones, S. J. (2005) Food insecurity affects school children's academic performance, weight gain, and social skills, *Journal of Nutrition*, **135**, 2831–9.

Kim, M., Garcia, P. and Leuthold, R. M. (2009) Managing price risks using local polynomial kernel forecasts, *Applied Economics*, **41**, 3015–26.

Klein, S., Burke, L., Bray, G., Blair, S., Allison, B., Pi-Sunyer, X., Hong, Y. and Eckel, R. H. (2004) Clinical implications of obesity with specific focus on cardiovascular disease: a statement for professionals from the American heart association council on nutrition, physical activity, and metabolism, *Circulation*, **110**, 2952–67.

Koplan, J., Liverman, C. and Kraak, V. (Eds) (2005) *Preventing Childhood Obesity: Health in the Balance*, National Academies Press, Washington, DC.

Krebs, N., Himes, J., Jacobson, D., Nicklas, T., Guilday, P. and Styne, D. (2007) Assessment of child and adolescent overweight and obesity, *Pediatrics*, **120**, S193–228.

Laraia, B., Siega-Riz, A., Gundersen, C. and Dole, N. (2006) Psychosocial factors and socioeconomic indicators are associated with household food insecurity among pregnant women, *Journal of Nutrition*, **136**, 177–82.

Lohman, B. J., Stewart, S., Gundersen, C., Garasky, S. and Eisenmann, J. C. (2009) Adolescent overweight and obesity: links to food insecurity and individual, maternal, and family stressors, *Journal of Adolescent Health*, **45**, 230–7.

Martin, K. and Ferris, A. (2007) Food insecurity and gender are risk factors for obesity, *Journal of Nutrition Education*, **39**, 31–6.

Matheson, D., Varady, J., Varady, A. and Killen, J. (2002) Household food security and nutritional status of Hispanic children in the fifth grade, *American Journal of Clinical Nutrition*, **76**, 210–17.

McIntyre, L., Glanville, T., Raine, K., Dayle, J., Anderson, B. and Battaglia, N. (2003) Do low-income lone mothers compromise their nutrition to feed their children?, *Canadian Medical Association Journal*, **168**, 686–91.

Mukhopadhyay, K. and Marsh, L. C. (2006) An approach to nonparametric smoothing techniques for regressions with discrete data, *Applied Economics*, **38**, 301–5.

Nord, M., Andrews, M. and Carlson, S. (2009) Household food security in the United States, 2008, Economic Research Report No. 83, US Department of Agriculture, Washington, DC.

Ogden, C., Carroll, M. and Flegal, K. (2008) High body mass index for age among US children and Adolescents, 2003–2006, *Journal of the American Medical Association*, **299**, 2401–5.

Ogden, C., Kuczmarski, R., Flegal, K., Mei, Z., Guo, S., Wei, R., Grummer-Strawn, L., Curtin, L., Roche, A. and Johnson, C. (2002) Centers for disease control and prevention 2000 growth charts for the United States: improvements to the 1977 National Center for Health Statistics Version, *Pediatrics*, **109**, 45–60.

Ozaki, V. A., Goodwin, B. K. and Shirota, R. (2008) Parametric and nonparametric statistical modeling of crop yield: implications for pricing crop insurance contracts, *Applied Economics*, **40**, 1151–64.

Panel Study of Income Dynamics (PSID) (2005) An overview of the panel study of income dynamics. Available at http://psidonline.isr.umich.edu/Guide/Overview.html (accessed 13 May 2005).

Patel, S. (2005) Shared genetic risk factors for obstructive sleep apnea and obesity, *Journal of Applied Physiology*, **99**, 1600–6.

Rose, D. and Bodor, J. (2006) Household food insecurity and overweight status in young school children: results from the early childhood longitudinal study, *Pediatrics*, **117**, 464–73.

Scheier, L. (2005) What is the hunger-obesity paradox, *Journal of the American Dietetic Association*, **105**, 883–6.

Skalicky, A., Meyers, A., Adams, W., Yang, Z., Cook, J. and Frank, D. (2006) Child food insecurity and iron deficiency anemia in low-income infants and toddlers in the United States, *Maternal and Child Health Journal*, **10**, 177–85.

Slack, K. and Yoo, J. (2005) Food hardship and child behavior problems among low income children, *Social Service Review*, **79**, 511–36.

Srinivasan, S., Myers, L. and Berenson, G. (2002) Predictability of childhood adiposity and insulin for developing insulin resistance syndrome (syndrome X) in young adulthood: the Bogalusa heart study, *Diabetes*, **51**, 204–9.

Statacorp (2007) *Stata Statistical Software: Release 10 Manual*, Statacorp LP, College Station, TX.

US Department of Agriculture, Food and Nutrition Service (1999) *Annual Historical Review: Fiscal Year 1997*, US Department of Agriculture, Washington, DC.

Whitaker, R., Phillips, S. and Orzol, S. (2006) Food insecurity and the risks of depression and anxiety in mothers and behavior problems in their preschool-aged children, *Pediatrics*, **118**, e859–68.

Appendix

Table A1. Core Food Security Module (CFSM)

1. 'We worried whether our food would run out before we got money to buy more'. Was that **often, sometimes** or never true for you in the last 12 months?
2. 'The food that we bought just didn't last and we didn't have money to get more'. Was that **often, sometimes** or never true for you in the last 12 months?
3. 'We couldn't afford to eat balanced meals'. Was that **often, sometimes** or never true for you in the last 12 months?
4. 'We relied on only a few kinds of low-cost food to feed our children because we were running out of money to buy food'. Was that **often, sometimes** or never true for you in the last 12 months?
5. In the last 12 months, did you or other adults in the household ever cut the size of your meals or skip meals because there wasn't enough money for food? (**Yes**/No)
6. 'We couldn't feed our children a balanced meal, because we couldn't afford that'. Was that **often, sometimes** or never true for you in the last 12 months?
7. In the last 12 months, did you ever eat less than you felt you should because there wasn't enough money for food? (**Yes**/No)
8. (If yes to Question 5) How often did this happen – **almost every month, some months but not every month**, or in only 1 or 2 months?
9. 'The children were not eating enough because we just couldn't afford enough food'. Was that **often, sometimes** or never true for you in the last 12 months?
10. In the last 12 months, were you ever hungry, but didn't eat, because you couldn't afford enough food? (**Yes**/No)
11. In the last 12 months, did you lose weight because you didn't have enough money for food? (**Yes**/No)
12. In the last 12 months, did you ever cut the size of any of the children's meals because there wasn't enough money for food? (**Yes**/No)
13. In the last 12 months did you or other adults in your household ever not eat for a whole day because there wasn't enough money for food? (**Yes**/No)
14. In the last 12 months, were the children ever hungry but you just couldn't afford more food? (**Yes**/No)
15. (If yes to Question 13) How often did this happen – **almost every month, some months but not every month**, or in only 1 or 2 months?
16. In the last 12 months, did any of the children ever skip a meal because there wasn't enough money for food? (**Yes**/No)
17. (If yes to Question 16) How often did this happen – **almost every month, some months but not every month**, or in only 1 or 2 months?
18. In the last 12 months did any of the children ever not eat for a whole day because there wasn't enough money for food? (**Yes**/No)

Note: Responses in bold indicate an 'affirmative' response.

Socio-economic characteristics and obesity in underdeveloped economies: does income really matter?

Awudu Abdulai

Department of Food Economics and Consumption Studies,
University of Kiel, Olshausenstrasse 40, 24118 Kiel, Germany

Available evidence suggests that overweight and obesity prevalence is increasing worldwide at an alarming rate in both developed and developing countries. This study focuses on the determinants of overweight in mothers and children, using a unique dataset collected in urban Accra, in Ghana. The findings show that mothers' education, employment status and ethnicity significantly exert influence on the generation of body weight. In particular, those who attained secondary and tertiary education had lower body mass indices and were much less likely to be overweight or obese, lending support to the notion that more educated women normally have better health knowledge and are more likely to consume healthy foods and also engage in physical exercises that help to control weight gain. Mother's education was also found to exert a negative and significant impact on the weight status of children. Furthermore, household expenditure was found to exert a positive and significant impact on the probability of a mother being overweight or obese, but no significant impact on the probability of a child being overweight.

I. Introduction

The high and rising overweight and obesity rates world-wide is increasingly gaining attention from both researchers and policy-makers (WHO, 2000; Monteiro *et al.*, 2001). In particular, obesity has reached epidemic proportions globally, with more than 1 billion adults overweight. Often coexisting in developing countries with under-nutrition, obesity is a complex condition, with serious social and psychological dimensions, affecting virtually all ages and socio-economic groups (WHO, 2004).

Martorell (2000) argues that obesity is not a problem everywhere in the developing world, but appears to become a problem as income increases, particularly in urban households. Available estimates indicate that over 40% of the populations in Colombia and Chile are overweight, while the corresponding figures for Ghana and Togo are 18 and 20%, respectively (WHO, 2000). A recent survey of 300 households consisting of 1243 persons in a township near Cape Town in South Africa revealed that 75% of the women in the sample were either overweight or obese (Case and Deaton, 2005). The WHO asserts that childhood obesity is already an epidemic in some areas and is on the rise in others, with about 22 million children under five estimated to be overweight worldwide. This gives cause for concern, given that childhood overweight and obesity are important predictors of adult overweight and obesity.

Available evidence indicates that more than 40% of 5 to 7 year old overweight children remain overweight or become obese (Power *et al.*, 1997).

Traditionally, major causes of illness and death in developing countries have been linked to infectious diseases and under-nutrition, and these are still major public health problems in several regions of the world. But recent projections by the World Health Organization (2000) indicate that in 20 years, noncommunicable diseases will account for over 60% of the disease burden and mortality in the developing world. Obesity is recognized as an underlying risk factor for many of these chronic conditions. It is a major risk factor for diabetes, hypertension, cardiovascular disease, stroke, gall bladder disease, respiratory dysfunction, osteoarthritis and some forms of cancer (Costa-Font and Gil, 2005). Furthermore, a recent large scale study of US cancer deaths concluded that adults being overweight or obese accounted for about 14% of all deaths from cancer in men and 20% of those in women (Calle *et al.*, 2003). Baum and Ford (2004) also show in their study that obesity has a statistically significant negative effect on the wage of young men and women, but the penalty is larger for women's than men's wage. Hence, human obesity translates with a time lag into future human health problems, including morbidity and mortality, reduced labour productivity and increased demand for health care. Overweight and obesity in children and adolescents may also have more immediate impacts, particularly on mental health because of social rejection and low self esteem (Costa-Font and Gil, 2005).

Although the genetic explanation for obesity is generally acceptable, the recent trends in overweight and obesity suggest that other factors may be equally significant. Recent research has therefore, focused on the role of environmental factors, including socio-economic status (Popkin *et al.*, 1995; Martorell *et al.*, 1998; Nayga, 2000; Danielzik *et al.*, 2002; Anderson *et al.*, 2003; Cutler *et al.*, 2003; Chou *et al.*, 2004; Costa-Font and Gil, 2004). The studies have generally reported a significant relationship between socio-economic status and overweight or obesity. Other environmental factors like technological innovation and television watching have also been found to be influencing overweight and obesity. For example, Gortmaker *et al.* (1996) report a positive correlation between television viewing and being overweight among children in the United States. The United States Center for Disease Control (2000) recently argued that the growing obesity rates are an indication of a growing long-term imbalance between an individual's energy intake from food and drink and energy use in basal metabolism, work and leisure,

and seem to have little to do with the gene pool of the population, which is fixed.

As in developed societies, the risk of obesity in developing countries is also strongly influenced by diet and lifestyle, which are changing dramatically as a result of the economic and nutrition transition. The globalization of food markets has resulted in the introduction of mass-produced, low-cost foods to the domestic food supply of many developing countries. This change, along with advertising campaigns, may have a powerful effect on food choices and dietary patterns of low-income families. For example, the introduction of low-cost vegetable oils from industrialized countries greatly increased the proportion of fat calories in the average diet in countries undergoing the nutrition transition (Caballero, 2005).

Although, the few published literature on this topic tend to suggest a positive relationship between socio-economic status and overweight in both men and women, (Popkin *et al.*, 1995; Nayga, 2000; Costa-Font and Gil, 2004) that may not be true for all developing countries. For example, an empirical analysis of women of childbearing ages from Latin America and the Caribbean, using national data in the mid-1990s revealed a negative association between education levels and obesity in five of nine countries (Martorell *et al.*, 1998). As pointed out by Monteiro *et al.* (2001), it is reasonable to expect that in any developing society, it is only up to a certain level of economic and technological development that the level of material wealth can remain the basic determinant of how much food an individual may obtain and how much energy he or she will spend along the day. Beyond that level, income differences will determine distinct access to several commodities but not necessarily to food, and energy expenditure during work might tend to converge to low or moderate values in all social classes. Under such circumstances, both rich and poor will be equally exposed to overweight.

Very few studies have empirically examined the determinants of overweight and obesity in developing countries and particularly in sub-Saharan Africa. This is in contrast to the huge literature on the topic in developed economies. Given the increasing significance of this phenomenon in this part of the world, additional work needs to be done to shed more light on the factors contributing to overweight and obesity problems in the society and to provide appropriate recommendations for public policy.

This study focuses on the determinants of overweight and obesity in mothers and children, using a unique dataset collected in urban Accra, in Ghana. Given that the dataset is cross sectional, we are only able to examine the impact of individual and household characteristics on the probability that a mother is overweight or obese, as well as household and child characteristics on the probability that a child is overweight. The article may be outlined as follows. Section II presents a simple behavioural model of the determinants of overweight, using a health production theoretical framework. Section III discusses the data employed and the specification used in the empirical analysis, while Section IV presents the empirical findings and discussion of the results. Concluding remarks are presented in the final section.

II. Conceptual Framework

The conceptual framework underpinning our empirical analysis of the determinants of overweight and obesity derives from the well-known household production model in the tradition of Becker (1981). This framework has also been employed by Nayga (2000) to examine the effect of schooling and health knowledge on obesity. The framework assumes that households maximize utility, which is dependent on the consumption of commodities and services, C_i, leisure, L_i and health status H_i of each household (of which body weight, is one dimension). Without considering the household decision-making process, assume that the household maximizes utility U, represented as:

$$U = U(H_i, C_i, L_i; K, Z_i) \qquad (1)$$

where K and Z, respectively represent individual and household characteristics, some of which are unobserved. The production of a household member's health may be described by the production function

$$H_i = g(I_i, K, Z, \mu_i) \qquad (2)$$

where I denotes the current inputs into the production function, such as nutrient intake, energy output, health care practices and illness and μ_i represents the unobservable determinants of H. Household allocation choices are made conditional on the budget constraint for purchased goods

$$\sum_i P_i C_i = Y \qquad (3)$$

where P_i is a vector of exogenous prices and Y is exogenous money income. Individual characteristics, K, such as age, employment or work status of the individual and education, ethnicity as well as household characteristics, Z, such as education of household head or mother, household income and

household composition may affect health outcomes through their impact on allocation decisions or directly through the health production function. Maximization of Equation 1 subject to the constraints (2) and (3) result in the household reduced form demand for goods

$$C_i = C(I_i, K, Z, Y, P_i, \mu_i) \qquad (4)$$

The reduced form demand function in the present study for health outcome H_i, of the households may be expressed as (Lancaster, 1971; Nayga, 2000)

$$H_i = f(I_i, K, Z, Y, P_i, \mu_i) \qquad (5)$$

III. The Empirical Specification

With prices held constant, the health outcome Equation 5 can be used to specify the overweight and obesity equations as

$$H_i = f(I_i, K, Z, Y, \varepsilon_i) \qquad (6)$$

where ε_i represents unobservable determinants of H. The above specification is employed to examine the determinants of health outcomes such as overweight and obesity of mothers and children in the household.

The key outcome variable, an indicator for whether the individual is overweight, is based on the body mass index (BMI). BMI is defined as weight in kilograms divided by height in meters square (kg/m^2) and is a commonly used measure to define overweight and obesity in individuals. Optimal BMI levels are generally believed to lie between 20 and 25. BMI below 20 is considered thin, BMI between 25 and 30 is overweight and BMI above 30 is obese.

Given that the survey include only height and weight measures for children and mothers, we use the height and weight measures for the children and mothers to calculate the BMI of these groups. There has not been a level of agreement over the classification of overweight and obesity in children as in adults. In particular, there has been some confusion both in terms of a globally applicable reference population and of the selection of appropriate cut-off points for designating a child as overweight or obese. Most authors therefore, use percentile distributions as cut-off points. For example, Dietz and Bellizzi (1999) conclude from their study that a BMI above the 85th percentile for a child's age and sex group is likely to accord with the adult definition of overweight, and above the 95th percentile with the adult definition of obese. Following Langnaese et al. (2002), we classify those children with a BMI above the 90th percentile ($17.7 \, kg/m^2$) of this distribution (for their sex-age group) as 'overweight'.

The theory predicts several possible relationships between income and weight, which are positive, negative or inverted U-shaped. Demand for food, that raises weight, could increase with income increases. Continued growth in weight, however, would depend on whether income growth encourages weight control or not. Weight could decline if rising income leads to reduced demand for food and food consumption. Philipson and Posner (1999) argue that in technologically less-developed economies, in which the share of income spent on food is large because food is expensive to produce, a positive relation between income and weight will be expected because richer individuals care more about their health. For the same reason, in technologically advanced economies, in which income is high relative to the price of food, income and weight will exhibit a negative relation.

Given that a major motivation of the study is to examine the relationship between socio-economic factors and overweight, it is essential that household resource availability is adequately measured. As argued by Thomas et al. (1996), nonwage income is normally very difficult to measure, and is not likely to reflect long-run resources. Besides, if households smooth consumption over income shocks, then expenditure is likely to be a better indicator of long-run resources.[1]

The mother's work status, which tends to affect her physical activity, will be expected to influence her weight. Lakdawalla and Philipson (2002) and Cutler et al. (2003) stress the significance of energy spent on the job and in commuting to work in explaining the increase in obesity over time. The amount of time that one works and the character of the work affects weight in two respects: the first is through increasing earned income, which as explained above, has an effect on weight. The second is through affecting the amount of calories expended on the job.[2]

The number of children in the family may also influence the mother's work status, since a mother may continue to work outside home with only one child, and choose to stay home when there are several children. For biological reasons, age could have an effect on the probability of being overweight. Specifically, people may gain weight as they approach middle age, but then begin to lose weight as they enter old age, resulting in an inverted U-shape relation between weight and age.

Education and ability may affect both the individual's employment patterns and health. Schooling, which is connected with health knowledge, may affect overweight and obesity in a number of ways. It potentially increases the efficiency of health production by expanding knowledge concerning what constitutes a healthy diet. Nayga's (2000) findings for the US indicate that schooling's effect on relative weight and the probability of being obese are explained by differences in knowledge. Komlos et al. (2004) also suggest that education may also influence an individual's BMI by altering time preference. An individual's consumption level has been shown to depend on the rate at which future health benefits are discounted in the individual's consumption decisions, with individual fitness being negatively associated with a high rate of time preference (or impatience). Thus, if individuals are less willing to trade current benefit (utility) for potential future health benefits, then they will most likely consume more calorie-dense foods and engage in more sedentary leisure pursuits despite the future adverse consequences. Smith et al. (2005) hypothesize that an increase in the marginal rate of time preference has contributed to increasing obesity. In contrast, Cutler et al. (2003), argue that little of the differences in health behaviours, including obesity, can be explained by variations in time preference and are instead largely due to variations in genetics and situational influences.

With regard to children, individual as well as the maternal and household characteristics described above may affect the likelihood of a child being overweight. Mother's weight status may reflect either the impact of genetics on the child's likelihood of being overweight or the effects of common home environment on the family's weight status. Moreover, popular opinion consistently draws a direct link between mothers working and poor health outcomes for children. There are a number of ways through which children's eating habits and level of physical activity may be affected by having parents who work outside the home. Parents who work outside home may serve more high-calorie prepared or fast foods, and unsupervised children may make poor nutritional

---

[1] While the reported mean total expenditure per capita per year of the households used in this study was 1 028 000 Cedis, the reported mean total income per capita per year was 536 300 Cedis, revealing that on average, households consumed more than they earned, most probably as a result of transfers from other family members and friends or under-reporting of earned income.

[2] It is interesting to note that some authors suggest that increased numbers of women at work have increased the demand for eating outside and for eating less healthy food. However, Cutler et al. (2003) reject this theory of obesity and rather propose a theory of obesity based on reductions in the time cost of food, which in turn has allowed more frequent food consumption of greater variety and thus, resulted in higher weight gains.

choices when preparing their own after-school meals or snacks. Unsupervised children may also spend a great deal of time indoors, watching television or playing video games rather than engaging in more active outdoor pursuits (Anderson *et al.*, 2003). Alternatively, there may not be any adverse effects of parents working on childhood weight problems. Parents' participation in the labour market may even have a negative impact on children's probability of being overweight if households where mothers work earn enough money to purchase more healthy meals. Children from such households may also be more likely to participate in after-school sports, thereby increasing their activity levels.

In addition to the socio-economic factors discussed above, the socio-cultural environment may also influence an individual's weight status. Given that overweight and obesity are household-produced goods, an individual's self-image and social interactions are likely to play a role in determining his or her weight. Several studies report that blacks and Hispanics in the United States tolerate, and may even encourage, larger body size than do whites (Becker *et al.*, 1999). Anderson *et al.* (2003) show in their study that black children are significantly more likely to be overweight than other groups, while Lakdawalla and Philipson (2002) report that black women tend to be much heavier than white and Hispanic women. Some authors also discuss the role of matching markets (marriage and dating markets) in determining weight. For example, Philipson and Posner (1999) argue that if weight affects one's ability to match, unmarried people today would be expected, as consumers in the marriage market, to be thinner than married people. Marital status may also affect the time available for household chores and active leisure in a variety of ways.

Given that a mother that is obese is also overweight, although an overweight mother may not be obese, unobservable variables may affect both the propensity to be overweight and obese. A full information maximum likelihood bivariate probit model was therefore, employed for the mother's specification, instead of two single probit estimations. However, a probit model was used to examine the probability of a child being overweight.

In estimating the child equation, mother's overweight and obesity status are included as explanatory variables. However, mothers who are overweight or obese are likely to differ from mothers who are not both in observable and unobservable ways. These omitted variables may bias the relationship between a mother's health outcome and children's overweight status across the sample. In particular, given that mothers and children share food and family resources together, there may be some unobserved factors that influence both a mother's and a child's weight problems simultaneously.[3] While the probit model used in the analysis can account for observable differences across individuals, there may still be unobservable differences that bias the relationship between a mother's weight and her child's weight. To account for this potential bias, a two-stage instrumental variable procedure is implemented to produce consistent estimates for the model (Davidson and Mackinnon, 1993). The first stage involves estimating probit models for mother being overweight and obese. In the second stage, where the child equation is estimated, the predicted values are used in place of the observed values for mother being overweight and obese.

IV. Data

The empirical work in this article is based on a survey conducted by the International Food Policy Research Institute (IFPRI) between January and April 1997. The survey team adopted a two-stage sampling strategy to select 559 households distributed among 16 enumeration areas within the Accra, Ga and Tema districts. The survey team made use of the primary sampling units that had been mapped out by the Ghana Statistical Service for the Greater Accra area. This sampling frame included 879 urban and 33 peri-urban enumeration areas. Cluster sampling was then employed to select 36 households in the 16 enumeration areas, for a total of 576 households. The basic sampling units for the survey were households with children under the age of three. The sample, therefore, did not include urban residents who do not live in households – that is, street children or homeless population.

Five of the twenty-five enumerators that were used in the survey were selected for specialized training in anthropometric measurement. The height and weight of children and mothers were directly measured by the trained enumerators. This is an advantage of the survey, compared to data on self-reported anthropometric measures. It is well known that self-reported anthropometric variables contain measurement error with heavier persons more likely to under-report their weight. Detailed information on the sampling design and data collection is available in Maxwell *et al.* (2000).

---

[3] The author is grateful to an anonymous reviewer for drawing his attention to this point.

The survey gathered information on demographic indicators, such as household headship, age structure and dependency ratio, available labour in the household, education and ethnicity. Livelihood indicators collected include reported total per capita household expenditure (used as proxy measure of income at household level), the primary income-generating activity of the head of household and maternal employment status and place of work, marital status, as well as other household variables such as the availability of a television set and piped water.

About 15% of the children in the sample fall in this category. The weight and BMI for mothers are skewed to the right, indicating that overweight and obesity is present in the sample (Fig. 1). About 37% of women had a BMI > 25, while 13% showed a BMI ≥ 30, lending support to the growing concern that obesity is an emerging problem among adults in many large urban areas in developing countries, including Africa (WHO, 2000).

The data also show a direct relationship between age and BMI. Overweight and obesity is quite prominent in the age group of 24–40 years. The mean age of overweight women was observed to be 32.8 years whereas that of the nonoverweight was 28 years. Overweight households were also larger and had higher per capita expenditures than the nonoverweight category. While the mean monthly household expenditure of overweight households was 599 359 Cedis, the average for the nonoverweight group was 488 120 Cedis. Definitions, means and SDs of all variables employed in the regressions are contained in Table 1. The per capita household expenditure is used as a proxy for income or wealth. The predominant ethnic group is the Ga/Adangbe tribe, who traditionally, are home in Accra and its surroundings.

V. Empirical Results

The reduced form bivariate probit estimates of the probability of a mother being overweight and obese are presented in Table 2, while the single equation probit estimates of the probability of child being overweight are presented in Table 3. The results in Table 2 show that the estimate of ρ (correlation between the errors) that maximized the bivariate probit likelihood function was 2.81 and was significantly greater than 0 at the 1% level. This suggests a positive correlation between the unobservables that determine overweight and obesity status. This result

also provides a justification for using a bivariate probit model in estimating the equation for overweight and obesity.[4] The marginal effects of the regressors on the probability of being overweight or obese, which are calculated by multiplying the coefficient estimates $\hat{\gamma}$ by $\phi(\hat{\gamma}'X)$ at the mean values of X, are also reported with the coefficient estimates.

The log-likelihood ratio statistic was significant at the 1% level, suggesting that the independent variables taken together influence weight status. The McFadden R^2, an indication of goodness-of-fit and the log-likelihood statistics (indicator of the significance of all covariates) are also presented in each Table. The results show that household expenditure exerts a positive and significant impact on both the probability of being overweight and obese, with nonlinear effects. That is, the probability of being overweight or obese first increases with increasing expenditure and later declines with additional per capita household expenditures, a result that contradicts with some findings based on US data (e.g. Stunkard, 1996), but is in line with findings reported by Costa-Font and Gil (2004) for Spain. As argued by Philipson and Posner (1999) in less-developed economies, where the share of income spent on food is large, income will tend to exert a positive impact on weight.

The results also indicate that at younger ages an increase in age increases the risk of overweight and obese with the maximum effect occurring at 39.5 years for overweight and 39 years for obesity. At older ages, the risk of overweight and obesity decreases as age increases. This finding is consistent with the results reported by Costa-Font and Gil (2004) for Spain.

Education generally has little effect on weight of women with primary or middle education, but with women who have secondary and tertiary education, schooling tends to reduce the likelihood of being overweight or obese. The marginal effects of secondary and tertiary education for overweight are 0.09 and 0.11, respectively. The corresponding figures for obese are 0.10 and 0.15, respectively. These later findings are consistent with results reported by Cutler et al. (2003), who show that obesity for US women is negatively associated with education. As argued earlier, more educated women generally have more health knowledge and as such are more likely to consume healthy foods and also engage in physical exercises that help to control weight gains. A test of the null hypothesis

---

[4] We also estimated comparable models using BMI as a continuous measure as dependent variable and obtained qualitatively similar results.

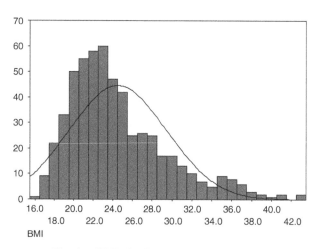

Fig. 1.   BMI distribution of mothers, 1997

Table 1. Definitions, means and SDs of variables

Variable	Variable description	Sample mean	SD
Dependent variables			
Mother overweight	1 if BMI $\geq$ 25 but less than 30, 0 otherwise	0.24	—
Mother obese	1 if BMI $\geq$ 30, 0 otherwise	0.13	—
Child overweight	1 if weight of child falls outside the 90th percentile of the sampled children, 0 otherwise	0.16	—
Independent variables			
Household size	Total number of people in household	5.1	2.3
Mother's age	Age of mother in completed years	29.76	7.69
Mother married	1 if mother is married, 0 otherwise	0.75	—
Child's age	Age of children between 0 and 6 years in months	17.55	9.91
No school	If primary care giver has no school education	0.11	—
Primary school	If primary care giver has primary school education	0.23	—
Middle/Islamic	If respondent has middle or Islamic school education	0.40	—
Secondary school	If primary care giver has some secondary or Islamic school education	0.16	—
Tertiary	If primary care giver has tertiary school education	0.10	—
Ga/Adangbe	If primary care giver is GA or Adangbe	0.37	—
Ewe	If primary care giver is Ewe	0.28	—
Akan	If primary care giver is Akan/Ashanti/Fanti	0.22	—
Other	If primary care giver is a different tribe	0.13	—
Age at 0–4	Household members between 0–4 years	0.26	0.11
Age at 5–14	Household members between 5–14 years	0.23	0.13
Age at 15–39	Household members between 15–39 years	0.39	0.21
Age at 40 and older	Household members of age 40 years and older	0.31	0.29
Farm or garden	1 if mother works on a farm or garden, 0 otherwise	0.69	—
Shop/factory/office	1 if mother works in a shop, factory or office, 0 otherwise	0.59	—
Street or market	1 if mother sells items on the street or in the market, 0 otherwise	1.15	—
FRUITCAL	Daily per head calorie consumption of fruit calories	50.42	127.8
TV	If TV present in household, 0 otherwise	0.50	—
Household expenditure	Log of per capita household monthly expenditure	8.73	0.50

Table 2. Bivariate estimates of whether mother is overweight or obese

Variable	Overweight Coefficient		Marginal probability		Obese Coefficient		Marginal probability
Intercept	−1.9851***	(−4.7007)			−1.4851***	(−4.1014)	
Mother's education							
Primary school	0.0985	(0.8686)	0.0291		0.0941	(0.8743)	0.0324
Middle/Islamic school	0.0674	(1.6180)	0.0198		0.1334	(1.2916)	0.0459
Secondary school	−0.2937**	(−2.1713)	−0.0865		−0.3078**	(−2.3827)	−0.1061
Tertiary education	−0.3761**	(−2.3268)	−0.1108		−0.4382***	(−2.8609)	−0.1510
Ethnicity							
Ga/Adangbe	0.4019**	(2.4697)	0.1184		0.3515**	(2.8044)	0.1211
Akan/Ashanti/Fanti	0.2528**	(2.0035)	0.0745		0.2671**	(2.12361)	0.0920
Ewe	0.0356	(1.3159)	0.0104		0.1752	(1.1443)	0.0604
Household characteristics							
Per capita household expenditure	0.0443**	(2.2477)	0.0131		0.0768**	(2.4336)	0.0265
Per capita household expenditure squared	−0.0055*	(−1.9730)	—		−0.0163*	(−1.8772)	—
Calories from fruits	−0.0278	(−1.2141)	−0.0082		−0.0958	(−1.37391)	−0.0329
Household members between 0–4 years	−0.1954*	(−1.8763)	0.0576		−0.0514*	(−1.7391)	−0.0177
Household members between 5–14 years	−0.1103	(−1.3547)	0.0325		−0.0117	(−1.1414)	−0.0040
Household members between 15–39 years	0.1965	(0.3448)	0.0571		0.0148	(1.2208)	0.0051
Household members of age 40 years and older	0.0091	(0.7144)	0.0027		0.0599	(0.9595)	0.0206
Married	0.0884	(1.2049)	0.0260		0.0145	(1.0651)	0.0049
Mother's age in years	0.0015**	(−2.6340)	0.0005		0.0014**	(2.5214)	0.0005
Mother's age squared	−0.0019**	(2.1053)	—		−0.0018**	(−2.0658)	—
Mother's work							
Farm or garden	−0.3184***	(−2.7691)	−0.0938		−0.3672**	(−2.4950)	−0.1265
Shop or factory or office	−0.2087*	(−1.9276)	−0.0615		−0.2265	(−1.3717)	−0.0781
Street or market	−0.1493*	(−1.6884)	−0.0439		−0.1384*	(−1.7892)	0.0477
Rho (1, 2)				0.281 (2.57)			
McFadden R^2				0.396			
Log-likelihood ratio				176.72			
Observations				555			

Notes: *t*-values errors are in parentheses.
* , ** and *** denote significance variables at 10, 5 and 1% level, respectively.

that the coefficients of the four education variables are jointly equal to zero is rejected for both overweight and obese. The sample value of the Wald statistics distributed as χ^2_4, are 16.59 and 17.56, with a critical value of 13.3.[5]

Work status appears to be associated with the risk of overweight and obesity. All the variables representing type of work are negative and statistically significant, implying that relative to their unemployed counterparts, women engaged in the labour market are less likely to be overweight or obese. The marginal effects suggest that relative to their counterparts in other employments, women working on farms or gardens (marginal effect of −0.09 and −0.13) are least likely to be overweight and obese. The negative and

highly significant coefficients of the variables representing work on farm or garden suggests that women engaged in these activities expend large amounts of energy and are therefore, less likely to be overweight and obese. The same applies to the variables for working in the market or street. Compared to women who are not engaged in the labour market, this group of women spend some time commuting to work and also engage in some work exercises. Although women at home might spend some time cooking, they are not likely to expend as much energy as those who commute to work and engage in physical activities on the job, that require substantial amounts of calories. A test of the null hypothesis that the coefficients of the three work-status variables are

[5] Note that obtaining tertiary education involves going through primary, middle and secondary schools.

Table 3. Probit estimates of whether child is overweight[a]

Variable	Coefficient	t-Value	Marginal probability
Intercept	−3.1667***	−2.2804	—
Child' age	0.2081	1.5862	0.0813
Mother's education			
Primary school	−0.0287	−1.1266	−0.0112
Middle/Islamic school	−0.1126	−1.3974	−0.0438
Secondary school	−0.3492**	−2.1807	−0.1360
Tertiary education	−0.5628**	−2.4218	−0.2192
Ethnicity			
Ga/Adangbe	0.4716**	2.1879	0.1837
Akan/Ashanti/Fanti	0.4380*	1.7684	0.1706
Ewe	0.2647	1.0952	0.1031
Household characteristics			
Household members between 0–4 years	−0.1683**	−2.4628	−0.0655
Household members between 5–14 years	−0.2174	−1.3964	−0.0847
Household members between 15–39 years	0.0156	0.0875	0.0061
Household members of age 40 years and older	0.0972	1.3379	0.0379
Mother is overweight[b]	0.1486**	2.4758	0.0409
Mother is obese[b]	0.3677**	2.5473	0.1284
Presence of a TV set	0.0729	1.5472	0.0316
Per capita expenditure	0.1653	1.6298	0.0655
Mother's work			
Farm or garden	0.1096	1.4963	0.0427
Shop or factory or office	0.1762*	1.6678	0.0686
Street or market	0.0873	1.0229	0.0341
Mother married	−0.0644	0.8716	−0.0322
Wald test statistics for joint significance			
Mother's education		$\chi^2_4 = 19.02$	
Mother's work status		$\chi^2_3 = 16.38$	
McFadden R^2		0.379	
Log-likelihood ratio		160.62	
Observations		724	

Notes: * , ** and *** denote significance variables at 10, 5 and 1% level, respectively.
[a] The dependent variable is a binary variable = 1 if child's BMI is above the 90th percentile for his/her age.
[b] The predicted values of these variables are used in place of the observed values.

jointly equal to zero is rejected for both overweight and obesity. The sample value of the Wald statistics distributed as χ^2_3, are 13.97 and 14.29 for overweight and obesity, respectively, with a critical value of 11.30.

The effects of ethnicity are also quite significant for overweight and obesity, with the Ga/Adangbe and Akan/Fanti/Ashante more likely to be overweight and obese than the other ethnic groups, with substantial marginal effects. In particular, Ga/Adangbes have significantly higher measures of outcomes. This finding is not surprising, given the fact that members of this ethnic group is generally known to be heavier than other ethnic groups in the country. Compared to other ethnic groups, Ewes do not seem to be significantly more likely to be overweight or obese.

In contrast to the findings of Costa-Font and Gil (2004), who report a notable effect of marital status on body mass in Spain, the results here reveal no significant effect of marriage on the probability of being overweight or obese. Although we do not focus on their coefficients, we also control for other variables such as household composition and household consumption of calories derived from fruits. While the negative, albeit insignificant coefficients of the variable for calories from fruits might indicate that greater quantities of fruits consumed tend to reduce the likelihood of overweight and obese, there is a question as to how the coefficients of the household composition variables may be interpreted. For example, the negative and significant (at the 10% level) coefficients of the variable for children under the age of five may either be linked to maternal employment patterns or household resources.[6]

[6] As argued earlier, if the presence of younger children in the household compels the mother to stay more at home, her presence may ensure that children eat more healthy foods that would reduce the likelihood of the child being overweight or obese. Particularly in a poor developing country, larger household size may be associated with budget limitations, resulting in reduced intake of calories.

Table 3 reports the results on the influence of individual and household effects on the probability of a child being overweight. A striking result is the impact of mother's weight on the child's weight status. To capture the differential impact of overweight and obese status of the mother, we include variables for obese and overweight mothers.[7] Both variables exert positive and significant impacts on the probability of a child being overweight, although the impact is greater for obese mothers. Given that obese mothers (BMI of at least 30) are also overweight (BMI of at least 25) in the present study, the marginal effect of a mother being obese is 0.16, which is the sum of the two marginal probabilities. This finding is in line with the notion that BMI has large genetic components, although it might also reflect the effects of the common home environment. If mothers for some reasons rely on calorie-rich prepared and fast foods, then one would expect everyone in the family to be more likely to be overweight.

Mother's education also appears to influence the probability of a child being overweight. The variables representing secondary and tertiary education are both negative and significant, implying that children with mothers that have attained secondary and tertiary education are less likely to be overweight.[8] A test of the null hypothesis that the coefficients of mother's education variables are jointly equal to zero is rejected, with a sample value of a Wald statistic of $\chi_4^2 = 19$ against a critical value of 13.30. This last finding would seem to confirm evidence provided by Langnäse et al. (2002) on the role of education in contributing to the epidemic of child obesity in Germany. It is, however, interesting to note that interpretation of such a finding poses a question as to whether maternal education actually has an impact on children's weight, or mothers with more education have other attributes that are different and tend to reduce the likelihood that their children will be overweight. As argued by Nayga (2000), the better health information knowledge of more educated women is probably responsible for the negative impact of mother's education on overweight.

Although the maternal work status variables are all positive, only the variable for the category shop/factory/office category is marginally significant, suggesting that the mother merely working does not necessarily have an impact on the child's weight status. The positive and significant impact of the shop/factory/office variable may be reflecting income effects on weight status, since this category of workers generally earn higher wages than their counterparts working on farms and gardens. Anderson et al. (2003) attribute the positive and significant impact of maternal work status on the probability that a child is overweight to constraints on mother's time.

Several of the other coefficients are also worth noting. As in the estimates for mothers, ethnicity also appears to influence the weight status of children. Relative to other ethnic groups, Ga/Adangbe children are significantly more likely to be overweight. Children from larger families are less likely to be overweight, compared to those from smaller families. Similarly, children from households with greater number of children under 5 years are less likely to be overweight.

Interesting enough, per capita expenditure does not seem to have any significant impact on the likelihood of a child being overweight. This is probably because the socio-economic status of the mother is well controlled for by education, ethnicity, weight and work status. In particular, expanding labour market opportunities for women normally result in significant increases in families' command of real resources and higher living standards. In order to verify if the socio-economic variables were responsible for the insignificance of the expenditure variable, we run a regression without the variables, but with per capita expenditure. Not surprisingly, there is a positive and significant impact of per capita expenditure, confirming that the inclusion of the socio-economic status of the mother renders the expenditure term insignificant.

Another interesting observation is the positive, albeit insignificant relationship between the presence of television in a household and weight of the child. The insignificance of the variable is probably due to the fact that it is a dummy that captures the presence or absence of a TV set in the household and not the extent of TV viewing, as in other studies. Particularly in Accra and several towns in Ghana, people from households without TV sets normally move from their homes to watch television in other homes, implying that TV viewing is a better variable to capture the impact. Since, the data employed in the present study does not contain information on TV viewing, using the presence of TV in the household provides information on TV viewing.

---

[7] The predicted values of the variables are used in place of the observed values.
[8] As pointed out by Glewwe (1998), father's schooling, apart from its income effect, is less likely to be important for maintaining children's health.

VI. Summary and Conclusions

Researchers and policy-makers are presently concerned about the sharp increase in the number of overweight children and adults in recent decades. Although it is quite apparent that weight gain arises from taking in more energy than one expends, the reasons for the sharp divergence between energy intake and expenditure in the last few decades remain unclear. While the genetic explanation for being overweight or obese may be compelling, the recent rapid increase in overweight suggests that other factors may be important as well. In particular, socio-economic status and technological innovations are among the factors that have been considered as important contributors to overweight problems.

This article employed a unique dataset to examine the influence of individual and household characteristics on the overweight and obesity among women and children in urban Accra, in Ghana. The data reveal that around 36% of women had a BMI > 25, while 13% showed a BMI $\geq$ 30, lending support to the growing concern that obesity is an emerging problem among adults in many large urban areas in developing countries, including Africa. The empirical examination of the determinants of overweight and obesity suggests a significant role for public policy in influencing the weight problems of urban Ghanaians.

Consistent with previous research, we find that mother's work status significantly affects her BMI and probability of being overweight. In particular, women engaged in farm or garden work and market or street work were found to be much less likely to be overweight relative to those who were unemployed and stayed at home. This finding suggests that women working on farms or gardens or even market and street work must normally commute to work and probably engage in work-related exercise, and as such are less likely to be overweight or obese. Commuting to work and engaging in work-related exercise require larger amounts of energy, which contributes to a reduction in weight gains.

Our results further reveal that mothers who attained secondary and tertiary education had lower BMIs and were much less likely to be overweight, lending support to the notion that education is negatively related to the probability of being overweight or obese. As shown by Nayga (2000), more educated women normally have better health information knowledge and are more likely to consume healthy foods and also engage in physical exercises that help to control weight

gains. Mother's education was also found to exert a negative and significant impact on the weight status of children. Thus, children with mothers who had secondary and tertiary education were far less likely to be overweight than those with only primary education or no schooling.

Our results also indicate that household expenditure exerts a positive and significant impact on the probability of a mother being overweight or obese, but at a decreasing rate, suggesting the importance of the relationship between income and weight control. In contrasts to findings from studies with US data, which report a negative relationship between income and weight, this observation indicates that at lower income levels, weight increases with increasing income, but tends to decline after a certain level of income. However, we find no evidence that household resources expressed through household expenditure affects the likelihood of a child being overweight.

Children whose mothers are obese are also more likely to be overweight, as the coefficients for overweight and obese both turned out to be positive and significant. Ethnicity also appears to be an important determinant of overweight and obesity, with Ga/Adangbe women and children being more likely to be overweight, compared to other ethnic groups. Although a much higher percentage of the Ga/Adangbe women than the other ethnic groups are overweight, it is generally known that particularly among the less-educated groups in urban areas, thinness continues to be a signal of possible poverty and poor health, malnutrition or even bad habits such as alcoholism and AIDS. It is therefore, not altogether surprising that in spite of the increasing trend towards slenderness, some women still view increasing weight as a sign of attractiveness.

It is worth mentioning that in developing economies, overweight and obesity problems are emerging at a time when under-nutrition remains a significant problem. The nutrition transition appears to be facilitating rapid gains in body weight in low income and under-nourished populations. Hence, strategies that consider both under-nourishment and overweight problems will need to be considered. As pointed out by Cabarello (2001), unless there is a concurrent reduction in childhood stunting and an improvement in adult stature, normalizing BMIs might not confer the same reduction in mortality risk as that in developed-countries populations. Continuing gains in BMI beyond the normal range will increase the potential risk associated with low stature. While reducing the health risk associated with obesity in developed countries requires a focus on controlling excess body weight, the task in developing countries also demands an effort to combat childhood malnutrition that would increase the stature of future generations of adults.

With regards to overweight and obesity in developing economies, public interventions like education programmes with a focus on healthy food choices, incorporation of physical activity and a decrease in sedentary behaviour will all be important. Moreover, promoting healthy behaviours to encourage, motivate and enable individuals lose weight by eating more fruits and vegetables, as well as nuts and grains would be quite significant in reducing the incidence of overweight and obesity. Future research in this area will still need to consider a broader understanding of other contributors to weight problems. It would be particularly interesting to know more about adult's and children's opportunities for vigorous exercises and access to recreational facilities.

Acknowledgements

The author would like to thank Wallace Huffman and James Mueller for stimulating his interest in this topic and the International Food Policy Research Institute, Washington, DC for making the data available; Ingrid Franz for research assistance, as well as the Journal editor and an anonymous reviewer for helpful comments and suggestions on an earlier version of the article.

References

Anderson, P. M., Butcher, K. F. and Levine, P. B. (2003) Maternal employment and overweight children, *Journal of Health Economics*, **22**, 477–504.

Baum, C. L. and Ford, W. F. (2004) The wage effects of obesity: a longitudinal study, *Health Economics*, **13**, 885–99.

Becker, D., Yanek, L., Koffman, D. and Bronner, Y. (1999) Body image preferences among urban African Americans and whites from low income communities, *Ethnicity and Disease*, **9**, 377–86.

Becker, G. S. (1981) *A Treatise on the Family*, Harvard University Press, Cambridge, MA.

Cabarello, B. (2005) Introduction to symposium on obesity in developing countries: biological and ecological factors, *Journal of Nutrition*, **131**, 866S–70S.

Calle, E. E., Rodrigues, C., Walker-Thurmond, K. and Thun., M. J. (2003) Overweight, obesity, and mortality from cancer in a prospectively studied cohort of U.S. adults, *New England Journal of Medicine*, **348**, 1625–2638.

Case, A. and Deaton, A. (2005). Health and wealth among the poor: India and South Africa compared, *American Economic Review Papers and Proceedings*, **95**, 229–33.

Chou, S. Y., Grossman, M. and Saffer., H. (2004) An economic analysis of adult obesity: results from the behavioral risk factor surveillance system, *Journal of Health Economics*, **23**, 565–87.

Costa-Font, J. and Gil, J. (2004) Social interactions and the contemporaneous determinants of individuals' weight, *Applied Economics*, **36**, 2253–63.

Costa-Font, J. and Gil, J. (2005) Obesity and the incidence of chronic diseases in Spain: a seemingly unrelated probit approach, *Economics and Human Biology*, **3**, 188–214.

Cutler, D. M., Glaeser, E. L. and Shapiro., J. M. (2003) Why have Americans become more obese, *Journal of Economic Perspectives*, **17**, 93–118.

Danielzik, S., Langnäse, K., Mast, M., Spethmann, C. and Müller, M. J. (2002) Impact of parental BMI on the manifestation of overweight 5–7 year old children, *European Journal of Nutrition*, **41**, 132–8.

Davidson, R. and Mackinnon, J. G. (1993) *Estimation and Inference in Econometrics*, Oxford University Press, New York.

Dietz, W. H. and Bellizzi, M. C. (1999) workshop on childhood obesity. summary of the discussion, *American Journal of Clinical Nutrition*, **70**, 173S–5S.

Glewwe, P. (1998) Why does mother's schooling raise child health in developing countries?, *Journal of Human Resources*, **34**, 124–59.

Gortmaker, S. L., Must, A., Sobol, A. M., Peterson, K., Colditz, G. A. and Dietz, W. H. (1996) Television viewing as a cause of increasing obesity among children in the United States, 1986–1990, *Archives of Pediatrics & Adolescent Medicine*, **150**, 356–62.

Komlos, J., Smith, P. and Bogin, B. (2004) Obesity and the rate of time preference: is there a connection?, *Journal of Biosocial Science*, **36**, 209–19.

Lancaster, K., 1971. Consumer Demand: A New Approach. Columbia University Press, New York.

Lakdawalla, D. and Philipson, T. (2002). The growth of obesity and technological change: a theoretical and empirical examination, NBER Working Paper No. 8946, Available at http://www.nber.org/papers/w894-6 (visited July 2005).

Langnaese, K., Mast, M. and Mueller, M. J. (2002) Social class differences in overweight of prepubertal children in northwest Germany, *International Journal of Obesity*, **26**, 566–72.

Martorell, R., Khan, L., Hughes, M. L. and Grammer Strawn, L. M. (1998) Obesity in latin American women and children, *Journal of Nutrition*, **128**, 1464–73.

Martorell, R. (2000) Obesity: an emerging health and nutrition issue in developing countries. in *Obesity in Women from Developing Countries*, (Eds.) L. Grammer Strawn, L. Khan, M. Hughes and R. Martorell,

International Food Policy Research Institute, Washington, DC, IFPRI Vision 2020 Book Chapter, pp. 49–53.

Maxwell, D., Levin, C. Armar-Klemesu, M. Ruel, M. Morris, S. and Ahiadeke, C. (2000) Urban livelihoods and food security in Greater Accra, Ghana, International Food Policy Research Institute Research Report No. 112, IFPRI, Washington, DC.

Monteiro, C. A., Conde, W. L. and Popkin, B. M. (2001) Independent effects of income and education on the risk of obesity in the brazilian adult population, *Journal of Nutrition*, **131**, 881S–86.

Nayga, R. M. (2000) Schooling, health knowledge and obesity, *Applied Economics*, **32**, 815–22.

Philipson, T. and Posner, R. (1999). The long-run growth in obesity as a function of technological change, John Ohlin Program in Law and Economics Working Paper No. 78, University of Chicago Law School.

Popkin, B. M., Paeratakul, S. and Ge, K. (1995) A review of dietary and environmental correlates of obesity with emphasis on developing countries, *Obesity Research*, **3**, 145S–53S.

Power, C., Lake, D. K. and Cole, T. J. (1997) Measurement and long-term health risks of child and adolescent fatness, *International Journal of Obesity and Related Metabolism Disorder*, **21**, 507–26.

Smith, P. K., Bogin, B. and Bishai, D. (2005) Are time preferences and boby mass index associated? Evidence from the National Longitudinal Survey of Youth, *Economics and Human Biology*, **3**, 259–70.

Stunkard, A. J. 1996. Socioeconomic status and obesity. *Origins and Consequences of Obesity*, **201**, 174–87.

Thomas, D., Lavy, V. and Strauss, J. (1996) Public policy and anthropometric outcomes in Cote d'Ivoire, *Journal of Public Economics*, **61**, 155–92.

US Department of Health and Human Services, Center for Disease Control and Prevention (2000). Overweight and obesity factors contributing to obesity: Biological, behavioral and environmental factors associated with overweight and obesity. www.cdc.gov/nccdphp/ dnpa/obesity/state_programs/index.htm (visited July 2005).

World Health Organization (2000) Obesity: preventing and managing the global epidemic. WHO Technical Report No. 894.

World Health Organization (2004) WHO World Health Assembly adopts global strategy on diet, physical activity and health, (Press Release) Available at http://www.who.int/mediacentre/releases/2004/ wha3/en/ (visited December 2004).

Dollars and pounds: the impact of family income on childhood weight

Y. F. Chia

Department of Economics, Cleveland State University, 2121 Euclid Avenue, Cleveland, OH 44115, USA

This article examines the impact of family income on childhood weight status for children in the United States using matched mother-child data from the National Longitudinal Survey of Youth (NLSY 79). Instrumental variable (IV) models, family Fixed Effects (FE) models and family Fixed Effects IV (FEIV) models are estimated in order to control for causality. The results suggest that although the prevalence of childhood obesity is higher in low-income families in the sample, family income might be acting primarily as a proxy for other unobserved characteristics that determine the child's weight status rather having a major direct causative role in determining the child's weight status.

I. Introduction

Childhood obesity is fast becoming one of the most prevalent childhood health conditions in many countries, especially in developed countries like the United States. In 2003–2004, 17.1% of children and adolescents in the USA were obese (Ogden *et al.*, 2006). In contrast, only 4% of children between the ages of 6 and 11 and 5% of adolescents between the ages of 12 to 19 in the USA were obese back in the 1960s (Ogden *et al.*, 2002a).

The main reason as to why public health authorities are concerned about the increase in the prevalence of childhood obesity is that childhood obesity is known to have adverse health effects and these effects might prove to be costly to society in the long run. Some of the health issues associated with childhood obesity include increased likelihoods of developing physical health conditions such as sleep apnea, asthma, fatty liver disease, type II diabetes and either early or delayed puberty (Lobstein *et al.*, 2004). In addition, children who are at-risk-of-overweight or obese are more likely to grow up into overweight, or obese adults who have elevated risks for cardiovascular conditions (Srinivasan *et al.*, 1996).

There have been several studies in the economics literature that have examined the potential causes of the increase in obesity prevalence. Philipson and Posner (1999) and

Lakdawalla and Philipson (2002) argue that technological change has increased the cost of physical activity and lowered costs of calories, thus causing the increase in weight observed in the United States. Cutler *et al.* (2003) suggest that technological changes in food preparation in the USA have led to decreases in both fixed and marginal time costs of food production, thus leading to increased caloric consumption. Anderson *et al.* (2003) and Chia (2008) present evidence to suggest that increased maternal participation in the labour force can lead to an increase in the likelihood of childhood obesity.

The prevalence of childhood obesity has been observed to differ for different socio-economic segments of society. The relationship between family income and childhood obesity prevalence differs between developed countries and developing countries. In developed countries, children from lower-income families are at a higher risk of becoming obese (Wang *et al.*, 2002; Armstrong *et al.*, 2003). On the other hand, in developing countries, children from higher-income families are at a higher risk of being obese (de Onis and Blössner, 2000; Wang *et al.*, 2002).

Most of the studies that have examined the impact of family income on weight have produced statistical correlations rather than causal estimates. The main econometric issue involved with estimating the causal impact of family income on weight is that it is very likely that there are unobserved factors that affect both income and weight. Does income have a major direct causal impact on the determination of weight outcomes or does income act mostly a proxy for other factors that affect weight? In a recent article, Schmeiser (2009) uses exogenous variation in family income produced by state-level and federal-level changes in the maximum Earned Income Tax Credit (EITC) benefit amount available to families to investigate the causal impact of income on weight for low-income adults in the United States. This study produces estimates which suggest that an increase in income leads to an increase in the Body Mass Index (BMI) values for low-income adults in the United States (Schmeiser, 2009).

The main objective of this article is to examine the impact of family income on childhood weight outcomes for children in the United States using matched mother–child data from the National Longitudinal Survey of Youth (NLSY 79). In order to produce causal estimates, I adopt the Instrumental Variable (IV) strategy used by Dahl and Lochner (2005). One of the main sources of identification for this IV strategy is the exogenous changes made to the US federal income tax code (in particular, changes made to the federal EITC program) over the period of the time covered by the sample utilized in this article.

The organization of this article is as follows. Section II describes the main changes made to the federal EITC program that serve as one of the primary sources of identification for the IV strategy, as well as the econometric methods and the sample utilized in this study. Section III presents and discusses the results from the analysis and Section IV concludes the article.

II. Material and Methods

The EITC

The EITC started as a relatively modest anti-poverty program in 1975 and has since grown into the largest federally funded means-tested cash assistance program in the United States (Hotz and Schloz, 2003). The total real monetary amount of the refunded portion of the credit from the EITC program has increased from \$3.08 billion (2003 US dollars) in 1975 to \$30.9 billion in 2003 (US House of Representatives, 2004). The number of recipient families has also grown from 6.2 million in 1975 to 19.3 million in 2003 (US House of Representatives, 2004). The real average credit per family has increased from \$687 (2003 US dollars) in 1975 to \$1784 in 2003 (US House of Representatives, 2004). The changes made to the EITC program are of specific interest to my analysis because they provide exogenous sources of variation in after-tax, after-transfer family income over the time period covered by my sample.

The EITC is a refundable tax credit for low-income working taxpayers and taxpayers apply for it through their income tax returns. The credit takes the form of a specified percentage (credit rate) of earned income up to a maximum amount. The maximum amount is applicable for earned incomes in a specified income range. The credit is then phased out to zero over a certain income range (phase out range). The credit rates, phase out rates and income ranges eligible for the credit have changed several times since the inception of the program in 1975 and have resulted in the expansion of the EITC program (US House of Representatives, 2004). In 1987, the credit was indexed for inflation. In 1991, the EITC program was significantly expanded. The credit rate and the maximum credit were raised and the range of incomes eligible for the credit was increased significantly. Separate schedules were also established for families with one child and families with two or more children. Prior to 1991, families have faced the same EITC schedules regardless of the number of children in the family. Since 1991, families with two or more children have faced a more generous EITC schedule than families with fewer children. The EITC program was again extensively expanded in 1994, raising the credit rates, maximum credits and phase out rates significantly (US House of Representatives, 2004). Table 1 summarizes the main EITC parameters for the tax years that are applicable to the sample used in this article.

Econometric model and IV estimation strategy

The econometric model and IV estimation strategy used in this article are derived from Dahl and Lochner (2005). The notation used below is also derived from the notation used in the Dahl and Lochner's (2005) article.

The relationship between the child i's weight-related outcomes and family income in period t is represented by the following equation:

$$weight_{it} = \beta_0 + \beta_x X_i + \beta_w W_{it} + \theta I_{it} + \varepsilon_{it} \qquad (1)$$

where $weight_{it}$ represents the child's weight-related outcome, X_i consists of fixed characteristics that affect the child's weight, W_{it} represents time-varying characteristics that affect the child's weight and I_{it} is total after-tax and after-transfer family income.

I_{it} can be further decomposed into total pre-tax family income and net transfers

$$I_{it} = PI_{it} + \tau_t^{s_{it}}(PI_{it}) \qquad (2)$$

where PI_{it} is total pre-tax family income in period t and $\tau_t^{s_{it}}(PI_{it})$ represents net transfers under the federal tax code in period t. $\tau_t^{s_{it}}(\cdot)$ represents the federal tax function in period t and s_{it} denotes the federal tax schedule that is relevant for the child's family in period t based on family characteristics such as marital status and number of children in the family.[1]

Total pre-tax family income, PI_{it}, is in turn the sum of the different categories listed on the personal income tax forms such as wage and salary income (including self-employment income), nontaxable transfer income, unemployment compensation, other income and so on and can thus be denoted as

$$PI_{it} = \sum_{n=1}^{N} pi_{int} \qquad (3)$$

where n indexes the components of pre-tax family income, N is the total number of pre-tax family income categories listed on

---

[1] The tax burdens in this article are calculated using the TAXSIM interface on the National Bureau of Economic Research (NBER) website (http://www.nber.org/taxsim).

Table 1. EITC parameters (monetary values are nominal values unless otherwise stated)

Calender (tax) year		Credit rate (%)	Minimum income for maximum credit ($)	Maximum credit ($)	Phase out rate
1987		14.00	6080	851	10.00
1989		14.00	6500	910	10.00
1991	One child	16.70	7140	1192	11.93
	Two children	17.30	7140	1235	12.36
1993	One child	18.50	7750	1434	13.21
	Two children	19.50	7750	1511	13.93
1995	No children	7.65	4100	314	7.65
	One child	34.00	6160	2094	15.98
	Two children	36.00	8640	3110	20.22
1997	No children	7.65	4340	332	7.65
	One child	34.00	6500	2210	15.98
	Two children	40.00	9140	3656	21.06
1999	No children	7.65	4530	353	7.65
	One child	34.00	6800	2312	15.98
	Two children	40.00	9540	3816	21.06
2001	No children	7.65	4760	364	7.65
	One child	34.00	7140	2428	15.98
	Two children	40.00	10 020	4008	21.06
2003	No children	7.65	4990	382	7.65
	One child	34.00	7490	2537	15.98
	Two children	40.00	10 510	4204	21.06

Source: US House of Representatives (2004).

the income tax forms that I have data for[2] and pi_{int} is the nth component of pre-tax family income for child i's family in period t. In this article, PI_{it} is constructed from the income that the mother and her spouse (if present in the household) receive from various sources such as wages, salaries, tips, business income, farm income, military income, unemployment income, interest income, educational benefits, veteran benefits, disability benefits, social security income, welfare, Aid to Families with Dependent Children (AFDC), alimony, child support and other sources.

The IV strategy used to estimate Equation 1 is based on the approach used in Dahl and Lochner (2005) and relies on the fact that total after-tax, after-transfer family income is a function of family characteristics and the tax code. A subset (denoted as z_{it}) of the variables in X_i and W_{it} are exogenous variables that affect the components of pre-tax family income. This vector z_{it} consists of variables such as the mother's age, race, immigrant status, educational attainment at age 23 and Armed Forces Qualifying Test (AFQT) percentile score.[3] As such, the nth pre-tax income component can be written as

$$pi_{\text{int}} = \gamma_{nt}z_{it} + \upsilon_{\text{int}} \qquad (4)$$

where γ_{nt} is allowed to vary over time and component.

Thus, total after-tax family income can be expressed as

$$I_{it} = \sum_{n=1}^{N}(\gamma_{nt}z_{it} + \upsilon_{\text{int}}) + \tau_t^{s_{it}}\left(\sum_{n=1}^{N}(\gamma_{nt}z_{it} + \upsilon_{\text{int}})\right) \qquad (5)$$

The procedure for constructing the IV for total after-tax, after-transfer family income is as follows. I first estimate each component of pre-tax family income as a function of the exogenous characteristics z_{it} (i.e. I estimate Equation 4 for each of the N components of pre-tax family income) in order to obtain predicted values of each pre-tax income component ($\hat{pi} = \hat{\gamma}_{nt}z_{it}$) and predicted total pre-tax family income ($\hat{PI}_{it} = \sum_{n=1}^{N}\hat{\gamma}_{nt}z_{it}$). The construction of the IV in this article differs from that of Dahl and Lochner's (2005), in which I allow each of the N components of pre-tax income listed on the income tax forms to be determined differently by z_{it} while Dahl and Lochner (2005) allows only total pre-tax income to vary with z_{it}.[4] Using these predicted pre-tax income values, I then calculate the predicted net transfer $\tau_t^{s_{it}}(\hat{PI}_{it})$ using the tax schedule that the family faces in period t. Finally, I construct the predicted total after-tax, after-transfer family income $\hat{I}_{it}$, where $\hat{I}_{it} = \hat{PI}_{it} + \tau_t^{s_{it}}(\hat{PI}_{it})$. $\hat{I}_{it}$ is the IV used in this article for I_{it}.

[2] The components of N include wage and salary income (including self-employment income), nontaxable transfer income, unemployment compensation, other income. I set the values of the pre-tax family income categories, listed on the income tax forms that I do not have information, on to zero in order for the tax calculator in TAXSIM to be able to calculate the tax burdens.

[3] The AFQT consists of a battery of 10 tests that measure knowledge and skill in the following areas: (1) general science; (2) arithmetic reasoning; (3) word knowledge; (4) paragraph comprehension; (5) numerical operations; (6) coding speed; (7) auto and shop information; (8) mathematics knowledge; (9) mechanical comprehension and (10) electronics information. During the summer and fall of 1980, the AFQT was administered to the NLSY 79 respondents (the mothers of the children in my sample are drawn from the pool of NLSY 79 respondents) as part of the NLSY survey design. The mother's percentile score on the AFQT serves as a proxy for her level of human capital in this article.

[4] One of the reasons for this modification is that in order to calculate the tax burdens through the TAXSIM interface on the NBER website, I need to fill in the individual values for the various pre-tax family income categories listed on the TAXSIM interface.

The constructed IV $\hat{I}_{it}$ is a function of the exogenous maternal characteristics and the exogenously determined federal tax code. As such, there are two main sources of identification. The first source of identification comes from changes in returns to income sources attributable to various specific maternal characteristics that have occurred over the time period covered by the sample. The second source of identification comes from exogenous changes to the federal tax code. As noted in the previous section, the EITC program underwent large, nonlinear expansions at certain points in time over the time period covered by my sample. As such, changes in the EITC program serves as one of the main drivers of exogenous variation in the tax code.

Data and sample selection

This article makes use of the data from the public-use children files and adult files of the NLSY 79. The NLSY was started in 1979 as a survey of American youths between the ages of 14 and 21. Starting in 1986, the NLSY administrators started collecting data on children born to mothers who were part of the NLSY 1979 cohort. Follow-up surveys on these children have been conducted once in every 2 years since then. The data collected for the child can be matched up to data collected for the mother to create matched mother–child pairs. This article makes use of the data available for the matched mother–child pairs from the data cycles collected starting in 1988 and ending in 2004.[5] The sample is restricted to children in each cycle who are: (1) over the age of two, (2) still eligible to be interviewed as children in the NLSY and (3) for whom weight status and family income are available.

The NLSY contains information on the heights and weights of the children surveyed in the children files. Their weights and heights are recorded in two ways: they are either actual measured values measured by the interviewer or they are estimates given by the mother. As such, indicator variables for whether the height is based on the mother's estimate and for whether the weight is based on the mother's estimate are included as covariates in the regressions to account for this discrepancy. From the heights and weights of the children, I can calculate their BMI values. Based on the BMI values, I can determine whether a child is considered to be at-risk-of-overweight or obese by comparing the BMI of the child to the age and gender specific cutoffs from the Centres for Disease Control and Prevention (CDC). These cutoffs are percentile values from age and gender specific growth charts developed by the CDC based on data from five reference populations surveyed between 1963 and 1994 (Ogden et al., 2002b).[6]

The cutoffs are available for children between the ages of 2 to 20 years. Children who have BMIs between the 85th and 95th percentile values are classified as being at-risk-of-overweight. Children who have BMIs higher than the 95th percentile values are classified as being obese.[7]

The mothers are asked to provide detailed information on the amount of income that they and their spouses (if present in the household) receive from various different sources in the previous calendar year. These sources include wages, salaries, tips, business income, farm income, military income, unemployment income, interest income, educational benefits, veteran benefits, disability benefits, social security income, welfare, AFDC, alimony, child support and other sources. As such, it is possible to construct measures of pre-tax family income components and total pre-tax family income in the calendar year prior to the survey year from the sources available in the survey. The NLSY does not ask the respondents to report the amount of income taxes that they have paid. In order to calculate the federal income tax liabilities and EITC payments for the families in my sample, I make use of the TAXSIM program available from the NBER website.[8]

The NLSY also contains a wealth of information on other aspects related to the child. In particular, the NLSY contains data on the child's birthweight. Since weight at birth affects the child's future weight, birthweight is included as a control in my analysis. Studies from the medical literature also suggest that breastfeeding lowers the risk of childhood obesity (von Kries et al., 1999; Gillman et al., 2001; Armstrong et al., 2002). As such, I include an indicator for whether the child was breastfed as a control in the regressions. Additional child demographic controls that are included in my analysis are the child's age, gender, race and birth order.

Studies have suggested that overweight parents are more likely to have overweight children (Lake et al., 1997; Whitaker et al., 1997). The NLSY contains information on the mother's weight and height and I use this information to control for whether the mother is overweight and/or obese in the regressions.[9] I also control for other maternal characteristics such as the mother's educational attainment at the age of 23, AFQT percentile, age of the mother at the birth of the child, immigrant status, health status, marital status and an indicator for whether the mother lived with both biological parents at the age of 14.

In addition, family specific controls such as the number of children in the household, the number of adults in the household and an indicator for whether the area of residence is rural are also included as controls in my analysis.

---

[5] The relevant survey years are 1988, 1990, 1992, 1994, 1996, 1998, 2000, 2002 and 2004. Since the income data available is for the calendar year prior to the survey year, the tax years that are relevant for the sample used in this article are 1987, 1989, 1991, 1993, 1995, 1997, 1999, 2001 and 2003.

[6] The growth chart data can be found at: http://www.cdc.gov/nchs/about/major/nhanes/growthcharts/datafiles.htm.

[7] The terminology used in this article differs slightly from the terminology adopted by the CDC. Due to the perceived stigma attached to the term 'obese', the CDC has decided to avoid using 'obese' to describe children. Instead, the CDC has adopted a terminology in which children whose BMIs are greater than the 95th percentiles are described as being 'overweight'. However, the 95th percentile cutoffs are considered to be comparable to cutoffs used to define childhood obesity in other systems of classification such as the International Obesity Task Force (IOTF) classification system.

[8] The TAXSIM program can be found at http://www.nber.org/taxsim. For more information on the TAXSIM program, refer to Feenberg and Coutts (1993).

[9] The NLSY does not contain information on the father's weight and height.

Table 2. Summary of EITC-related characteristics for sample

Survey year	Tax year	Number of children	Average pre-tax income (2003 dollars)	Fraction eligible for EITC	Mean EITC payment if eligible (2003 dollars)
1988	1987	3958	38 731.61	0.26	649.72
1990	1989	3698	45 782.63	0.26	706.49
1992	1991	4100	48 244.37	0.25	936.16
1994	1993	3701	54 150.91	0.23	1084.22
1996	1995	3390	63 254.95	0.22	1813.41
1998	1997	3018	67 497.98	0.20	2068.62
2000	1999	2161	74 175.52	0.19	2358.15
2002	2001	2074	86 748.45	0.16	2009.66
2004	2003	1704	89 400.21	0.13	1905.54

Note: Weighted with child sampling weights.

III. Results and Discussion

Descriptive statistics

Table 2 describes the EITC-related characteristics of the sample for each survey year. Given the sampling design of the NLSY, it is not surprising that average family pre-tax income increases steadily throughout the sample period as a reflection of the mothers progressing through their lifecycles. The changes in the number of children meeting the sample selection requirements over the sample period also reflect the lifecycle progressions of the mothers. The number of children increases initially because the mothers are young mothers in the early survey years and are still giving birth to new children who enter the NLSY survey. The number of children eligible eventually decreases as the children grow older and start to move out of the mother's household. Since average pre-tax family income is steadily increasing throughout the sample period, it is not entirely surprising that the proportion of families eligible for the EITC actually falls in the later years of the sample period even though there were expansions in the EITC program happening simultaneously. However, for families which are eligible for the EITC, the magnitude of the average real EITC payment increases up till the tax year of 1999. The figures suggest that the changes made to the EITC program have created variation in the magnitude of the average EITC payment between survey years. Because of the expansion of the EITC program in the tax year 1991, the average EITC payment for eligible families in the sample jumps from $706 (2003 dollars) in the tax year 1989 to $936 (2003 dollars) in the tax year 1991, a difference of $230. The even more generous expansion of the EITC program in the tax year 1994 leads to an even larger increase in the average EITC payment for eligible families post expansion. In the last cycle prior to the 1994 expansion, the average EITC payment for eligible families in the sample is $1084 (2003 dollars). In the first cycle after the 1994 expansion, the average EITC payment for eligible families has increased to $1813 (2003 dollars).

Table 3 summarizes the main characteristics of the sample used in this article. A comparison of the characteristics of the children from the low-income, EITC-eligible families with the characteristics of the children from the higher-income families suggests that there are differences between the two groups outside of weight outcomes and family income. Children from the low-income families are more likely to be at-risk-of-overweight or obese than children from the higher-income families. 31.2% of the children from the low-income, EITC-eligible families are at-risk-of-overweight or obese compared to 28% of the children from the higher-income families. Children in the low-income sub-sample are much more likely to be Black than children in the higher-income sub-sample. They are also more likely to be Hispanic. Children from low-income families are also more likely to be born with low birthweight and are less likely to be breastfed as infants.

There are also several significant differences between the mothers of the children in the two sub-samples. The mothers in the low-income sub-sample are much less likely to be married and have a spouse present in the household compared to the mothers in the higher-income sub-sample. They also tend to be younger at the birth of the child. One of the things to note is that the mothers in the low-income sub-sample are more likely to be overweight or obese than mothers in the higher-income sub-sample, i.e. 50.3% of the mothers in the low-income sub-sample are overweight or obese compared to 44.6% of the mothers in the higher-income sub-sample.

One factor that might affect both the child's weight and family income is the mother's human capital. Mothers with high human capital are likely to earn higher wages. They might also provide better care for their children. If mothers with high human capital tend to be better informed on healthy nutritional practices and childhood activities, then the children of mothers with high human capital will be more likely to be within the healthy weight range. As such, maternal human capital should be accounted for when looking at the relationship between childhood weight and family income. In the NLSY, maternal educational attainment at the age of 23 and maternal AFQT score are available and can serve as proxies for maternal human capital. The figures presented in Table 3 suggest that there are significant differences in maternal educational attainment at the age of 23 and maternal AFQT score between mothers in the two sub-samples. Mothers in the low-income sub-sample have much lower AFQT scores and are also much less likely to be educated beyond high school at the age of 23 compared to the mothers in the higher-income sub-sample.

Table 3. Descriptive statistics for sample

	(1)	(2)	(3)	(4)
	Full sample	Eligible for EITC	Ineligible for EITC	(2)–(3)
Main variables				
Child is at-risk-of-overweight or obese	0.287	0.312	0.280	0.032
Child is at-risk-of-overweight	0.141	0.150	0.138	0.012
Child is obese	0.146	0.161	0.142	0.019
Pre-tax income (2003 dollars)	60 821.790	19 182.580	72 417.290	−53 234.710
After-tax income (2003 dollars)	52 858.080	20 187.890	61 955.920	−41 768.030
Child variables				
Age of child (years)	8.565	9.054	8.429	0.625
Child is male	0.513	0.507	0.514	−0.008
Child is Black	0.146	0.264	0.113	0.152
Child is Hispanic	0.068	0.087	0.063	0.024
Child is firstborn	0.423	0.388	0.433	−0.044
Birthweight (ounces)	118.767	115.235	119.762	−4.527
Low birthweight (birthweight < 5.5 lbs)	0.071	0.091	0.066	0.025
Child was breastfed	0.550	0.407	0.590	−0.183
Mother variables				
Age of mother at birth	26.116	24.561	26.549	−1.988
Current age of mother	34.663	33.594	34.961	−1.367
Mother is overweight or obese	0.458	0.503	0.446	0.057
Mother is obese	0.203	0.259	0.187	0.071
Mother has health limitations	0.064	0.081	0.059	0.023
Mother's AFQT percentile	46.630	32.128	50.669	−18.541
Mother is an immigrant	0.040	0.043	0.039	0.004
Mother lived with both parents at the age of 14	0.728	0.623	0.757	−0.134
Mother is married	0.716	0.332	0.822	−0.490
Mother's education at the age of 23				
Less than high school	0.145	0.252	0.116	0.136
High school graduate	0.482	0.568	0.458	0.110
Some college	0.217	0.159	0.234	−0.075
College graduate	0.155	0.021	0.193	−0.171
Family variables				
Number of children	2.496	2.516	2.496	0.020
Number of adults in household	2.200	1.880	2.200	−0.321
Area of residence is rural	0.285	0.293	0.285	0.009
Number of observations	27 804	7498	20 306	

Note: Weighted with child sampling weights.

OLS estimates

The results from the Ordinary Least Squares (OLS) specifications are summarized in Table 4.[10] In the basic OLS specification for the at-risk-of-overweight regression where additional child, household and maternal variables are not included as regressors, total after-tax family income is negatively associated with the probability that the child is at-risk-of-overweight. However, once the additional child, household and maternal variables are added as controls, the estimated coefficient on family income is no longer statistically significant. The decrease in statistical significance of the estimated coefficient on family income is not surprising since many of the additional household and maternal variables potentially affect both family income and child weight status.

For the OLS specifications where the outcome variable is the obese indicator, the estimated coefficients on total family income are always negative and statistically significant. In the basic OLS specification where additional child, household and maternal variables are not included as regressors, a $10 000 increase in family income is associated with a 0.75-percentage-point decrease in the likelihood that the child is obese. This correlation is statistically significant at the 1% level. However, once the additional child, household and maternal controls are included in the full OLS specification, the absolute magnitude of the estimated coefficient on family income falls considerably and the estimated coefficient is statistically significant only at the 10% level. In the OLS specification with the full set of controls, a $10 000 increase in family income is associated with a 0.20-percentage-point decrease in the likelihood that the child is obese. Overall, the OLS results provide some evidence to suggest that an increase in family income is associated with a decrease in the likelihood that the child is obese.

[10] The equations of interest were also estimated using logit and probit. The results from the logit and probit regressions are similar to those from the OLS regressions and are available upon request. Since one of the objectives of this article is to report Fixed Effects (FE) and Fixed Effects Instrumental Variables (FEIV) estimates, I chose to implement a linear probability model instead of logit or probit. This decision was made because FE estimators of nonlinear panel models are known to have the potential to be severely biased (for an overview, see Greene, 2004).

Table 4. OLS estimates

	At-risk-of-overweight [Basic]	At-risk-of-overweight [Full]	Obese [Basic]	Obese [Full]
After-tax income ($10 000)	−0.00134	0.0001	−0.00748	−0.00195
	[1.75]*	[0.10]	[8.23]***	[1.81]*
Mother's education: High school		−0.01036		−0.01517
		[0.95]		[1.10]
Mother's education: Some college		−0.01678		−0.01101
		[1.26]		[0.67]
Mother's education: College graduate		−0.01592		−0.0527
		[0.87]		[2.65]***
Mother's AFQT percentile		−0.0001		−0.0006
		[0.55]		[2.56]**
Constant	0.11094	0.06602	0.17948	−0.00644
	[6.71]***	[1.24]	[9.04]***	[0.10]
Observations	27 650	23 430	27 650	23 430
R-squared	0.01	0.02	0.03	0.06

Notes: Robust *t*-statistics are in brackets. Regressions are weighted with child sampling weights. All specifications are estimated with year FE and with dummies for the child's age, gender and region of residence. The full set of controls also includes the child's birthweight, a dummy for low birthweight, a dummy for whether the child was breastfed, the number of adults in the household, number of children, age of mother at birth of child, dummy for firstborn status, dummies for the child's race, dummies for the mother having health limitations, for the mother being an immigrant, for the mother being married, for the mother being overweight or obese, for the mother living with both parents at the age of 14 and a dummy for the area of residence being rural.
*, ** and *** denote significance at 10, 5 and 1% levels, respectively.

Table 5. IV estimates

	At-risk-of-overweight [Basic]	At-risk-of-overweight [Full]	Obese [Basic]	Obese [Full]
After-tax income ($10 000)	−0.00258	0.00101	−0.02291	0.00192
	[1.50]	[0.08]	[10.50]***	[0.15]
Mother's education: High school		−0.01053		−0.01587
		[0.94]		[1.14]
Mother's education: Some college		−0.01751		−0.0141
		[1.06]		[0.73]
Mother's education: College graduate		−0.01814		−0.06207
		[0.53]		[1.71]*
Mother's AFQT percentile		−0.00012		−0.00066
		[0.40]		[1.98]**
Constant	0.11701	0.06723	0.25463	−0.00131
	[6.61]***	[1.20]	[11.28]***	[0.02]
Observations	27 650	23 430	27 650	23 430
R-squared	0.01	0.02		0.06

Notes: See notes in Table 4.

However, the inclusion of additional child, household and maternal variables as controls does decrease the absolute magnitude and the level of statistical significance of the estimated coefficient on total family income. This suggests that family income might be mostly a proxy for other unobserved characteristics that affect the child's weight status rather than having a major direct causative impact on the child's weight status itself.

IV estimates

Table 5 summarizes the results from the IV specifications where predicted total after-tax, after-transfer family income acts as an instrument for actual total after-tax, after-transfer family income. The IV specifications are estimated in order to control for time-variant unobserved heterogeneity that might

affect both family income and the child's weight outcomes. The first-stage regressions suggest that predicted total after-tax family income is a strong predictor of actual total after-tax family income (see the Appendix, Table A1).

For the specifications where the dependent variable is the at-risk-of-overweight indicator, the IV estimates of the coefficient on total family income are not statistically significant.

In the basic IV specification where the dependent variable is the obese indicator and where additional child, household and maternal variables are not included as controls, the estimated coefficient on family income is negative and statistically significant at the 1% level. However, once the additional child, household and maternal variables are included as controls, the IV estimate of the coefficient on total family income becomes positive and statistically insignificant.

Table 6. Family FE estimates

	At-risk-of-overweight [Basic]	At-risk-of-overweight [Full]	Obese [Basic]	Obese [Full]
After-tax income ($10 000)	−0.00053	0.00011	−0.0008	−0.00177
	[0.46]	[0.08]	[0.72]	[1.35]
Constant	0.1758	0.41658	0.14373	−0.20422
	[5.69]***	[1.99]**	[5.15]***	[1.12]
Observations	27 650	23 430	27 650	23 430
R-squared	0.2	0.22	0.32	0.34

Notes: Robust *t*-statistics are in brackets. Regressions are weighted with child sampling weights. All specifications are estimated with year FE and with dummies for the child's age, gender and region of residence. The full set of controls also includes the number of adults in the household, number of children, dummies for the mother having health limitations, for the mother being married, for the mother being overweight or obese and a dummy for the area of residence being rural.
** and *** denote significance at 5 and 1% levels, repectively.

Table 7. Family FEIV estimates

	At-risk-of-overweight [Basic]	At-risk-of-overweight [Full]	Obese [Basic]	Obese [Full]
After-tax income ($10 000)	0.00445	0.01955	0.00689	0.03185
	[0.37]	[0.72]	[0.59]	[1.22]
Constant	0.12806	0.19598	0.14862	−0.44382
	[2.04]**	[0.00]	[2.44]**	[0.00]
Observations	27 650	23 430	27 650	23 430

Notes: Robust *t*-statistics are in brackets. Regressions are weighted with child sampling weights. All specifications are estimated with year FE and with dummies for the child's age, gender and region of residence. The full set of controls also includes the number of adults in the household, number of children, dummies for the mother having health limitations, for the mother being married, for the mother being overweight or obese and a dummy for the area of residence being rural.
** Denotes significane at 5% level.

To summarize, the IV estimates of the coefficients on total family income are not statistically significant in the specifications with the full set of controls for all of the weight-related indicators studied. This might suggest that family income acts mostly as a proxy for other characteristics that determine the child's weight rather than family income playing a major direct causative role in the determination of the child's weight.

Family FE estimates

Table 6 summarizes the results from the family FE specifications. The family fixed effects specifications control for the time-invariant unobserved heterogeneity at the family level that might affect both family income and the child's weight outcomes. The family FE models are identified off for changes in family income over time. Although the family FE estimates of the coefficients on family income generally have the same signs as the corresponding OLS estimates, they are not statistically significant for any of the weight indicators being studied. This might be further evidence to suggest that family income is acting mainly as a proxy for unobserved characteristics that affect the child's weight rather than acting as a major causative agent that directly affects the child weight.

Family FEIV estimates

Table 7 summarizes the family FEIV results. The FEIV models in effect control for time-variant and time-invariant

unobserved heterogeneity at the family level that might affect both family income and the child's weight outcomes. The first-stage regressions for the FEIV model suggest that predicted total after-tax family income is a strong predictor of actual total after-tax family income (see the Appendix, Table A2).

Similar to the family FE estimates presented in the previous sub-section, the FEIV estimates of the coefficients on family income are never statistically significant for any of the weight indicators being studied. This provides more evidence that family income might be mainly a proxy for unobserved characteristics that determine the child's weight rather than being a major causative agent in the determination of the child's weight.

IV. Conclusions

This article has attempted to examine the impact of family income on childhood weight for children in the United States. The descriptive statistics support the common perception that the prevalence of childhood obesity is higher in low-income families than in higher-income families in the United States. However, when examined together, the results from the various different estimation procedures suggest that family income might act primarily as a proxy for other characteristics that determine the child's weight, rather having a major direct causative role in determining the child's weight.

The OLS results provide some evidence to suggest that an increase in family income is associated with a decrease in the likelihood that the child is obese. However, the inclusion of additional child, household and maternal variables as controls in the OLS specifications does decrease the absolute magnitude and level of statistical significance of the estimated coefficient on total family income, raising the possibility that family income might be acting mainly as a proxy for unobserved factors that affect both income and the child's weight.

In order to account for unobserved family characteristics that might affect both family income and the child's weight status, IV models, family FE models and family FEIV models are also estimated. The IV estimates of the coefficients on total family income are not statistically significant in the specifications with the full set of controls for all of the weight-related indicators studied. The family FE estimates and the FEIV estimates of the coefficients on family income are never statistically significant for any of the weight indicators studied. Thus, when examined together, the results from the various estimation procedures seem to suggest that family income might be acting primarily as a proxy for other characteristics that determine the child's weight rather than having a major direct causative impact in determining the child's weight.

This article presents a preliminary attempt to examine the causal impact of family income on childhood weight. Many questions about the relationships between socio-economic factors and the childhood obesity epidemic remain to be answered through future research.

Acknowledgements

I would like to thank Mark Stabile, Michael Baker and Phil Oreopolous for their guidance and helpful suggestions. I would also like to thank seminar participants at the Midwest Economics Association Conference and at the University of Akron for their comments and suggestions. All errors are my own.

References

Anderson, P. M., Butcher, K. F. and Levine, P. B. (2003) Maternal employment and overweight children, *Journal of Health Economics*, **22**, 477–504.

Armstrong, J., Dorosty, A. R., Reilly, J. J. and Child Health Information Team and Emmett, P. M. (2003) Coexistence of social inequalities in undernutrition and obesity in preschool children: population based cross sectional study, *Archives of Disease in Childhood*, **88**, 671–5.

Armstrong, J., Reilly, J. J. and Child Health Information Team (2002) Breastfeeding and lowering the risk of childhood obesity, *Lancet*, **359**, 2003–4.

Chia, Y. F. (2008) Maternal labour supply and childhood obesity in Canada: evidence from the NLSCY, *Canadian Journal of Economics*, **41**, 217–42.

Cutler, D. M., Glaeser, E. L. and Shapiro, J. M. (2003) Why have Americans become more obese?, *Journal of Economic Perspectives*, **17**, 93–116.

Dahl, G. B. and Lochner, L. (2005) The impact of family income on child achievement, NBER Working Paper No. 11279, National Bureau of Economic Research.

de Onis, M. and Blössner, M. (2000) Prevalence and trends of overweight among preschool children in developing countries, *The American Journal of Clinical Nutrition*, **72**, 1032–9.

Feenberg, D. and Coutts, E. (1993) An introduction to the TAXSIM model, *Journal of Policy Analysis and Management*, **12**, 189–94.

Gillman, M. W., Rifas-Shiman, S. L., Camargo Jr, C. A., Berkey, C. S., Frazier, A. L., Rockett, H. R., Field, A. E. and Colditz, G. A. (2001) Risk of overweight among adolescents who were breastfed as infants, *Journal of the American Medical Association*, **285**, 2461–7.

Greene, W. H. (2004) The behaviour of the maximum likelihood estimator of limited dependent variable models in the presence of fixed effects, *Econometrics Journal*, **7**, 98–119.

Hotz, V. J. and Scholz, J. K. (2003) The earned income tax credit, in *Means-Tested Transfer Programs in the United States* (Ed.) R. Moffitt, University of Chicago Press, Chicago, pp. 141–98.

Lakdawalla, D. and Philipson, T. (2002) The growth of obesity and technological change: a theoretical and empirical examination, NBER Working Paper No. 8946, National Bureau of Economic Research.

Lake, J. K., Power, C. and Cole, T. J. (1997) Child to adult body mass index in the 1958 British birth cohort: associations with parental obesity, *Archive of Diseases in Childhood*, **77**, 376–81.

Lobstein, T., Baur, L. and Uauy, R. (2004) Obesity in children and young people: a crisis in public health, *Obesity Review*, **5**, 157s–62s.

Ogden, C. L., Carroll, M. D., Curtin, L. R., McDowell, M. A., Tabak, C. J. and Flegal, K. M. (2006) Prevalence of overweight and obesity in the United States, 1999–2004, *Journal of the American Medical Association*, **295**, 1549–55.

Ogden, C. L., Flegal, K. M., Carroll, M. D. and Johnson, C. L. (2002a) Prevalence and trends in overweight among US children and adolescents, 1999–2000, *Journal of the American Medical Association*, **288**, 1728–32.

Ogden, C. L., Kuczmarski, R. J., Flegal, K. M., Mei, Z., Guo, S., Wei, R., Grummer-Strawn, L. M., Curtin, L. R., Roche, A. F. and Johnson, C. L. (2002b) Centre for Disease Control and Prevention 2000 growth charts for the United States: improvements to the 1977 National Centre for Health Statistics Version, *Pediatrics*, **109**, 45–60.

Philipson, T. J. and Posner, R. A. (1999) The long-run growth in obesity as a function of technological change, NBER Working Paper No. 7423, National Bureau of Economic Research.

Schmeiser, M. D. (2009) Expanding waistlines and wallets: the impact of family income on the BMI of women and men eligible for the earned income tax credit, *Health Economics*, **18**, 1277–94.

Srinivasan, S. R., Bao, W., Wattigney, W. A. and Bereson, G. S. (1996) Adolescent overweight is associated with adult overweight and related multiple cardiovascular risk factors: the Bogalusa Heart Study, *Metabolism*, **45**, 234–40.

US House of Representatives (2004) *Background Materials and Data on Programs Within the Jurisdiction of the Committee on Ways and Means*, Government Printing Office, Washington, DC.

von Kries, R., Koletzko, B., Sauerwald, T., von Mutius, E., Barnert, D., Grunert, V. and von Voss, H. (1999) Breast feeding and obesity: cross sectional study, *British Medical Journal*, **319**, 147–50.

Wang, Y., Monteiro, C. and Popkin, B. M. (2002) Trends of obesity and underweight in older children and adolescents in the United States, Brazil, China and Russia, *The American Journal of Clinical Nutrition*, **75**, 971–7.

Whitaker, R. C., Wright, J. A., Pepe, M. S., Seidel, K. D. and Dietz, W. H. (1997) Predicting obesity in young adulthood from childhood and parental obesity, *New England Journal of Medicine*, **337**, 869–73.

Appendix

Table A1. First stage regressions for cross-sectional IV strategy

	(1) Income	(2) Income	(3) Income	(4) Income	(5) Income	(6) Income	(7) Income	(8) Income	(9) Income	(10) Income	(11) Income
Predicted after-tax income	0.95153 [19.65]***	0.86833 [15.44]***	0.84126 [15.14]***	0.80955 [14.66]***	0.79065 [14.66]***	0.78863 [14.67]***	0.7386 [10.03]***	0.80587 [10.11]***	0.82117 [10.18]***	0.8175 [10.16]***	0.42619 [5.48]***
Child is male	-0.01259 [0.15]	-0.03388 [0.41]	-0.0397 [0.48]	-0.04368 [0.53]	-0.05487 [0.68]	-0.04887 [0.60]	-0.0526 [0.65]	-0.05213 [0.64]	-0.05256 [0.65]	-0.05262 [0.65]	-0.06393 [0.83]
Child is Black		-0.43691 [3.23]***	-0.50675 [3.51]***	-0.51897 [3.60]***	-0.36684 [2.50]**	-0.40247 [2.72]***	-0.48917 [2.80]***	-0.45332 [2.71]***	-0.43815 [2.62]***	-0.38138 [2.23]**	0.14237 [0.65]
Child is Hispanic		0.00947 [0.06]	-0.16699 [1.01]	-0.17553 [1.06]	-0.08285 [0.50]	-0.09095 [0.55]	-0.13671 [0.80]	-0.14712 [0.85]	-0.07603 [0.43]	-0.06847 [0.39]	0.09306 [0.91]
Child is firstborn		0.19215 [2.33]**	0.27403 [3.76]***	0.36225 [4.61]***	0.37325 [4.79]***	0.3627 [4.70]***	0.35662 [4.59]***	0.35666 [4.60]***	0.35779 [4.61]***	0.35271 [4.55]***	0.23788 [0.56]
Birthweight (ounces)		0.00123 [0.39]	0.00086 [0.27]	0.00109 [0.35]	0.00348 [1.11]	0.00366 [1.15]	0.00381 [1.20]	0.00384 [1.20]	0.00393 [1.23]	0.00387 [1.21]	0.00088 [0.29]
Low birthweight		-0.20582 [0.81]	-0.22785 [0.89]	-0.2389 [0.93]	-0.18296 [0.73]	-0.12711 [0.49]	-0.12467 [0.48]	-0.126 [0.48]	-0.12299 [0.47]	-0.14189 [0.54]	-0.1389 [0.55]
Child was breastfed		0.28428 [1.98]**	0.26056 [1.83]*	0.25329 [1.79]*	0.21673 [1.53]	0.21606 [1.51]	0.21992 [1.56]	0.22806 [1.60]	0.2322 [1.63]	0.23476 [1.65]*	0.15566 [1.13]
Number of adults in household			0.61727 [7.59]***	0.61549 [7.61]***	0.62363 [7.76]***	0.61371 [7.40]***	0.61967 [7.49]***	0.61516 [7.48]***	0.61844 [7.48]***	0.61249 [7.41]***	0.06758 [0.98]
Number of children			0.05945 [0.91]	0.06786 [1.03]	0.08539 [1.31]	0.10388 [1.56]	0.1025 [1.52]	0.09738 [1.45]	0.09644 [1.44]	0.09756 [1.46]	0.06175 [0.93]
Area of residence is rural			-0.46951 [3.43]***	-0.46071 [3.38]***	-0.43697 [3.26]***	-0.47114 [3.49]***	-0.47057 [3.49]***	-0.47297 [3.52]***	-0.48344 [3.59]***	-0.48423 [3.60]***	-0.54667 [4.18]***
Age of mother at birth				0.09112 [2.66]***	0.09003 [2.64]***	0.09413 [2.86]***	0.0973 [2.97]***	0.09764 [2.98]***	0.09776 [2.98]***	0.09495 [2.88]***	0.08232 [2.60]***
Mother is overweight or obese					-0.39868 [2.37]**	-0.36869 [2.14]**	-0.36463 [2.13]**	-0.3662 [2.14]**	-0.36869 [2.15]**	-0.37295 [2.18]**	-0.38872 [2.29]**
Mother is obese					-0.57547 [3.77]***	-0.58867 [3.83]***	-0.58982 [3.84]***	-0.58782 [3.83]***	-0.58655 [3.83]***	-0.58655 [3.84]***	-0.54687 [3.65]***
Mother has health limitations						-0.82607 [4.70]***	-0.83163 [4.71]***	-0.83116 [4.71]***	-0.83003 [4.70]***	-0.82618 [4.70]***	-0.62538 [3.86]***
Mother's education: High school							-0.07036 [0.45]	-0.09854 [0.65]	-0.11814 [0.77]	-0.14218 [0.91]	-0.12092 [0.84]
Mother's education: Some college							0.06204 [0.22]	-0.01076 [0.04]	-0.03955 [0.15]	-0.07402 [0.28]	0.09151 [0.36]
Mother's education: College graduate							0.26328 [0.60]	0.07759 [0.19]	0.01673 [0.04]	-0.01015 [0.02]	0.87028 [2.15]*
Mother's AFQT percentile								-0.00355 [0.89]	-0.00416 [1.05]	-0.00423 [1.06]	0.00608 [1.65]+
Mother is an immigrant									-0.44279 [1.69]*	-0.46635 [1.79]*	-0.50283 [2.12]**
Mother lived with both parents at the age of 14										0.21168 [1.54]	0.05496 [0.43]
Mother is married											2.78176 [27.04]***
Constant	0.75958 [2.30]**	1.00964 [2.08]**	-0.09513 [0.18]	-2.37596 [2.36]**	-2.43102 [2.44]**	-2.51123 [2.60]***	-2.39539 [2.52]**	-2.45529 [2.58]***	-2.4783 [2.60]***	-2.49474 [2.63]***	-1.56922 [1.73]*
Observations	27650	25068	24524	24524	24524	23481	23481	23481	23481	23430	23430
R-squared	0.31	0.31	0.32	0.32	0.33	0.33	0.33	0.33	0.33	0.33	0.39

Notes: Robust *t*-statistics are in brackets. Regressions are weighted with child sampling weights. All specifications are estimated with year FE and with dummies for the child's age, gender and region of residence.

*, **, and *** denote significance at 10, 5 and 1% levels, respectively.

Table A2. First stage regressions for feiv strategy

	(1) Income	(2) Income	(3) Income	(4) Income	(5) Income	(6) Income	(7) Income	(8) Income	(9) Income	(10) Income	(11) Income
Predicted after-tax income	0.37322	0.33639	0.28915	0.28914	0.28883	0.28551	0.28551	0.28551	0.28551	0.2843	0.18325
	[14.20]***	[12.42]***	[10.42]***	[10.42]***	[10.41]***	[10.01]***	[10.01]***	[10.01]***	[10.01]***	[9.96]***	[6.69]***
Child is male	−0.00617	0.00233	0.00573	0.00574	0.00545	0.00559	0.00559	0.00559	0.00559	0.0058	−0.00772
	[0.20]	[0.07]	[0.17]	[0.17]	[0.16]	[0.16]	[0.16]	[0.16]	[0.16]	[0.17]	[0.23]
Child is firstborn		−0.03789	−0.06263	−0.06283	−0.06309	−0.05675	−0.05675	−0.05675	−0.05675	−0.05588	−0.08408
		[0.94]	[1.53]	[1.54]	[1.54]	[1.35]	[1.35]	[1.35]	[1.35]	[1.33]	[2.09]*
Birthweight (ounces)		−0.00043	−0.00026	−0.00026	−0.00026	−0.00038	−0.00038	−0.00038	−0.00038	−0.00039	−0.00018
		[0.33]	[0.20]	[0.20]	[0.20]	[0.28]	[0.28]	[0.28]	[0.28]	[0.29]	[0.14]
Low birthweight		−0.03399	−0.03875	−0.03863	−0.03945	−0.0312	−0.0312	−0.0312	−0.0312	−0.03148	−0.03469
		[0.39]	[0.44]	[0.44]	[0.44]	[0.34]	[0.34]	[0.34]	[0.34]	[0.34]	[0.39]
Child was breastfed		0.09123	0.0723	0.07235	0.07098	0.07968	0.07968	0.07968	0.07968	0.08052	0.04129
		[1.57]	[1.23]	[1.23]	[1.21]	[1.31]	[1.31]	[1.31]	[1.31]	[1.33]	[0.71]
Number of adults in household			0.32804	0.32805	0.32657	0.33512	0.33512	0.33512	0.33512	0.33483	0.09258
			[14.40]***	[14.40]***	[14.33]***	[14.21]***	[14.21]***	[14.21]***	[14.21]***	[14.18]***	[3.98]***
Number of children			0.13951	0.13949	0.14027	0.16437	0.16437	0.16437	0.16437	0.16399	0.12684
			[5.24]***	[5.24]***	[5.27]***	[5.88]***	[5.88]***	[5.88]***	[5.88]***	[5.86]****	[4.73]***
Area of residence is rural			−0.05391	−0.05387	−0.05379	−0.07323	−0.07323	−0.07323	−0.07323	−0.07294	−0.11183
			[0.95]	[0.95]	[0.95]	[1.26]	[1.26]	[1.26]	[1.26]	[1.25]	[2.00]*
Age of mother at birth				−0.00329	−0.00282	0.00085	0.00085	0.00085	0.00085	0.00113	0.0015
				[0.09]	[0.08]	[0.02]	[0.02]	[0.02]	[0.02]	[0.03]	[0.04]
Mother is overweight or obese					0.15668	0.14881	0.14881	0.14881	0.14881	0.14269	0.0434
					[3.06]***	[2.80]***	[2.80]***	[2.80]***	[2.80]***	[2.68]***	[0.85]
Mother is obese					0.03241	0.00276	0.00276	0.00276	0.00276	0.00519	−0.10194
					[0.55]	[0.05]	[0.05]	[0.05]	[0.05]	[0.08]	[1.73]+
Mother has health limitations						−0.05692	−0.05692	−0.05692	−0.05692	−0.05671	−0.02659
						[0.78]	[0.78]	[0.78]	[0.78]	[0.78]	[0.38]
Mother is married											2.39849
											[43.26]***
Constant	3.34065	3.50348	2.76583	2.84827	2.77804	2.74829	2.74829	3.04814	3.04814	2.98317	1.61597
	[18.46]***	[14.28]***	[10.64]***	[2.94]***	[2.87]***	[2.76]***	[2.76]***	[0.00]	[0.00]	[0.00]	[0.00]
Observations	27 650	25 068	24 524	24 524	24 524	23 481	23 481	23 481	23 481	23 430	23 430
R-squared	0.78	0.77	0.78	0.78	0.78	0.78	0.78	0.78	0.78	0.78	0.8

Notes: See notes in Table A1.

Race and gender differences in the cognitive effects of childhood overweight

Susan L. Averett and David C. Stifel

Department of Economics, Lafayette College, Easton, PA 18042, USA

The increase in the prevalence of overweight children (ages 6–13 years) in the United States over the past two decades is likely to result in adverse public health consequences. We use data from the children of the National Longitudinal Survey of Youth 1979 cohort to investigate an additional consequence of childhood overweight – its effect on relative cognitive development. To control for unobserved heterogeneity, we estimate individual (child) fixed effect (FE) models and instrumental variable (IV) models. Although recent research suggests that there is a negligible effect of childhood overweight on cognitive ability, our results demonstrate that the effects are uncovered when examining the relationship separately by race. In particular, we find that overweight white boys have math and reading scores approximately an SD lower than the mean. Overweight white girls have lower math scores whereas overweight black boys and girls have lower reading scores. Our results suggest that in addition to well-documented health consequences, overweight children may also be at risk in terms of experiencing adverse education outcomes, which could lead to lower future wages.

I. Introduction

In the United States the prevalence of overweight children has increased dramatically over the past two decades creating public health problems (Dietz, 1998; Schwimmer *et al.*, 2003; Hedley *et al.*, 2004). Recent research has concluded that being overweight has little to no effect on cognitive development (Kaestner and Grossman, forthcoming). We use data from the children of the National Longitudinal Survey of Youth 1979 cohort (NLSY79) to demonstrate that there is an effect that varies by the race and gender of the child.

II. Data

We use data from the NLSY79 (http://www.bls.gov/nls/nlsy79.htm), a panel study of approximately 12 000 individuals who were first interviewed in 1979 when they were between the ages of 14 and 22 years and were re-interviewed annually from 1979 to 1992 and bi-annually since 1994. Our analysis focuses on the children (ages 6–13 years) of the original NLSY79 female respondents and includes data through the 2002 survey year when the mothers were between the ages 37 and 45 years and the children ranged in age from 3 to 15 years. Anthropometric measures of height and weight were recorded bi-annually for each child beginning in 1986. We exclude from the analysis the approximately 20% of the cases in which these were not measured but were reported by the child's mother. We measure overweight with the body mass index (BMI), a standard metric in the literature. To compare BMI across age and gender cohorts, normalized BMI z-scores (BMIZ) are calculated using the

Nutstat module of the CDC's Epi-Info software. An overweight child has a BMIZ score in excess of 1.65.

Our measures of cognitive development are the math and reading recognition scores from the Peabody Individual Achievement Tests (Dunn and Barkwardt, 1970) administered to children aged 5 years and over. The Peabody Individual Achievement Tests are among the most widely used brief assessments of academic achievement and are individually administered measures of academic achievement. Given that we use standardized scores for both these tests (i.e. the age-specific mean is 100 and the SD is 15), the appropriate way to interpret them is as a measure of performance relative to normal development.

III. Childhood Overweight and Cognitive Development

There are various avenues through which childhood overweight may affect relative cognitive development. Overweight children may suffer from deficiencies of nutrients that are understood to be important for the physical development of the brain (Nead et al., 2004; Taras, 2005). Sleep apnea and asthma are also more common among overweight children and may interfere with cognitive performance (Luder et al., 1998). Low self-esteem that may follow from being overweight can lead to lower academic performance or to a perceived inability to perform well in school (Davison and Birch, 2001; Swartz and Puhl, 2003; Datar et al., 2004). In addition, overweight children are more likely to be more socially isolated compared with adolescents who are not overweight (Strauss and Pollack, 2003), more likely to have behaviour problems (Datar and Sturm, 2004) and more likely to act as bullies and to be bullied (Janssen et al., 2004). Finally, the social functioning of overweight children is likely to be reduced so much that Schwimmer et al. (2003) compare their quality of life to those of children with cancer.

IV. Theory and Estimation Strategy

The theoretical foundations for modelling cognitive ability are based on integrating health and cognitive ability production functions into a common-preference model of household decision-making in the tradition of Becker (1981). The full model is presented in Averett and Stifel (2007). Our estimation strategy can be summarized by the following equation:

$$c_{it} = \alpha + X'_{it}\beta + w'_{it}\gamma + \varepsilon_{it} \qquad (1)$$

where c_{it} is a measure of the relative cognitive ability for child i at time t, X_{it} is a vector of individual-level, family-level and community-level observables and w_{it} is a vector of measures of BMI for child i at time t. The vector of parameters of interest is γ. We estimate (1) by Ordinary Least Squares (OLS) where BMIZ enters as a dummy variable indicating whether the child is overweight (i.e. BMIZ > 95th percentile).

However, OLS estimates of model (1) provide unbiased estimates of γ only if the child's BMIZ is exogenous, that is, it is uncorrelated with the error term (i.e. $E(\epsilon|w) = 0$), and the direction of causality goes from BMIZ to cognitive development. If these conditions do not hold, then the OLS estimator will be biased. There are two general reasons why we might expect such a bias.

First, there may be omitted variables such as those unobserved characteristics that simultaneously determine cognitive ability and BMIZ. In such a situation, changes in these unobservable characteristics lead to coincidental changes in BMIZ and cognitive development, leading us to find a spurious relationship between BMIZ and test scores. An example of one such unobservable is parental behaviour. Datar et al. (2004) found that overweight kindergartners were more likely to come from poor families in which the parents did not read to their children or encourage good academic performance. This makes it difficult to determine whether being overweight is truly the cause of the poor academic performance, or whether poor parenting or some other factor is the cause of both the overweight and the poor academic performance. Unobserved school characteristics may also lead to biased estimates as they may be an important determinant of both academic achievement and BMIZ (Crosnoc and Mueller, 2004). To deal with this unobserved heterogeneity, we estimate individual FE models. In an individual FE model, Equation 1 becomes

$$c_{it} = \alpha + \mu_i + X'_{it}\beta + w'_{it}\gamma + \varepsilon_{it} \qquad (2)$$

where μ_i is a child-specific dummy variable and X_{it} now includes only those explanatory variables that are not fixed over time. The effectiveness of the FE estimator in reducing the bias in γ depends on the unobservable characteristics that affect both nutritional outcomes and cognitive development being fixed over time and consequently differenced out.[1]

Second, the direction of causality may go both ways. For example, although being overweight may cause low self-esteem, depression or other adverse health outcomes and consequently low cognitive development, depression (which may stem from low cognitive ability) may be a cause of overweight (Goodman and Whitaker, 2002). Another method of establishing causality is IV estimation. This method involves estimating a (set of) first-stage equation(s),

$$w_{it} = \theta + X'_{it}\varphi + Z'_{it}\lambda + v_{it} \qquad (3)$$

where w is the child's BMIZ score and Z is a set of IVs that are excluded from Equation 1. Values for BMIZ predicted using the parameter estimates from the first-stage estimation (3), $\hat{w}_{it}$, are then used as an explanatory variable in model (1) instead of observed BMIZ, w_{it},

$$c_{it} = \alpha + X'_{it}\beta + \hat{w}'_{it}\gamma_{iv} + \varepsilon_{it} \qquad (4)$$

This approach not only addresses the concern of reverse causality, but also, because the instruments are uncorrelated with the error term, it removes biases in the estimator because of unobserved heterogeneity. The difficulty, of course, is finding suitable instruments that explain nutritional outcomes but not academic achievement.

The strong genetic component of child weight (Stunkard *et al.*, 1986; Volger *et al.*, 1995; Cawley, 2004) indicates that a potential instrument is the mother's BMI. To minimize the possibility that mother's BMI is correlated with the error term in the second stage, we use a historical measure of mother's BMI from 1981.[2] For nearly all of the cases in our sample, this BMI measurement was taken before the birth of the mother's first child, and as such is more likely to measure the genetic component of child weight than does the contemporaneous measure of mother's BMI. A simple regression of mother's contemporaneous BMI on her 1981 BMI reveals that only 42% of the variation in current BMI is explained by historical levels. Nonetheless, we also include as control variables proxies for unobserved household environment and mother's unobserved abilities and attitudes that may be more/less favourable to cultivating higher academic achievement. These proxies include a dummy variable indicating whether the child was breastfed, average household income since the child was born and the mother's AFQT score and education level. Parental weight status is also used by an instrument for child's BMI by Sabia (2007) in his examination of the effect of adolescent obesity on GPA.

V. Results

Our estimating sample consists of 20 856 child years. Table 1 presents the results from estimates from the naïve OLS estimates that ignore the potential endogeneity of BMI, individual FE estimates that net out time-invariant heterogeneity and IV models that also control for reverse causality.

The OLS results indicate that overweight black and white children have lower math scores and that overweight black children also have lower reading scores. In the FE models, the coefficients are smaller and insignificant with the sole exception of black girls who score significantly lower on reading tests if they are overweight. The IV models indicate that overweight white girls and boys have lower math scores. For white boys, the coefficient is quite large at −18.74, but for white girls, it is −5.96. Overweight white boys also have standardized reading scores 11.44 points lower than white boys who are not overweight. But overweight white girls do not have reading scores that are statistically different from white girls who are not overweight. Overweight black girls and boys do not have significantly lower math scores, and the coefficients are much smaller than those for whites. But their reading scores are about 12 points lower on average than their nonoverweight counterparts.

The validity of our IV results depends on how well our instruments perform. In the first stage of the IV

---

[1] We also estimated sibling FE models, the results of which were qualitatively similar to the individual FE models presented here. The motivation for this approach is that differences between siblings remove variance in weight attributable to a shared family environment. However, Cawley (2004) argues that this is not an appropriate way to remove unobserved heterogeneity citing evidence that shared family environments explain a negligible proportion of the variance in weight across siblings. However, others have noted that an obesogenic family environment is an important predictor of children's changes in BMI (Davison *et al.*, 2005). These estimates are available upon request.

[2] Following the suggestion by Klepinger *et al.* (1995), we began with a set of potential instruments that included the district density of fast-food outlets, district mean fast-food prices, and mother's historical BMI and sibling BMI. However, Sargan tests repeatedly rejected the overidentification restrictions. As such, we limited the instruments to mother's historical BMI as this is the strongest of the excluded variables as measured by significance in the first-stage equations.

Table 1. OLS, fixed-effects and IV estimates of the effect of being overweight on math and reading scores by race and gender (ages 6–13 years)

	White Girls						White Boys					
	OLS		Fixed Effects		IV		OLS		Fixed Effects		IV	
	Coeff.	t-Stat.	Coeff.	t-Stat.	Coeff.	t-Stat.	Coeff.	t-Stat.	Coeff.	t-Stat.	Coeff.	t-Stat.
PIAT Math												
Overweight dummy (BMIZ > 1.6449)	−1.85	−2.09**	−0.76	−1.22	−5.96	−1.96**	−1.93	−2.04**	−1.18	−1.85*	−18.74	−4.03***
R^2	0.17		0.01		0.14		0.14		0.03		0.03	
Partial r^2					0.04						0.02	
F-text of excluded instruments (p-value)					0.000						0.000	
Weak identification statistics												
Cragg–Donald statistic					85.73						42.35	
– Stock and Yogo critical value					19.93						19.93	
Anderson–Rubin F-text (p-value)					0.00						0.01	
PIAT Reading Recognition												
Overweight dummy (BMIZ > 1.6449)	−0.56	−0.78	0.04	0.07	−5.14	−1.60	−1.22	−1.50	−0.57	−0.98	−11.44	−4.18***
R^2	0.15		0.01		0.14		0.16		0.01		0.03	
Partial r^2					0.04						0.02	
F-text of excluded instruments (p-value)					0.000						0.000	
Weak identification statistics												
Cragg–Donald statistic					83.9						40.9	
– Stock and Yogo critical value					19.93						19.93	
Anderson–Rubin F-text (p-value)					0.000						0.000	
Number of observations	4351		4351		4351		4563		4563		4563	

	Black Girls						Black Boys					
	OLS		Fixed Effects		IV		OLS		Fixed Effects		IV	
	Coeff.	t-Stat.	Coeff.	t-Stat.	Coeff.	t-Stat.	Coeff.	t-Stat.	Coeff.	t-Stat.	Coeff.	t-Stat.
PIAT Math												
Overweight dummy (BMIZ > 1.6449)	−2.10	−3.14***	−0.98	−1.33	−2.44	−1.00	−1.48	−1.99**	**−0.73**	−1.00	−0.54	−0.79
R^2	0.17		0.02		0.17		0.17		0.01		0.17	
Partial r^2					0.05						0.06	
F-text of excluded instruments (p-value)					0.000						0.000	
Weak identification statistics												
Cragg–Donald statistic					73.7						101.5	
– Stock and Yogo critical value					19.93						19.93	
Anderson–Rubin F-text (p-value)					0.08						0.08	
PIAT Reading Recognition												
Overweight dummy (BMIZ > 1.6449)	**−1.67**	−1.77*	**−1.10**	−1.68	−12.23	−4.48	**−0.68**	−0.94	**−0.12**	−0.19	−11.79	−3.06***
R^2	0.19		0.05		0.08		0.18		0.09		0.12	
Partial r^2					005						0.4	
F-text of excluded instruments (p-value)					0.000						0.000	
Weak identification statistics												
Cragg–Donald statistic					75.1						57.5	
– Stock and Yogo critical value					19.93						19.93	
Anderson–Rubin F-text (p-value)					0.000						0.000	
Number of observations	3095		3095		3095		2966		2966		2966	

Notes: Mother's BMI and BMI-squared in 1981 used as instruments.
*, ** and *** denote significance at 10, 5 and 1% levels, respectively.

estimation (results available upon request), mother's BMI and BMI squared (measured in 1981) are significant predictors of a child's BMIZ score both individually and jointly. The p-values on the F-statistics testing their joint significance are all less than 1%. Furthermore, the other coefficient estimates in the first stage for the IV model are of the expected signs and magnitudes. The large Cragg–Donald statistics and Anderson–Rubin F-statistics suggest that IV estimation is predictable enough to provide consistent parameter estimates (Stock and Yogo, 2005; Murray, 2006). Because we use an early measure of the mother's BMI, it is not surprising that it passes the overidentifying restrictions tests. And, we note that mother's BMI has been successfully used as an instrument for child's BMI by Sabia (2007) in an examination of the effect of adolescent obesity on adolescent GPA. Although the coefficients in the IV models for whites are larger than the FE and OLS coefficients, they are not unreasonably large. Given that we use the standardized scores, they are telling us that scores are roughly 1 SD lower for overweight children. Our first-stage F-statistics are large enough that the finite-sample bias of IVs – which biases the IV estimate towards the OLS estimate – is unlikely to be a serious problem in our IV regressions.

The parameter estimates for the other explanatory variables are as we might expect and are available upon request.

VI. Concluding Remarks

We used data from children born to the women in the NLSY79 to address whether being overweight *causes* lower cognitive ability. Our IV estimates suggest that obese white boys have math and reading test scores that are on average about 1 SD below those of their peers. Overweight white girls also have lower math scores, but the magnitude of the effect is about one-third that of overweight white boys. Overweight black boys and girls have significantly lower reading scores but not lower math scores. These findings underscore the importance of disaggregating by race and gender when examining the effect of childhood overweight on cognitive ability. A fruitful path for future research would be to determine the mechanism behind the path from overweight to lower test scores. Is it depression or discrimination from teachers? Is it a lack of essential nutrients brought on by eating a diet too high in fat and calories but nutritionally empty? These are important questions for future research.

References

Averett, S. and Stifel, D. (2007) Food for Thought: The Cognitive Effects of Childhood Malnutrition in the United StatesMimeo. Available at http://ww2.lafayette.edu/~stifeld/papers/averett_stifel_obesity_june_2007.pdf (accessed 22 September 2009).

Becker, G. S. (1981) *A Treatise on the Family*, Harvard University Press, Cambridge, MA.

Cawley, J. (2004) The impact of obesity on wages, *Journal of Human Resources*, **39**, 451–74.

Centers for Disease Control (2000) Growth charts. Available at http://www.cdc.gov/nchs/about/major/nhanes/growthcharts/clinical_charts.htm (accessed 24 August 2009).

Crosnoe, R. and Mueller, C. (2004) Body mass index, academic achievement, and school context: examining the educational experiences of adolescents at risk of obesity, *Journal of Health and Social Behavior*, **45**, 393–407.

Datar, A. and Sturm, R. (2004) Childhood overweight and parent- and teacher-reported behavior problems. Evidence from a prospective study of kindergartners, *Archives of Pediatrics and Adolescent Medicine*, **158**, 804–10.

Datar, A., Sturm, R. and Magnabosco, J. L. (2004) Childhood overweight and academic performance: national study of kindergartners and first-graders, *Obesity Research*, **12**, 58–68.

Davison, K. K. and Birch, L. L. (2005) Weight status, parent reaction, and self-concept in 5 year old girls' *Pediatrics*, **107**, 46–53.

Davison, K. K., Francis, L. A. and Birch, L. L. (2005) Reexamining obesogenic families: parent's obesity-related behaviors predict girls' change in BMI, *Obesity Research*, **13**, 1980–90.

Dietz, V. M. (1998) Health consequences of obesity in youth: childhood predictors of adult disease, *Pediatrics*, **101**, 518–25.

Dunn, L. M. and Barkwardt, F., Jr. (1970) *Peabody Individual Achievement Test Manual*, American Guidance Service, Inc., Circle Pines, MN.

Goodman, E. and Whitaker, R. C. (2002) A prospective study of the role of depression in the development and persistence of adolescent obesity, *Pediatrics*, **110**, 497–504.

Hedley, A. A., Ogden, C. L., Johnson, C. L., Carroll, M. D., Curtin, L. R. and Flegal, K. M. (2004) Prevalence of overweight and obesity among US children, adolescents, and adults, 1999–2002, *Journal of the American Medical Association*, **291**, 2847–50.

Janssen, I., Craig, W. M., Boyce, W. F. and Pickett, W. (2004) Associations between overweight and obesity with bullying behaviors in school-aged children, *Pediatrics*, **113**, 1187–94.

Kaestner, R. and Grossman, M. Effects of weight on children's educational achievement, *Economics of Education Review*. DOI: 10.1016/j.econedurev.2009.03.002.

Klepinger, D., Lundberg, S. and Plotnick, R. (1995). Instrument selection: the case of teenage childbearing and women's educational attainment, Discussion Paper No. 1077-95, Institute for Research on Poverty, University of Wisconsin, Madison.

Luder, E., Melnik, T. A. and Dimaio, M. (1998) Association of being overweight with greater asthma symptoms in inner city black and Hispanic children, *Journal of Pediatrics*, **132**, 699–703.

Murray, M. P. (2006) Avoiding invalid instruments and coping with weak instruments, *Journal of Economic Perspectives*, **20**, 111–32.

Nead, K., Halterman, J., Kaczorowski, J., Auinger, P. and Weitzman, M. (2004) Overweight children and adolescents: a risk group for iron deficiency, *Pediatrics*, **114**, 104–8.

Sabia, J. J. (2007) The effect of body weight on adolescent academic performance, *Southern Economic Journal*, **73**, 871–900.

Schwimmer, J. B., Burwinkle, T. M. and Varni, J. W. (2003) Health-related quality of life of severely obese children and adults, *Journal of the American Medical Association*, **289**, 1813–9.

Stock, J. H. and Yogo, M. (2005) Testing for weak instruments in linear IV regressions, in *Identification and Inference for Econometric Models: Essays in Honor of Thomas Rothenberg*, (Eds) D. W. K. Andres and J. H. Stock, Cambridge University Press, Cambridge, pp. 80–108.

Strauss, R. S. and Pollack, H. A. (2003) Social marginalization of overweight children, *Archives of Pediatric and Adolescent Medicine*, **157**, 746–52.

Stunkard, A., Sorensen, T., Hanis, C., Teasdale, T., Chakraborty, R., Schull, W. and Schulsinger, F. (1986) An adoption study of human obesity, *New England Journal of Medicine*, **314**, 193–8.

Swartz, M. B. and Puhl, R. (2003) Childhood obesity: a societal problem to solve, *Obesity Reviews*, **4**, 57–71.

Taras, H. (2005) Nutrition and student performance at school, *Journal of School Health*, **75**, 199–213.

Volger, G., Sorensen, T., Stunkard, A., Srinivasan, M. and Rao, D. (1995) Influences of genes and shared family environment on adult body mass index assessed in an adoption study by a comprehensive path model, *International Journal of Obesity*, **19**, 40–5.

The relationship between smoking, quitting smoking and obesity in Australia: a seemingly unrelated probit approach

N. Au[a], K. Hauck[b] and B. Hollingsworth[a]

[a]*Centre for Health Economics, Monash University, Melbourne, VIC 3800, Australia*
[b]*Imperial College London, Business School, London, SW7 2AZ, UK*

Smoking and obesity are two leading causes of preventable death. Further understanding of the relationship between these two risk factors can assist in reducing avoidable morbidity and mortality. This study investigates the empirical association between obesity and the propensity to smoke and to quit smoking, using a Seemingly Unrelated (SUR) probit approach that takes into consideration the potential for reverse causality and unobserved heterogeneity. Using Australian health survey data, this article demonstrates the usefulness of the SUR probit approach in generating information on the relationship between unobserved factors influencing both smoking behaviour and obesity, and in providing estimates of the conditional probabilities of each risk factor. Results suggest the two risk factors are not independent. The presence, size and direction of correlation between the unobserved factors are found to vary by smoking behaviour and by gender. Estimates of conditional probabilities demonstrate smokers have a lower probability of obesity, particularly among females, and ex-smokers have a higher probability of obesity, particularly among males. These findings suggest that health policies targeted at one risk factor may have unintended implications for the other.

I. Introduction and Background

Smoking and obesity are two leading preventable causes of death and disease in high-income countries (Mokdad *et al.*, 2004), and the detrimental health consequences associated with both smoking and obesity, such as heart disease and cancer are well-known. Smoking prevalence in most high-income nations has declined over the past few decades. For example, in the United States and Australia, adult smoking rates have fallen considerably since the early 1970s from around 37% to 20% in the United States (Centers for Disease Control and Prevention,

2009) and from 37% to 16% in Australia (Woodward, 1984; Australian Institute of Health and Welfare, 2008). Over the same period of time, there has been a dramatic increase in obesity prevalence, with the United States, the United Kingdom and Australia among the heaviest Organization for Economic Co-operation and Development (OECD) nations (OECD, 2009). Adult obesity prevalence in the United States increased from around 15% in the 1970s to over 30% in 2008 (Flegal *et al.*, 2002, 2010). In Australia, it has risen from below 10% in 1989–1990 to 25% in 2008 (Australian Bureau of Statistics, 2009). With obesity now considered at epidemic

75

proportions in many nations, there is a strong incentive for better understanding of the factors determining obesity (Popkin and Doak, 1998).

Weight gain fundamentally occurs as a result of an energy imbalance between the amount of calories consumed and expended, yet the exact causes of the rapid rise in obesity rates remain unclear. Researchers have begun to investigate the role of social and economic changes in explaining rising obesity rates. Declines in the cost of food due to technological advances in mass food production (Philipson, 2001; Cutler et al., 2003), greater access to fast-food outlets and restaurants (Chou et al., 2004), longer work hours (Ruhm, 2005; Courtemanche, 2009a), urban sprawl (Ewing et al., 2003; Garden and Jalaludin, 2009) and social interactions (Costa-Font and Gil, 2004; Christakis and Fowler, 2007) are some of the changes suggested to have contributed to weight gain over recent decades.

It has also been hypothesized that the decline in smoking prevalence, which can be attributed to tobacco control policies, may have contributed to the rise in obesity prevalence (Flegal et al., 1995; Chou et al., 2004). The fall in smoking prevalence and contemporaneous rise in obesity rates may, of course, be purely coincidental. However, medical evidence suggests smoking is typically associated with a lower Body Mass Index (BMI) and smoking cessation with weight gain (Filozof et al., 2004; Chiolero et al., 2008). These associations have been explained by metabolic effects and loss of appetite associated with nicotine (Perkins, 1992), and the tendency to consume more calories while expending less after quitting smoking (Stamford et al., 1986). Further understanding of the relationship between smoking, quitting and obesity is of great potential value to public health policy. If obesity has occurred as a result of tobacco control policies, potential quitters may benefit from targeted assistance with regards to post-cessation weight gain. Conversely, if smoking cessation were not associated with obesity, such evidence may prove useful in allaying fears of weight gain that may be preventing current smokers from quitting.

It is difficult to present convincing evidence of the impact of smoking behaviour on obesity in the absence of experimental data. The presence of unobserved or unmeasured characteristics such as concern about body weight, time-preference or self-control may confound the relationship between smoking behaviour and body weight (Chiolero et al., 2008; Robb et al., 2008), leading to biased estimates when ordinary linear regression methods are used. Furthermore, the direction of influence is unclear. While the medical literature suggests smoking can affect metabolism and appetite, it is also possible for body weight to influence smoking behaviour. For example, overweight or obese individuals may decide to smoke as a form of weight-control (French and Jeffery, 1995; Cawley et al., 2004).

Although Instrumental Variable (IV) techniques can be used to estimate casual relationships when endogeneity is a concern, they rely on the availability of suitable instruments. A number of studies have used IV techniques to estimate the effect of smoking on obesity, using cigarette prices and taxes as instruments for smoking (Chou et al., 2004; Rashad and Grossman, 2004; Gruber and Frakes, 2006; Rashad, 2006; Baum, 2009; Courtemanche, 2009b; Fang et al., 2009; Nonnemaker et al., 2009). However the results appear to be

highly sensitive to specification and instruments used, with conclusions spanning from a positive effect (smoking cessation leads to obesity), no effect, through to a negative effect (smoking cessation leads to lower levels of obesity). The conflicting results may be due to the fact that cigarette costs are poor instruments for cigarette consumption, particularly for certain age groups (Liu, 2010). The more recent smoking literature finds that demand for cigarettes is relatively price inelastic, which implies that the correlation between smoking (the endogenous variable) and price (the instrument) is small, and in turn results in price being a weak instrument for consumption (for a review see Gallet and List, 2003). In summary, it seems that at present no clear conclusions about the relationship between smoking behaviour and obesity can be drawn from IV techniques.

The potential for common unobserved factors to affect both smoking and obesity implies further information on the association between smoking behaviour and obesity can be efficiently obtained by allowing for a correlation between the unobserved factors affecting both smoking and obesity. This study seeks to exploit the information inherent in the data to better understand the empirical association between obesity and the propensity to smoke and to quit smoking, without imposing assumptions on the direction of the possible relationship between these two lifestyle choices. We utilize a Seemingly Unrelated (SUR) regression approach to model jointly obesity and smoking behaviour, using health survey data from Australia. The SUR approach enables us to determine the presence, size and direction of the correlation between unobserved factors that affect smoking behaviour and the probability of obesity. Such information is useful for gaining further insight into the factors that commonly influence smoking and obesity, as well as for understanding how unobserved heterogeneity may affect studies that fail to account for the endogeneity of smoking in models of obesity.

In addition, the SUR model allows estimation of probabilities of obesity conditional on smoking status, and vice versa, which provides evidence on the association between obesity and smoking behaviour. It further informs policy makers on the implications of a policy intervention that targets only one lifestyle choice on the other choice. For example, a policy that reduces the probability of smoking may in turn affect the probability of obesity conditional on smoking. Our model allows calculating the change in the probability of obesity that is associated with a change in the probability of smoking.

The SUR approach is commonly used when it is probable that two or more variables of interest are affected by some common, unobserved factors, and has been applied to a wide spectrum of research questions, for models with either continuous or binary dependent variables. Examples of the application of the SUR approach are diverse, and include the relationships between obesity and several chronic diseases (Costa-Font and Gil, 2005), between the demands for various food commodities (Jensen and Manrique, 1998), between several indicators of health system performance (Hauck and Street, 2006), and between access to different types of physician services (Atella et al., 2004). Unlike a structural model using IV techniques, the SUR probit does not allow inference on a direct causal relationship between obesity and smoking. At the same time though, an advantage of the SUR model is that it does not impose (potentially erroneous) assumptions on the direction of the relationship, and it does not require instruments.

II. Model

The SUR probit estimates two binary probits jointly, allowing for correlation between the error terms of the two equations. For each SUR model, we specify two reduced-form equations, one for the probability of being obese and another for the probability of either smoking or quitting. This enables investigation of the relationship between obesity and smoking, and between obesity and quitting smoking. Joint estimation of the equations exploits additional information inherent in the correlation between unobserved factors which affect the two dependent variables.

We specify the models as follows:

$$Obese_i^* = \beta_1 X_i + \mu_{1i}$$
$$Smoker_i^* = \delta_1 X_i + \mu_{2i} \tag{1}$$

$$Obese_i^* = \beta_1 X_i + \varepsilon_{1i}$$
$$Quitter_i^* = \delta_1 X_i + \varepsilon_{2i}, \tag{2}$$

where $Obese_i^*$ is an unobserved latent variable that takes the value of one if the individual i has a BMI of 30 or more and zero otherwise, and $Smoker_i^*$ is an unobserved latent variable that takes the value of one if the individual i smokes and zero if i has never smoked. Model (1) investigates the relationship between smoking and obesity. Here, ex-smokers are dropped from the sample to ensure smokers are compared with persons who have never smoked. Model (2) investigates the relationship between obesity and quitting smoking. Here, we run two separate models: Model A drops never-smokers from the sample to allow ex-smokers to be compared with current smokers. Model B drops smokers from the sample to allow ex-smokers to be compared with never-smokers. For (2), $Quitter_i^*$ is therefore an unobserved latent variable that takes the value of one if individual i is an ex-smoker and zero if a smoker for Model A, and zero if a never-smoker for Model B.

X is a vector of observed demographic, socioeconomic and lifestyle factors that are likely to influence obesity and smoking behaviour and μ_{1i}, μ_{2i}, ε_{1i} and ε_{2i} are stochastic error terms. It is assumed that the error terms have a bivariate normal distribution, which allows for a nonzero correlation between the errors. The correlation coefficients ρ and λ measure the strength and direction of any relation between the errors μ_{1i} and μ_{2i}, and ε_{1i} and ε_{2i} respectively, such that $\rho = \text{cov}(\mu_{1i}, \mu_{2i})$, and $\lambda = \text{cov}(\varepsilon_{1i}, \varepsilon_{2i})$. Correlation between the error terms implies independent estimation of univariate probits would result in inefficient parameter estimates. We test for correlation between the error terms in the models ($\rho = 0$ or $\lambda = 0$) with a Wald test. Models are estimated separately for males and females.

The size and significance of ρ and λ determine whether the factors influencing smoking and obesity, and quitting smoking and obesity are related. The signs on ρ and λ indicate the overall direction of the relationship. For example, there may be unobserved factors which increase both an individual's likelihood to smoke and to be obese, such as a tendency to follow addictive behaviour (Wang *et al.*, 2004). This would imply a *positive* correlation between the error terms in the *smoker* and *obese* equations. On the other hand, there may be unobserved factors which influence the decision to smoke and the probability of obesity in opposing directions, such as weight-concern (French and Jeffery, 1995). This would imply a *negative* correlation between the error terms in the *smoker* and *obesity* equations.

We further calculate the probabilities of being obese conditional on smoking status and on being a quitter, accounting for unobserved heterogeneity. This allows us to compare, for example, conditional probabilities of the probability of being obese given smoking and never-smoking across subgroups such as men and women, or differences in conditional probabilities that may arise from policy interventions that target one specific lifestyle choice.

III. Data and Variables

Data

This study uses pooled cross-sectional data from four years (2002–2005) of the Victorian Population Health Survey (VPHS), a representative survey of adults (18 and over) in the Australian state of Victoria. The VPHS is an annual telephone survey that includes extensive information on health, demographic and socioeconomic indicators. Detailed information on the VPHS sampling methods can be found in the VPHS report by the Victorian Government Department of Human Services (2003), pp. 5–8. Our total sample consists of 10 989 males and 16 906 nonpregnant females. Summary statistics on the variables used in the analyses are provided in Table 1.

Smoking, quitting smoking and obesity

The outcome variables *Obese*, *Smoker* and *Quitter* are based on self-reported height, weight and smoking status,[1] therefore there is potential for measurement bias. However, it has been shown that the reporting bias in the VPHS is comparably small (Morgan, 2007) therefore we do not adjust for potential reporting bias.

Covariates

We control for demographic, socioeconomic and lifestyle factors that are likely to influence the propensity for smoking, quitting and obesity. The covariates include continuous measures of *age* and *age*^{2} and indicators for marital status consisting of *never-married, divorced, widowed* (*married* is the reference group). To account for ethnic differences in the determinants of smoking and obesity, such as ideal body size, social expectations and influences, we include indicator

---

[1] Participants in the VPHS were asked: 'Which of the following best describes your smoking status? 1. I smoke daily; 2. I smoke occasionally; 3. I don't smoke now but I used to; 4. I've tried it a few times but never smoked regularly; or, 5. I've never smoked'. Respondents are classified as smokers if they answered 1 or 2, ex-smokers if they answered 3, and never-smokers if they answered 4 or 5.

Table 1. Definitions and summary statistics of variables

Variable	Definition	Males Mean (SE)	Females Mean (SE)
Obese	α has BMI ≥ 30	0.149 (0.004)	0.158 (0.004)
Smoker	α smokes	0.242 (0.006)	0.201 (0.004)
Quitter	α has quit smoking	0.290 (0.006)	0.226 (0.004)
Never-smoker	α has never smoked	0.468 (0.006)	0.573 (0.005)
Age	Age of respondent	44.57 (0.213)	45.61 (0.191)
Rural	α lives in a rural area	0.273 (0.004)	0.269 (0.003)
Single	α has never married	0.236 (0.006)	0.178 (0.005)
Widowed	α is widowed	0.060 (0.002)	0.094 (0.003)
Divorced	α is divorced or separated	0.021 (0.001)	0.077 (0.002)
Uni	α attained university level education	0.305 (0.006)	0.277 (0.005)
TAFE	α attained Technical and Further Education or vocational training	0.201 (0.005)	0.145 (0.004)
Primary	α attained primary level education	0.029 (0.002)	0.033 (0.002)
Student	α is currently a student	0.059 (0.004)	0.064 (0.003)
Retired	α is retired	0.179 (0.004)	0.205 (0.004)
Unemployed	α is unemployed, unable to work or home duties	0.075 (0.003)	0.218 (0.004)
Inc $20–40K	α has household income between A$20 000 and A$40 000	0.175 (0.005)	0.219 (0.004)
Inc $40–60K	α has household income between A$40 000 and A$60 000	0.272 (0.006)	0.240 (0.004)
Inc $60–80K	α has household income between A$60 000 and A$80 000	0.160 (0.005)	0.144 (0.004)
Inc > $80K	α has household income greater than A$80 000	0.245 (0.006)	0.176 (0.004)
Asian	α is from Asia or both parents from Asia	0.078 (0.004)	0.065 (0.003)
NW European	α is from North West Europe or both parents from North West Europe	0.114 (0.004)	0.112 (0.003)
SE European	α is from South East Europe or both parents from South East Europe	0.104 (0.004)	0.105 (0.004)
Other ethnic	α is from other ethnic group	0.090 (0.004)	0.083 (0.003)
No walks	α does not walk continuously for at least 10 mins in a week	0.156 (0.004)	0.142 (0.004)
Walks 7 +	α walks continuously for at least 10 mins, seven or more times per week	0.359 (0.006)	0.316 (0.005)
No exercise	α does not exercise vigorously in a week	0.573 (0.006)	0.558 (0.005)
Exercise 3 +	α does vigorous exercise three or more times per week	0.205 (0.005)	0.184 (0.004)
Risky drinker	α is a risky drinker	0.129 (0.004)	0.039 (0.002)
Non-drinker	α does not drink alcohol	0.127 (0.004)	0.215 (0.004)

Notes: Sample size is 10 989 and 16 906 for males and females, respectively. VPHS sample weights are used in calculating the mean and SD. α = dichotomous variable that equals 1 if respondent.

variables *Asian, South-East European, North-West European* and *other ethnicity* (Australian *native* is the reference).[2]

A socioeconomic gradient for smoking and obesity has been consistently reported (Ball and Crawford, 2005; Laaksonen *et al.*, 2005). It is suggested that schooling may lead to healthier behaviours by improving health knowledge (Kenkel, 1991; Nayga, 2000), or by raising levels of cognitive ability (Cutler and Lleras-Muney, 2010). Therefore, the model includes indicator variables for highest level of education achieved, including *primary school*, *TAFE* (Technical and Further Education or vocational training) and *university* (completion of *secondary school* is the reference). Employment indicators include *unemployed* or *out of the labour force*, *retired* and full-time *student* (*employed* as reference). Also included is a binary variable, *rural*, that indicates whether the respondent lives in a rural or remote area. To account for income, we include a measure of annual *household income*. The VPHS collects data on income bands. Missing values are imputed with the median income band based on gender, marital status

and education.[3] We include indicators of annual household income categories as defined by the VPHS: A$20 – <40 000, A$40 – <60 000, A$60 – <80 000 and ≥A$80 000 (<A$20 000 is the reference group).

We include two measures of physical activity (walking and vigorous exercise) in the *Obese* equations to approximate energy expenditure, and in the *Smoker* and *Quitter* equations because evidence suggests smoking is associated with lower levels of physical activity (Chiolero *et al.*, 2008). The physical activity variables are measured according to the number of times the respondent exercises vigorously or walks for 10 minutes or more per week. The model includes binary variables for *no-walks*, *walks ≥7 times* (reference is *walks 1–6 times*), *no-exercise* and *exercise ≥3* times (reference is *exercises 1–2 times*). We include measures of alcohol intake as alcohol is estimated to contribute more than 10% of calorie intake among drinkers (Williamson *et al.*, 1987) and smoking is known to be associated with alcohol consumption (Bien and Burge, 1990). Binary variables, *risky drinker* and *non-drinker*

[2] Variables for ethnicity are based on the country of birth of the respondents and their parents. For example, a person is considered *Asian* if born in Asia *or* if born in Australia with both parents born in Asia. Respondents are considered Australian *native* if they and at least one parent was born in Australia.
[3] Following similar methodology to Rhum (2005), household incomes are assumed to be at the midpoint of each income band and 125% of the (unbounded) top category. Median incomes are calculated for 32 groups stratified by gender (male or female), marital status (married, never-married, divorced, widowed) and education (primary, high-school, TAFE, University).

Table 2. SUR probit results: marginal effects for males

	Obese[a]		Smoker		Quitter (Model A)[b]		Quitter (Model B)[b]	
Age	0.016	(0.000)	0.011	(0.001)	0.007	(0.076)	0.014	(0.000)
Age^2 (10^{-2})	−0.018	(0.000)	−0.019	(0.000)	0.009	(0.027)	−0.006	(0.032)
Single	−0.012	(0.382)	0.028	(0.212)	−0.148	(0.000)	−0.103	(0.000)
Divorced	0.018	(0.381)	0.128	(0.000)	−0.128	(0.000)	0.006	(0.808)
Widowed	0.013	(0.742)	0.154	(0.004)	−0.179	(0.000)	−0.042	(0.210)
Primary	0.075	(0.078)	−0.020	(0.692)	0.009	(0.837)	−0.023	(0.562)
TAFE	−0.005	(0.670)	−0.062	(0.001)	0.077	(0.001)	−0.007	(0.715)
Uni	−0.036	(0.002)	−0.168	(0.000)	0.097	(0.000)	−0.084	(0.000)
Asian	−0.075	(0.000)	−0.018	(0.611)	0.007	(0.895)	0.018	(0.620)
NW European	0.003	(0.836)	0.033	(0.195)	0.026	(0.358)	0.086	(0.000)
SE European	0.042	(0.026)	0.077	(0.006)	−0.065	(0.043)	0.045	(0.101)
Other ethnic	0.005	(0.772)	0.060	(0.044)	−0.029	(0.425)	0.060	(0.052)
Rural	0.011	(0.259)	−0.026	(0.069)	0.005	(0.765)	−0.003	(0.811)
Student	−0.043	(0.045)	−0.236	(0.000)	0.081	(0.267)	−0.143	(0.002)
Retired	0.005	(0.833)	0.001	(0.977)	0.004	(0.924)	0.004	(0.866)
Unemployed	0.037	(0.101)	0.101	(0.001)	−0.079	(0.010)	0.023	(0.455)
Inc $20–40K	−0.006	(0.740)	−0.048	(0.059)	0.011	(0.726)	−0.056	(0.015)
Inc $40–60K	0.000	(0.981)	−0.125	(0.000)	0.067	(0.037)	−0.064	(0.009)
Inc $60–80K	−0.014	(0.480)	−0.118	(0.000)	0.082	(0.024)	−0.043	(0.132)
Inc > $80K	−0.018	(0.342)	−0.129	(0.000)	0.051	(0.164)	−0.088	(0.001)
No walks	−0.003	(0.793)	0.046	(0.044)	−0.052	(0.051)	0.011	(0.587)
Walks 7 +	−0.018	(0.099)	0.042	(0.013)	−0.038	(0.061)	0.008	(0.607)
No exercise	0.005	(0.663)	0.038	(0.045)	−0.044	(0.069)	0.005	(0.777)
Exercise 3 +	−0.021	(0.130)	0.004	(0.855)	0.016	(0.585)	0.012	(0.603)
Risky drinker	−0.016	(0.250)	0.261	(0.000)	−0.129	(0.000)	0.129	(0.000)
Non-drinker	0.049	(0.006)	−0.093	(0.000)	−0.042	(0.204)	−0.131	(0.000)

Notes: [a]*Obese* equation results are taken from Obese-Smoker model.
[b]Model A = quitters compared with smokers; Model B = quitters compared with never-smokers.
p-values are in parentheses. All models also contain year dummies.
All estimations incorporate VPHS sample weights.

(reference group is *low-risk drinker*) account for alcohol intake according to the Australian National Health and Medical Research Council Alcohol Guidelines (NHMRC, 2001). In addition, the models include year dummies to take account of exogenous time effects.

IV. Results

SUR probit results

The results from the SUR probit model for males and females are shown in Tables 2 and 3, respectively. Reported are the marginal effects, evaluated at the means of all continuous explanatory variables and evaluated for a discrete change of all dummy variables from 0 to 1, on the marginal probability of obesity and smoking behaviour. For brevity, the *Obese* equation results from only the Obese-Smoker model are shown. Results for the *Obese* equation from the Obese-Quitter models do not differ greatly from those shown (available from the corresponding author upon request). Our estimates on education and household income confirm previous evidence that the propensity for both smoking and obesity are higher among groups with lower socioeconomic status (Nayga, 2000; Ball and Crawford, 2005; Laaksonen *et al.*, 2005). For example, a university educated male has a 0.168 lower marginal probability of being a smoker and a 0.036 lower marginal probability of being obese than a male who

only completed high-school. A female with an annual income of A$80 000 or more has a 0.102 lower marginal probability of being a smoker and a 0.074 lower marginal probability of being obese than her counterpart who earns less than A$20 000. Quitting smoking is more likely among those with higher socioeconomic standing when compared with continuing smoking, while a comparison with never-smokers shows the likelihood of being a former smoker is lower for those with a higher socioeconomic standing. This may be due to a lower probability of being a smoker in the first place.

Walking seven or more times per week is negatively associated with obesity, but vigorous exercise is not a significant determinant. As expected, not walking and not exercising is associated with a higher propensity to smoke. Walking seven or more times per week is positively associated with smoking for males only, which is a counterintuitive result. Marital status is not significantly related to obesity, but plays an important role in determining smoking behaviour – married persons are less likely to be smokers and more likely to have quit smoking (among those who are either current or former smokers). To illustrate, a married female has a 0.054 lower marginal probability of being a smoker and a 0.156 higher probability of quitting smoking compared with single females. Nondrinkers have a 0.049 and 0.064 higher marginal probability of obesity compared with low-risk drinkers for males and females, respectively. This is consistent with previous evidence of an inverse association between alcohol consumption and BMI (Williamson *et al.*, 1987). As expected, drinking at risky

79

Table 3. SUR probit results: marginal effects for females

	Obese[a]		Smoker		Quitter (Model A)[b]		Quitter (Model B)[b]	
Age	0.014	(0.000)	0.009	(0.000)	0.005	(0.144)	0.011	(0.000)
Age^2 (10^{-2})	−0.015	(0.000)	−0.017	(0.000)	0.005	(0.221)	−0.012	(0.000)
Single	0.007	(0.651)	0.054	(0.004)	−0.156	(0.000)	−0.049	(0.011)
Divorced	−0.010	(0.419)	0.151	(0.000)	−0.140	(0.000)	0.057	(0.003)
Widowed	0.018	(0.326)	0.089	(0.001)	−0.093	(0.010)	0.029	(0.176)
Primary	0.050	(0.049)	−0.019	(0.515)	−0.063	(0.224)	−0.047	(0.065)
TAFE	−0.008	(0.479)	−0.058	(0.000)	0.092	(0.000)	−0.005	(0.765)
Uni	−0.020	(0.050)	−0.142	(0.000)	0.143	(0.000)	−0.054	(0.000)
Asian	−0.104	(0.000)	−0.201	(0.000)	0.064	(0.437)	−0.211	(0.000)
NW European	−0.023	(0.062)	0.024	(0.185)	0.044	(0.078)	0.068	(0.000)
SE European	0.000	(0.972)	−0.023	(0.215)	−0.086	(0.007)	−0.093	(0.000)
Other ethnic	−0.020	(0.177)	−0.011	(0.574)	−0.037	(0.248)	−0.037	(0.057)
Rural	0.007	(0.390)	−0.011	(0.241)	−0.005	(0.721)	−0.010	(0.280)
Student	−0.078	(0.000)	−0.109	(0.000)	0.039	(0.430)	−0.080	(0.004)
Retired	0.039	(0.043)	−0.049	(0.026)	0.081	(0.023)	−0.002	(0.933)
Unemployed	0.028	(0.010)	0.020	(0.131)	−0.011	(0.576)	0.012	(0.387)
Inc $20–40K	−0.021	(0.072)	−0.044	(0.004)	−0.006	(0.825)	−0.026	(0.115)
Inc $40–60K	−0.041	(0.000)	−0.065	(0.000)	0.014	(0.622)	−0.037	(0.027)
Inc $60–80K	−0.064	(0.000)	−0.076	(0.000)	0.051	(0.121)	−0.028	(0.167)
Inc > $80K	−0.074	(0.000)	−0.102	(0.000)	0.036	(0.300)	−0.067	(0.001)
No walks	0.005	(0.694)	0.085	(0.000)	−0.096	(0.000)	0.029	(0.079)
Walks 7+	−0.028	(0.002)	0.005	(0.696)	−0.010	(0.573)	0.000	(0.992)
No exercise	−0.001	(0.942)	0.016	(0.200)	−0.033	(0.102)	−0.006	(0.634)
Exercise 3+	−0.011	(0.359)	0.016	(0.306)	0.009	(0.699)	0.017	(0.297)
Risky drinker	0.027	(0.331)	0.294	(0.000)	−0.180	(0.000)	0.133	(0.000)
Non-drinker	0.064	(0.000)	−0.104	(0.000)	−0.037	(0.141)	−0.131	(0.000)

Notes: [a]Obese equation results are taken from Obese-Smoker model.
[b]Model A = quitters compared with smokers; Model B = quitters compared with never-smokers.
p-values are in parentheses. All models also contain year dummies.
All estimations incorporate VPHS sample weights.

Table 4. SUR probit results: Wald test for correlation in error terms

Model	Obese-Smoker		Obese-Quitter (Model A)[a]		Obese-Quitter (Model B)[a]	
	Males	Females	Males	Females	Males	Females
Sample (n)	7386	12 797	6184	7693	8408	13 322
Correlation coefficient	−0.036	−0.057*	0.127**	0.088**	0.102**	0.018
Wald χ^2	1.176	4.677	13.003	8.639	11.761	0.552
p-value	(0.278)	(0.031)	(0.000)	(0.003)	(0.001)	(0.458)

Notes: [a] Model A = quitters compared with smokers; Model B = quitters compared with never-smokers.
* and ** denote significance at 5 and 1% levels, respectively.

levels is positively associated with smoking and negatively associated with quitting (among those who are either current or former smokers). Ethnicity plays a significant role in determining obesity and smoking behaviour. For example, Asians females have a 0.104 lower marginal probability of being obese and a 0.201 lower marginal probability of being a smoker than their native counterparts.

The relationship between smoking and obesity

The correlation coefficients (ρ and λ) and results from the Wald-tests are presented in Table 4. For the Obese-Smoker models, ρ is weakly negative but statistically insignificant from zero for males. This suggests that, for males, unobserved factors impacting on smoking and obesity are not related.

For females, we find a statistically significant negative correlation between the unobserved factors ($\rho = -0.057$). This indicates there are one or more unobserved factors impacting positively on smoking and negatively on obesity (or vice versa), or in other words, unobserved factors which increase the probability of smoking will at the same time decrease the probability of obesity (and vice versa).

We can only speculate which factors drive the negative correlation, but our finding supports the notion that body weight concern may be the unobserved factor that increases the propensity to smoke while decreasing the likelihood of obesity through careful dieting. Studies have found the association between smoking initiation and weight concern to be stronger among females than males, and that women smokers report greater concern about weight gain if they quit smoking than men (French and Jeffery, 1995). Such findings could explain why ρ is significant for females but insignificant for males.

It is also possible that the unobserved factor may be time-preference, self-control, addictive tendency, depression or concern for health. However such factors are likely to influence both smoking and obesity in the same direction, i.e. we would expect to see a positive correlation coefficient. Therefore, it seems unlikely that such factors are driving the correlation between the error terms in the two equations.

The relationship between quitting smoking and obesity

The Obese-Quitter models confirm a negative correlation between the two lifestyle choices smoking and obesity. In the context of these models the correlation is positive, implying that the probability of quitting smoking (i.e. the probability of becoming a nonsmoker) and obesity is affected in the same direction by one or more unobserved factors, for both males and females. For the Obese-Quitter Model A, which includes only ex-smokers and smokers, we observe a statistically significant positive correlation between the unobserved factors for both males and females. This time, the correlation is greater for males ($\lambda = 0.127$) than females ($\lambda = 0.088$). This indicates that there are one or more unobserved factors affecting the probability of quitting and obesity in the same direction, i.e. either positively or negatively. We cannot identify what these unobserved factors are, but the results again support the notion that concern about weight gain may be a factor that is reducing both the probability of quitting smoking and the likelihood of being obese. However, λ is larger for males than females, suggesting other factors are likely to play a role here, particularly for males. Such factors may be related to a higher calorie intake which is positively associated with both obesity and quitting smoking (Chiolero et al., 2008).

Model B, which includes only ex-smokers and never-smokers, finds for males there is again a statistically significant positive correlation between the unobserved factors ($\rho = 0.102$). For females, Model B results show no correlation between the error terms, suggesting there is no correlation between unobserved factors affecting obesity and quitting when comparing quitters to never-smokers.

Predicted probabilities of obesity

A key advantage of estimating SUR probits is that it allows us to predict joint and conditional probabilities, taking account of the correlations between the unobservable factors – information which would not be available if smoking and obesity were analysed separately. Joint probabilities allow us to estimate the probability of two states occurring in conjunction (such as being obese and smoking), whereas conditional probabilities allow us to estimate the probability of one state occurring (such as being obese), given the occurrence of another state (such as smoking). Such predicted probabilities give additional information on the relationship between obesity and smoking behaviour.

Table 5 shows the marginal and conditional probabilities of obesity using the SUR probit estimates. The results for the Obese-Smoker model show that a typical male has a 0.135

Table 5. Predicted probabilities of obesity

	Males Mean	Females Mean
Obese-Smoker		
Sample includes smokers and never-smokers		
pr(obese)	0.135	0.154
Pr(obese|smoker)	0.127	0.137
Pr(obese|never-smoker)	0.139	0.159
Obese-Quitter (Model A)		
Sample includes quitters and smokers		
pr(obese)	0.164	0.159
Pr(obese|quitter)	0.187	0.175
Pr(obese|smoker)	0.137	0.141
Obese-Quitter (Model B)		
Sample includes quitters and never-smokers		
pr(obese)	0.152	0.162
Pr(obese|quitter)	0.176	0.166
Pr(obese|never-smoker)	0.137	0.160

Note: All SEs are < 0.001 and estimates are significantly different from each other at 1% level.

probability of being obese while a typical female has a higher probability of being obese at 0.154. If the male is a smoker, the probability of being obese is lower at 0.127, but if he has never-smoked, the probability of being obese is highest at 0.139, which is about 10% higher than for a smoker. The pattern for females is even more pronounced: females who have never-smoked have a 16% higher probability of obesity compared with smokers. These findings are consistent with the evidence of increased metabolism and suppressed appetite resulting from cigarette smoking (Chiolero et al., 2008), and with results from longitudinal studies that have found weight gain to be associated with smoking cessation compared with continuing smoking (Williamson et al., 1991). The more pronounced result for females is also supportive of evidence that smoking initiation is associated with weight concern particularly among females (French and Jeffery, 1995).

The results from the Obese-Quitter Model A reveal that a male ex-smoker has a 0.187 chance of being obese. This probability is 37% higher than if he were a continuing smoker. For females there is a similar pattern, with the probability of obesity for an ex-smoker 24% higher compared with that of a smoker. These results confirm earlier findings of a negative relationship between smoking and obesity and support studies that have shown quitting smoking to be associated with increased appetite, decreased resting metabolic rate, increased adipose tissue lipoprotein lipase activity and weight gain (Chiolero et al., 2008). From the results of the Obese-Quitter Model B, we find for males the probability of being obese is 28% higher for quitters compared with never-smokers. For females the probability of being obese is only 4% higher for quitters compared with never-smokers.

V. Discussion and Conclusion

There are several limitations to this study. BMI and smoking status variables are self-reported and may therefore suffer from measurement error. Ideally we would like to include information on calorie intake in our model, but like most surveys, this level of detail is not collected by the VPHS. We cannot uncover what the unobservable factors in evidence are explicitly; this would require further research, on a more extensive dataset with, for example, information on the genetic make-up of respondents or detailed information on psychological aspects to uncover tendencies for addictive behaviour, time-preference or body weight concern. Despite these limitations, we can derive several conclusions from our study.

Our empirical results suggest that accounting for the correlation between unobserved factors when examining the determinants of obesity and smoking behaviour is important. We find that joint estimation is more efficient than univariate analyses because unobserved factors impacting on both smoking and obesity are significantly correlated. Joint estimation of the determinants for smoking and obesity consistently reveals a negative relationship between the two lifestyle choices. In summary, we find a negative correlation between the probabilities of smoking and obesity for females, and a positive correlation between the probability of quitting (i.e. being a nonsmoker) and obesity for both genders, though the correlation is greater for men. This implies that for females, there are unobserved factors which influence obesity and smoking in opposing directions, and further, that there are unobserved factors which influence the probabilities of both quitting and obesity in the same direction.

The results from the predicted probabilities show that smokers are less likely to be obese, and quitters are more likely to be obese. However, the odds of obesity given smoking status differ considerably by gender and by the smoking status of the comparison group. The estimates of the conditional probabilities confirm previous results in the literature that there is a negative relationship between smoking and obesity and a positive relationship between quitting and obesity (Flegal et al., 1995; Chou et al., 2004; Baum, 2009). This implies that a policy which is designed to reduce smoking could unintentionally increase obesity, and likewise, a policy designed to reduce obesity could increase the probability of smoking. Policy makers may want to consider that there are potential knock-on effects when designing targeted public health policies.

The considerably higher probability of obesity for male ex-smokers compared with never-smokers highlights an important area for further research into the underlying causes of this relationship. This may indicate that prospective male quitters may benefit from targeted advice and assistance regarding post-cessation weight gain. The finding that female quitters have only a marginally higher probability of obesity than never-smokers suggests weight gain following smoking cessation may not be a problem, at least not when comparing with women who have never smoked. This may be because female ex-smokers are concerned about possible weight gain and take appropriate steps (such as dieting) to minimize weight gain following smoking cessation.

The strength of our study is that it demonstrates the value of the SUR probit for the analysis of the complex interrelation between two important risk factors, smoking and obesity, where endogeneity is a concern but the reliability of IV techniques is questionable. We further show how the SUR model can be used to predict the wider implications of targeted public health policies. Our results highlight there are factors which do warrant further analysis in the relationship between

smoking, smoking cessation and obesity, and that such research may benefit from more detailed data being collected, with more extensive follow up.

Acknowledgements

We are grateful to the Victorian Department of Human Services for providing us with the data and an anonymous referee for helpful comments.

References

Atella, V., Brindisi, F., Deb, P. and Rosati, F. C. (2004) Determinants of access to physician services in Italy: a latent class seemingly unrelated probit approach, *Health Economics*, **13**, 657–68.

Australian Bureau of Statistics (2009) *National Health Survey, Summary of Results, 2007–08*, Cat. No. 4364.0. Available at www.abs.gov.au (accessed 5 February 2010).

Australian Institute of Health and Welfare (2008) *Australia's Health 2008*. Available at http://www.aihw.gov.au/publications/index.cfm/title/10585 (accessed 3 March 2009).

Ball, K. and Crawford, D. (2005) Socioeconomic status and weight change in adults: a review, *Social Science and Medicine*, **60**, 1987–2010.

Baum, C. L. (2009) The effects of cigarette costs on BMI and obesity, *Health Economics*, **18**, 3–19.

Bien, T. and Burge, R. (1990) Smoking and drinking: a review of the literature, *The International Journal of the Addictions*, **25**, 1429–54.

Cawley, J., Markowitz, S. and Tauras, J. (2004) Lighting up and slimming down: the effects of body weight and cigarette prices on adolescent smoking initiation, *Journal of Health Economics*, **23**, 293–311.

Centers for Disease Control and Prevention (2009) *Trends in Current Cigarette Smoking Among High School Students and Adults, United States, 1965–2007*. Available at http://www.cdc.gov/tobacco/data_statistics/tables/trends/cig_smoking/index.htm (accessed 23 January 2010).

Chiolero, A., Faeh, D., Paccaud, F. and Cornuz, J. (2008) Consequences of smoking for body weight, body fat distribution, and insulin resistance, *The American Journal of Clinical Nutrition*, **87**, 801–9.

Chou, S. Y., Grossman, M. and Saffer, H. (2004) An economic analysis of adult obesity: results from the Behavioral Risk Factor Surveillance System, *Journal of Health Economics*, **23**, 565–87.

Christakis, N. A. and Fowler, J. H. (2007) The spread of obesity in a large social network over 32 years, *New England Journal of Medicine*, **357**, 370–9.

Costa-Font, J. and Gil, J. (2004) Social interactions and the contemporaneous determinants of individuals' weight, *Applied Economics*, **36**, 2253–63.

Costa-Font, J. and Gil, J. (2005) Obesity and the incidence of chronic diseases in Spain: a seemingly unrelated probit approach, *Economics and Human Biology*, **3**, 188–214.

Courtemanche, C. (2009a) Longer hours and larger waistlines? The relationship between work hours and obesity, *Forum for Health Economics and Policy*, **12**, 1–31.

Courtemanche, C. (2009b) Rising cigarette prices and rising obesity: coincidence or unintended consequence?, *Journal of Health Economics*, **28**, 781–98.

Cutler, D. M., Glaeser, E. L. and Shapiro, J. M. (2003) Why have Americans Become more obese?, *The Journal of Economic Perspectives*, **17**, 93–118.

Cutler, D. M. and Lleras-Muney, A. (2010) Understanding differences in health behaviors by education, *Journal of Health Economics*, **29**, 1–28.

Ewing, R., Schmid, T., Killingsworth, R., Zlot, A. and Raubenbush, S. (2003) Relationship between urban sprawl and physical activity, obesity, and morbidity, *American Journal of Health Promotion*, **18**, 47–57.

Fang, H., Ali, M. M. and Rizzo, J. A. (2009) Does smoking affect body weight and obesity in China?, *Economics and Human Biology*, **7**, 334–50.

Filozof, C., Pinilla, M. C. F. and Fernández-Cruz, A. (2004) Smoking Cessation and weight gain, *Obesity Reviews*, **5**, 95–103.

Flegal, K. M., Carroll, M. D., Ogden, C. L. and Curtin, L. R. (2010) Prevalence and trends in obesity among US adults, 1999–2008, *Journal of the American Medical Association*, **303**, 235–41.

Flegal, K. M., Carroll, M. D., Ogden, C. L. and Johnson, C. L. (2002) Prevalence and trends in obesity among US adults, 1999–2000, *Journal of the American Medical Association*, **288**, 1723–7.

Flegal, K. M., Troiano, R. P., Pamuk, E. R., Kuczmarski, R. J. and Campbell, S. M. (1995) The Influence of smoking cessation on the prevalence of overweight in the United-States, *The New England Journal of Medicine*, **333**, 1165–70.

French, S. A. and Jeffery, R. W. (1995) Weight concerns and smoking: a literature review, *Annals of Behavioral Medicine*, **17**, 234–44.

Gallet, C. A. and List, J. A. (2003) Cigarette demand: a meta-analysis of elasticities, *Health Economics*, **12**, 821–35.

Garden, F. L. and Jalaludin, B. B. (2009) Impact of Urban sprawl on overweight, obesity, and physical activity in Sydney, Australia, *Journal of Urban Health-Bulletin of the New York Academy of Medicine*, **86**, 19–30.

Gruber, J. and Frakes, M. (2006) Does falling smoking lead to rising obesity?, *Journal of Health Economics*, **25**, 183–97.

Hauck, K. and Street, A. (2006) Performance assessment in the context of multiple objectives: a multivariate multilevel analysis, *Journal of Health Economics*, **25**, 1029–48.

Jensen, H. H. and Manrique, J. (1998) Demand for food commodities by income groups in Indonesia, *Applied Economics*, **30**, 491–501.

Kenkel, D. S. (1991) Health behavior, health knowledge, and schooling, *The Journal of Political Economy*, **99**, 287–305.

Laaksonen, M., Rahkonen, O., Karvonen, S. and Lahelma, E. (2005) Socioeconomic status and smoking: analysing inequalities with multiple indicators, *European Journal of Public Health*, **15**, 262–9.

Liu, F. (2010) Cutting through the smoke: separating the effect of price on smoking initiation, relapse and cessation, *Applied Economics*, **42**, 2921–39.

Mokdad, A. H., Marks, J. S., Stroup, D. F. and Gerberding, J. L. (2004) Actual causes of death in the United States, 2000, *Journal of the American Medical Association*, **291**, 1238–45.

Morgan, L. (2007) *The Determinants of Obesity in a High-income Country: An Application with Respect to Country of Birth*, University of York, York, UK.

Nayga, R. M. (2000) Schooling, health knowledge and obesity, *Applied Economics*, **32**, 815–22.

NHMRC (2001) *Australian Alcohol Guidelines: Health Risks and Benefits*. Available at http://www.nhmrc.gov.au/publications/synopses/_files/ds9.pdf (accessed 4 November 2008).

Nonnemaker, J., Finkelstein, E., Engelen, M., Hoerger, T. and Farrelly, M. (2009) Have efforts to reduce smoking really contributed to the obesity epidemic?, *Economic Inquiry*, **47**, 366–76.

OECD (2009) *Health at a Glance: OECD Indicators 2009*. Available at http://www.sourceoecd.org/ (accessed 20 January 2009).

Perkins, K. A. (1992) Metabolic effects of cigarette smoking, *Journal of Applied Physiology*, **72**, 401–9.

Philipson, T. (2001) The world-wide growth in obesity: an economic research agenda, *Health Economics*, **10**, 1–7.

Popkin, B. M. and Doak, C. M. (1998) The obesity epidemic is a worldwide phenomenon, *Nutrition Reviews*, **56**, 106–14.

Rashad, I. (2006) Structural estimation of caloric intake, exercise, smoking, and obesity, *The Quarterly Review of Economics and Finance*, **46**, 268–83.

Rashad, I. and Grossman, M. (2004) The economics of obesity, *Public Interest*, Summer, **156**, 104–12.

Robb, C., Huston, S. and Finke, M. (2008) The mitigating influence of time preference on the relation between smoking and BMI scores, *International Journal of Obesity*, **32**, 1670–7.

Ruhm, C. J. (2005) Healthy living in hard times, *Journal of Health Economics*, **24**, 341–63.

Stamford, B. A., Matter, S., Fell, R. D. and Papanek, P. (1986) Effects of smoking cessation on weight gain, metabolic rate, caloric consumption, and blood lipids, *The American Journal of Clinical Nutrition*, **43**, 486–94.

Victorian Government Department of Human Services (2003) *Victorian Population Health Survey 2002*. Available at http://www.health.vic.gov.au/healthstatus/downloads/vphs/vphs2002.pdf (accessed 3 June 2010).

Wang, G.-J., Volkow, N. D., Thanos, P. K. and Fowler, J. S. (2004) Similarity between obesity and drug addiction as assessed by neurofunctional imaging, *Journal of Addictive Diseases*, **23**, 39–53.

Williamson, D. F., Forman, M. R., Binkin, N. J., Gentry, E. M., Remington, P. L. and Trowbridge, F. L. (1987) Alcohol and body weight in United States adults, *American Journal of Public Health*, **77**, 1324–30.

Williamson, D. F., Madans, J., Anda, R. F., Kleinman, J. C., Giovino, G. A. and Byers, T. (1991) Smoking cessation and severity of weight gain in a national cohort, *The New England Journal of Medicine*, **324**, 739–45.

Woodward, S. D. (1984) Trends in cigarette consumption in Australia, *Internal Medicine Journal*, **14**, 405–7.

Tobacco control and obesity: evidence from a cross section of countries

Craig A. Gallet

Department of Economics, California State University at Sacramento, 6000 J Street, Sacramento, CA 95819-6082, USA

Although several studies of highly developed countries find tobacco control efforts impact obesity rates, whether such results extend to less developed countries is unclear. Accordingly, this study re-examines this issue by using data from countries that lie across the development spectrum. Similar to the existing literature, evidence suggests higher cigarette prices increase the per cent of the population that is overweight or obese. Yet, other tobacco control efforts have less influence. A number of other factors, including health-care expenditure, urban concentration and undernourishment, are also found to influence population weight.

I. Introduction

Although numerous studies find tobacco control efforts reduce smoking prevalence, in light of the medical evidence of a negative correlation between smoking and body weight (e.g. Williamson *et al.*, 1991), several studies of highly developed countries have examined the link between obesity and tobacco control efforts.[1] However, since tobacco use and control efforts differ according to the level of development (Jha and Chaloupka, 2000; Jha *et al.*, 2000; Gallet, 2009a), a limitation of these studies is that it may be inappropriate to infer the global impact of tobacco control on obesity from results based on more affluent countries.

In this study, we re-examine the relationship between obesity and tobacco control using data from a cross section of countries that cover the development spectrum. Briefly, in addition to a number of other factors, our results suggest cigarette taxes influence the prevalence of male and female obesity, as obesity rates are higher in countries with higher cigarette prices. Yet, other tobacco control tools (i.e. smoking bans, advertising bans and the placement of warning labels on cigarette packages) do not appreciably influence obesity rates. In the sections that follow, the empirical model and estimation results are presented. This article concludes with a summary.

II. Empirical Model

The World Health Organization provides country-specific data for 2008 on the per cent of male and female populations with a Body Mass Index (BMI) of 25 or higher and 30 or higher. A BMI of 30 or higher is the conventional threshold for an individual to be considered obese, whereas a BMI of 25 or higher includes individuals considered to be either overweight or obese (Chou *et al.*, 2004; Gruber and Frakes, 2006; Baum, 2009). These two gender-specific

---

[1] For example, a number of studies (e.g. Chou *et al.*, 2004; Rashad and Grossman, 2004; Baum, 2009) find rising obesity rates are an unintended consequence of increasing taxes on cigarettes, whilst other studies (e.g. Gruber and Frakes, 2006; Nonnemaker *et al.*, 2009) fail to find such a link.

Table 1. Variable names, definitions and descriptive statistics

Variable	Definition	Mean	SD
BMI25F	Per cent of female population with BMI $\geq$ 25	46.26	17.82
BMI25M	Per cent of male population with BMI $\geq$ 25	43.42	20.95
BMI30F	Per cent of female population with BMI $\geq$ 30	20.68	11.45
BMI30M	Per cent of male population with BMI $\geq$ 30	14.13	9.48
CigPrice	Price of a pack of cigarettes (US $)	2.37	2.15
SmokeBan	= 1 if smoking banned in public places, 0 if not	0.64	0.48
AdBan	= 1 if tobacco advertising banned, 0 if not	0.74	0.44
Warning	= 1 if warning label required, 0 if not	0.66	0.47
Income	Per capita GDP (US thousand $)	13.69	20.34
HealthExp	Per capita health expenditures (US thousand $)	1.04	1.74
Urban	Per cent of population living in urban area	57.20	22.11
Age65	Per cent of population aged 65 and over	7.91	5.37
Under	Per cent of population undernourished	13.00	11.76

Notes: Data on the four BMI rates, CigPrice, SmokeBan, AdBan, Warning and HealthExp came from the World Health Organization (http://www.who.int/en/). Data on Income, Urban, Age65 and Under came from the World Bank (http://www.worldbank.org/). Missing observations limit the sample to 128 observations. BMI, Body Mass Index; GDP, Gross Domestic Product.

BMI percentages serve as dependent variables in a series of regressions.

Several factors are considered as possible determinants of our BMI measures. To begin, similar to studies of obesity in the United States (e.g. Chou *et al.*, 2004; Nonnemaker *et al.*, 2009), we include the price of cigarettes in the regression model. In addition, though, we also include a number of other tobacco control policies as determinants of higher BMI. Specifically, we include dichotomous variables to account for the presence of smoking bans (i.e. variable set equal to 1 if country bans smoking in health care, government, education or restaurant facilities; 0 if not), advertising bans (i.e. variable set equal to 1 if country bans tobacco advertising in various media; 0 if not) and warning labels (i.e. variable set equal to 1 if country requires warning labels be placed on cigarette packages; 0 if not).[2]

A number of socio-economic factors are also included as regressors. First, since studies link aggregate health outcomes to per capita income and healthcare spending (e.g. Hitiris and Posnett, 1992; Crémieux *et al.*, 1999; Gallet, 2009b), we include per capita Gross Domestic Product (GDP) and per capita health expenditures as determinants of high BMI rates.[3] Second, we include the per cent of the population living in urban areas. It may be, for instance, that greater urbanization reduces the need for a vehicle, thus increasing walking, and thereby reducing high

BMI percentages; or since there is less access to fresh produce and a greater concentration of fast-food restaurants in many urban areas, it could also be that greater urbanization increases high BMI rates (Zhao and Kaestner, 2010). Third, several studies (e.g. Chou *et al.*, 2004; Gruber and Frakes, 2006) find a positive correlation between BMI and age, and so we also include in the model the per cent of the population aged 65 and older. Finally, the per cent of the population that is undernourished is included as a determinant of our two rates, with the expectation that these rates are inversely related to undernourishment. See Table 1 for variable names, definitions and descriptive statistics.

III. Estimation Results

Gender-specific regressions are estimated for the two BMI measures, with the results provided in Table 2. Although R^2 is highest for the regressions specific to males, suggesting there are differences tied to gender, the coefficients are similar in sign and significance across the regressions. Accordingly, we focus the discussion on these similarities.

Concerning the role of tobacco control across all four regressions, the coefficient of the cigarette price is positive and significantly different from 0. Similar to studies of highly developed countries (e.g. Chou *et al.*,

[2] A number of studies (e.g. Meier *et al.*, 1997; Saffer and Chaloupka, 2000; Yurekli and Zhang, 2000) find smoking bans, advertising bans and warning labels reduce the demand for cigarettes. Accordingly, reductions in smoking prevalence resulting from such policies could also increase obesity. Indeed, Liu *et al.* (2010) find that workplace smoking bans in the United States contribute to rising obesity rates.

[3] Chou *et al.* (2004) and Gruber and Frakes (2006) find obesity rates are lower in higher income households, which could reflect the greater ability of wealthier households to have more healthy diets.

Table 2. Estimation results

Variables	BMI25F	BMI25M	BMI30F	BMI30M
CigPrice	3.08***	2.37***	1.96***	1.22***
	(3.42)	(3.05)	(3.03)	(3.20)
SmokeBan	−1.44	0.20	−1.18	0.12
	(−0.67)	(0.10)	(−0.79)	(0.11)
AdBan	−5.66*	−1.53	−3.12	−0.17
	(−1.73)	(−0.51)	(−1.45)	(−0.12)
Warning	0.47	−0.03	0.47	−0.57
	(0.16)	(−0.01)	(0.23)	(−0.44)
Income	0.21	0.44**	0.22	0.27**
	(0.70)	(2.06)	(1.09)	(2.25)
HealthExp	−6.85**	−7.04***	−5.67***	−3.96***
	(−2.23)	(−2.87)	(−2.63)	(−2.97)
Urban	0.36***	0.36***	0.20***	0.15***
	(4.24)	(4.88)	(3.61)	(4.36)
Age65	0.05	1.01***	0.05	0.52***
	(0.14)	(3.17)	(0.21)	(3.07)
Under	−0.64***	−0.58***	−0.42***	−0.22***
	(−5.26)	(−4.80)	(−4.77)	(−3.99)
Number of observations	128	128	128	128
R^2	0.57	0.72	0.51	0.70

Notes: White (1980) SEs are used to construct t-statistics (provided in parentheses below coefficient estimates).
***, ** and *Significant at 1%, 5% and 10% levels, respectively.

2004; Rashad and Grossman, 2004; Baum, 2009), therefore, we also find results which suggest raising taxes on cigarettes has an unintended consequence of elevating body weight.[4] In addition, with the exception of the marginally significant coefficient of the advertising ban variable in Column 1, other tobacco control policies have little impact on higher BMI rates. Accordingly, our finding that cigarette price has the most significant impact on obesity rates is consistent with studies of global tobacco use (e.g. Jha and Chaloupka, 2000), which suggest taxes on tobacco are the most effective means of reducing smoking prevalence.

As for the remaining variables, although insignificant in the female regressions, the positive coefficients of per capita income and the per cent of the population aged 65 and older suggest obesity rates are most pronounced among affluent countries with older populations. Lastly, across all four regressions, we find the per cent of the population with a higher BMI is lower in countries with higher rates of undernourishment and greater health-care expenditure, as well as countries with lower urban populations.

IV. Conclusions

Studies of wealthy countries find raising taxes on cigarettes increases obesity rates. Utilizing data from a multitude of countries that lie across the development spectrum, the results of this article also support this unintended consequence of cigarette taxation, as higher cigarette prices are found to increase the per cent of the population considered overweight or obese. Yet, we also find that smoking bans, advertising bans and cigarette warning labels collectively have negligible influence on the overweight and obese populations. Furthermore, a number of other factors, most notably health-care expenditure, urban concentration and undernourishment, are found to also influence higher weight in the population.

The intended use of our results is not to argue against tobacco control, particularly cigarette taxation. Rather, our results highlight the need to consider the broader impact of tobacco control when making policy recommendations. Indeed, if higher cigarette taxes elevate obesity rates, then policymakers may wish to consider tools to counterbalance the effect of cigarette taxes on obesity.

References

Baum, C. (2009) The effects of cigarette costs on BMI and obesity, *Health Economics*, **18**, 3–19.

Chou, S. Y., Grossman, M. and Saffer, H. (2004) An economic analysis of adult obesity: results from the behavioral risk factor surveillance system, *Journal of Health Economics*, **23**, 565–87.

Crémieux, P., Ouellette, P. and Pilon, C. (1999) Health care spending as determinants of health outcomes, *Health Economics*, **8**, 627–39.

Gallet, C. (2009a) Snuff the puff: international evidence on the determinants of anti-smoking laws, *Applied Economics Letters*, **16**, 1449–53.

Gallet, C. (2009b) The determinants of AIDS mortality: evidence from a state-level panel, *Atlantic Economic Journal*, **37**, 425–36.

Gruber, J. and Frakes, M. (2006) Does falling smoking lead to rising obesity?, *Journal of Health Economics*, **25**, 183–97.

Hitiris, T. and Posnett, J. (1992) The determinants and effects of health expenditure in developed countries, *Journal of Health Economics*, **11**, 173–81.

Jha, P. and Chaloupka, F. (2000) The economics of global tobacco control, *British Medical Journal*, **321**, 358–61.

Jha, P., Paccaud, F. and Nguyen, S. (2000) Strategic priorities in tobacco control for governments and international agencies, in *Tobacco Control in Developing*

[4] To put these results in context, the elasticity of each BMI rate with respect to the cigarette price was calculated at the mean. The average of the female and male elasticities corresponding to BMI $\geq$ 25 is 0.15, while for BMI $\geq$ 30 the average elasticity is 0.22. Hence, a given percentage increase in the price of cigarettes has the greatest impact on the population considered obese.

Countries (Eds.) P. Jha and F. Chaloupka, Oxford University Press, Oxford, pp. 449–64.

Liu, F., Zhang, N., Cheng, K., *et al.* (2010) Reduced smoking and rising obesity: Does smoking ban in the workplace matter?, *Economics Letters*, **108**, 249–52.

Meier, K. and Licari, M. (1997) The effect of cigarette taxes on cigarette consumption, 1955 through 1994, *American Journal of Public Health*, **87**, 1126–30.

Nonnemaker, J., Finkelstein, E., Engelen, M., *et al.* (2009) Have efforts to reduce smoking really contributed to the obesity epidemic?, *Economic Inquiry*, **47**, 366–76.

Rashad, I. and Grossman, M. (2004) The economics of obesity, *Public Interest*, **156**, 104–12.

Saffer, H. and Chaloupka, F. (2000) The effects of tobacco advertising bans on tobacco consumption, *Journal of Health Economics*, **19**, 1117–37.

White, H. (1980) A heteroskedasticity-consistent covariance matrix estimator and a direct test for heteroskedasticity, *Econometrica*, **48**, 817–38.

Williamson, D., Madans, J., Anda, R., *et al.* (1991) Smoking cessation and severity of weight gain in a national cohort, *New England Journal of Medicine*, **324**, 739–45.

Yurekli, A. and Zhang, P. (2000) The impact of clean indoor-air laws and cigarette smuggling on demand for cigarettes: an empirical model, *Health Economics*, **9**, 159–70.

Zhao, Z. and Kaestner, R. (2010) Effects of urban sprawl on obesity, *Journal of Urban Economics*, **29**, 779–87.

Obesity and heart disease awareness: a note on the impact of consumer characteristics using qualitative choice analysis[1]

RODOLFO M. NAYGA, JR.

This note examines the impact of socio-economic and demographic factors on the likelihood that an individual is aware of the link between being overweight and heart disease. Results indicate that nonwhites, lower educated individuals, and those with lower income are less likely to be aware of the link between being overweight and heart disease. Considering the extent of the obesity problem in the United States, these results should be used as a guide in the design of food policy and health education campaigns about obesity and heart disease.

I. INTRODUCTION

One of the greatest dangers associated with being overweight is the increased risk of coronary heart disease. Although obesity is technically not a disease, there is evidence that those who are overweight have an increased mortality risk due to cardiovascular disease (Wheelock, 1992). Coronary heart disease is now one of the leading causes of death in the United States. Despite the clear connection between being overweight and the risk of heart disease, more Americans are overweight than ever. More than one-fourth of American adults are overweight, with higher percentages among women in ethnic minorities (Senauer, et al.,1991). The percentages of people in various ethnic groups deemed to be overweight are given in Table 1. According to the Public Health Service, the percentage of overweight men has increased from 5% in 1980 to 16% in 1990 while the percentage of overweight women jumped from 2% to 10% during the same period (Tippett and Goldman, 1994). These figures are alarming since, as mentioned earlier, the risk of heart attack increases directly with excess weight. This issue is, therefore, a significant health problem for American consumers (Waldholz, 1990).

Education concerning obesity and its effect on health (e.g., heart disease) needs to be targeted at appropriate segments of the population (Senauer, et al., 1991). Knowledge of the influence of socioeconomic and demographic factors on the likelihood that a consumer is aware of the link between being overweight and heart disease (weight–heart disease relationship) is, therefore, necessary in the design and implementation of food and nutrition programmes. This knowledge will also provide food policy decision makers with the information about socioeconomic and demographic factors that affect weight–heart disease awareness. For instance, the relationship between certain socio-demographic factors and weight–heart disease awareness can be evaluated, and knowledge of these relationships can be utilized to develop policies or education programmes that focus on certain groups of individuals who are less likely to be aware of the link between heart disease and being overweight. No other study has focused on this issue in the past. The purpose of this short note is to assess the impact of various socioeconomic and demographic characteristics of the individual on the likelihood of being aware about the link between being overweight and heart disease.

II. MODEL SPECIFICATION

Scant information is available regarding the effect of socio-economic and demographic variables on the likelihood of weight–heart disease awareness. Conditioned on the data

Table 1. *Age adjusted percentage of overweight persons aged 20–74 years*

Ethnic Group	Male	Female
Mexican American	30.3	41.6
Cuban	27.6	31.6
Puerto Rican	25.6	40.2
Nonhispanic white	24.2	23.9
Nonhispanic black	26.0	44.4

Source: US Department of Health and Human Services, Public Health Service, 1989.

available in the 1991 Diet and Health Knowledge Survey (DHKS), the exogenous variables used in the analysis include presence of children, race, sex, employment status, urbanization, age, income, education, and region. The general model specification used is therefore:

$$WH_i = b_0 + b_1 \, child + b_2 \, black + b_3 \, race3 + b_4 \, male$$
$$+ b_5 \, employed + b_6 \, city + b_7 \, nonmetro + b_8 \, age$$
$$+ b_9 \, income + b_{10} \, education + b_{11} ne$$
$$+ b_{12} mw + b_{13} \, west$$

The description of these variables is given in Table 2.

To avoid the problem of perfect multicollinearity, one classification is eliminated from each group of variables for estimation purposes. The base group include individuals who satisfy the following description: those without children in the household, white, female, employed, those residing in suburban areas, and those who are in the south.

A qualitative choice (i.e. logit model) framework is used to estimate the model. Qualitative choice models are used in the

analysis due to the reason that the dependent variable is binary. The commonly used alternative specifications for the estimation of qualitative choice models are the linear probability model, the probit model, and logit model (Nayga, 1996). In estimating qualitative choice models, logit and probit models are preferred over linear probability models because the latter suffers from a number of weaknesses. The use of linear probability model results in biased estimates of standard errors of ordinary least squares due to heteroscedastic nature of the variance of the disturbance term. Moreover, the disturbance term of the model is not normally distributed. As a result, the classical statistical tests are not applicable. The use of linear probability model also results in predictions outside the interval between 0 and 1, which is inconsistent with the interpretation of the conditional expectation as a probability. The logit specification is chosen in this study. The logit model is estimated using maximum likelihood estimation as it results in large-sample properties of consistency and asymptotic normality of the parameter estimates. Conventional tests of significance are, therefore, applicable.

III. DATA

The data set used in this study is the 1991 DHKS from the US Department of Agriculture. The target individuals in this survey are the main-meal preparers or planners in households in the 48 conterminous states who participated in the 1991 Continuing Survey of Food Intakes by Individuals (CSFII). Data in this survey were collected by computer-assisted telephone interviews (in-person interviews for those without telephones). A total of 1925 individuals participated in the DHKS survey. Due to incomplete data in some of the variables, 1502 observations were used in the present analysis. The variables and their means are exhibited in Table 1. Since

Table 2. *Description and means of the variables used in the analysis*

Name	Description	Mean
Dependent variable		
WH	1 if individual is aware of the link between being overweight and heart disease; 0 otherwise	0.63
Independent variables		
child	presence of children	0.41
black	1 if individual is black; 0 otherwise	0.14
race3	1 if individual is of some other race; 0 otherwise	0.04
male	1 if individual is male; 0 otherwise	0.19
employed	1 if individual is employed; 0 otherwise	0.45
city	1 if individual resides in the city; 0 otherwise	0.30
nonmetro	1 if individual resides in nonmetro area; 0 otherwise	0.31
age	age of the individual in years	48.52
income	household income (in $1000)	23.47
education	highest year of regular school attended	11.78
ne	1 if residence is in the Northeast; 0 otherwise	0.17
mw	1 if residence is in the Midwest; 0 otherwise	0.25
west	1 if residence is in the West; 0 otherwise	0.21

Table 3. *Maximum likelihood estimates of the variables in the model*

Variable	Parameter	Standard error
intercept	−0.516	0.402
child	0.168	0.142
black	−0.277*	0.017
race3	−0.612*	0.285
male	−0.116	0.145
employed	0.048	0.133
city	−0.068	0.149
nonmetro	−0.144	0.140
age	−0.005	0.004
income	0.012*	0.003
education	0.101*	0.021
ne	−0.242	0.166
mw	−0.009	0.149
west	0.156	0.163
Sample size	1502	
McFadden R^2	0.051	
Correct prediction (%)	89.6	

* Statistically significant at the 0.05 level.

the data are from a household sample, sample statistics cannot be compared to the population individual statistics of the US. Nevertheless, the DHKS sample was determined to be representative at the household level (Lin, 1995). Moreover, the means of the variables seem typical of the nation except the possible under-representation of males and employed individuals. However, it should be remembered that the respondents being analysed in this study are household main meal planners.

IV.   EMPIRICAL RESULTS

The maximum likelihood estimates of the model are given in Table 3. Results indicate that blacks are less likely to be aware of the link between being overweight and heart disease. Moreover, individuals of other races are also less likely to be aware of the weight–heart disease linkage. These results are critical and particularly troublesome considering that about one-third of the black and Hispanic population are obese (US Department of Health and Human Services, 1989).

As expected, education is positively related to the likelihood of being aware of the link between being overweight and heart disease. This finding implies that lower educated individuals are less likely to be aware of the link between being overweight and heart disease. Income is positively related to

the likelihood of being aware of the link between weight and heart disease. This finding means that lower income individuals are less likely to be aware of the connection between being overweight and heart disease. This result is critical since the percentage of people overweight is far higher among those below the poverty level than those above it (US Department of Health and Human Services, 1989). These findings further underscore the importance of targeting health education campaigns toward those who are less educated and poor.

V.   CONCLUDING COMMENTS

This study examines how the socio-economic and demographic variables affect the likelihood of weight–heart disease awareness. No known study concerning this topic has been published. Results of the present study suggest that nonwhites, those who are lower educated and those with lower income generally are less likely to be aware of the link between being overweight and heart disease. These results have some important implications for government and public health programmes. The findings in this study could be used as a guide to direct government information programmes toward specific population subgroups, specifically nonwhites, lower educated, and the poor. The results of this study are critical considering that a significant percentage of these population subgroups are obese.

REFERENCES

Lin, C.T.J. (1995) Demographic and socioeconomic influences on the importance of food safety in food shopping. *Agricultural and Resource Economics Review*, 24,190–8.
Nayga, Jr., R.M.(1996) Consumer demand for poultry at home and away from home: a discrete choice analysis. *Applied Economics Letter*, 3, in press.
Senauer, B., Asp, E. and Kinsey J. (1991) *Food Trends and the Changing Consumer*. Eagan Press, St. Paul, MN.
Tippett, K. and Goldman, J. (1994) Diets more healthful, but still fall short of dietary guidelines. *Food Review*, 17, 8–14.
US Department of Health and Human Services, Public Health Service (1989). *Nutrition Monitoring in the United States*. DHHS Publ. 89-1255, Hyattsville, MD.
Waldholz, M. (1990) Weight is cardiac risk in women. *Wall Street Journal*, 29 March.
Wheelock, V. (1992) Healthy eating: the food issue of the 1990s. *British Food Journal*, 94, 3–8.

Social interactions and the contemporaneous determinants of individuals' weight

JOAN COSTA-FONT and JOAN GIL‡

LSE Health and Social Care, London School of Economics, London, UK and
‡Departament de Teoria Econòmica & CAEPS, Universitat de Barcelona, Barcelona

Obesity and overweight are central issues in the public health debate in most developed countries. In this debate, some of the socio-economic determinants of obesity and overweight are still relatively unexplored. This paper presents an empirical examination of the possible influence of social interactions on contemporaneous obesity and (over)underweight. A joint estimation model for obesity and self-image is applied to a sample for Spain taken from the European Union household panel for 1998. The results suggest that obesity might be in part a social phenomenon connected to individuals' social life.

I. INTRODUCTION

Obesity is one of the major health problems in developed and developing societies (Wang *et al.*, 2002). Its prevalence has risen three-fold since 1980 in areas of North America, the UK, Eastern Europe, the Pacific Islands, Australasia and China.[1] The WHO (2003b) estimates that obesity rates have increased by 10–40% in most European countries over the past 10 years and that the condition is relatively common among women and in southern and eastern European countries (Table 1). Childhood obesity is also escalating alarmingly, especially in southern Europe, where rates are 10–20% higher than in the north.[2]

Obesity is an important issue because it is responsible for numerous health complications, ranging from non-fatal debilitating conditions such as osteoarthritis, respiratory difficulties, skin problems and infertility, to life-threatening chronic diseases such as Coronary Heart Disease, type II diabetes, and certain cancer.[3] Obesity may also have psychological consequences, including lowered self-esteem and clinical depression. Further, from the economic perspective, it is estimated that treatment for obesity accounts for between 2 and 8% of the overall health budgets in western countries. In addition to the direct economic impact, the indirect costs of obesity may be far greater if one includes workdays lost, visits to doctors, disability pensions, loss of wages and productivity, and premature mortality. Proposals to deal with the problem range from the provision of education to formal incentives or punishments such as the recent plan (2003) drawn up by the British NHS to oblige the obese population to sign a contract by which they commit themselves to a healthy lifestyle in order to receive health care.

Like other developed countries, Spain is experiencing a rise in obesity, in both adults and children. Between 29–35% of six- and seven-year-olds suffer from overweight and between 8–16% from obesity. Among the Spanish population aged 2–24, overweight is running at 21.4% and obesity at 5.8%. Overweight children often become overweight adults; indeed, obesity has become a major health

---

[1] The World Health Organization (2003a) estimates that obesity has reached epidemic proportions around the globe, with more than 1000 million overweight adults, at least 300 million of whom are obese.
[2] Cf. The reports of the International Obesity Task Force—IOTF (2002) and (2003).
[3] For instance, in the analyses carried out for the World Health Report 2002, approximately 58% of diabetes, 21% of ischaemic heart disease and 8–42% of certain cancers were attributable to a body mass index above 21 Kg/m².

Table 1. *Prevalence of obesity in some EU member states*

EU Country	Obese men (in %)	Obese women (in %)
Belgium	12.1	18.4
Denmark	10	9
France	9.6	10.5
Germany	17.2	19.3
Italy	6.5	6.3
The Netherlands	8.4	9.3
Spain	11.5	15.2
Sweden	10	11.9
UK	17	20

Source: International Obesity Task Force, 1999.

policy issue, responsible for some 28 000 deaths a year (8.5% of the total). Causes of obesity include genetic inheritance and poor diet, and, increasingly, sedentary behaviour. According to the latest available data from the Spanish Ministry of Health (2003), 50% of the Spanish population have a sedentary lifestyle. Interestingly, this behaviour is more common among female adults (52%) than among males (41%) and the share of the population that devotes more than 5 hours a week to sports is the second lowest in the EU, after Portugal.

In spite of this aggregate evidence, the determinants of obesity are relatively unknown. Among them, the social determinants arc the ones that have been tested the least. Social determinants are frequently country-specific and often present highly complex interactions with social behaviour patterns. Empirical evidence shedding light on the impact of social interaction on body weight is crucial for the design of health policies such as information campaigns, promoting advice from doctors, and so on. Effective policies for controlling obesity require an understanding of the complex processes underpinning body mass composition which not only involve biological and genetic endowments but are associated with socio-economic, cultural and behavioural factors (Sundquist and Johansson, 1998; Zhang and Wang, 2004). These studies identify income and ethnicity as responsible for a higher prevalence of obesity. Interestingly, there is an apparent inverse association between obesity and income in the US white population while it is just the contrary in minority groups. Socio-economic position is believed to affect attitudes towards food and body weight status (Cahnman, 1968). Other factors are time preference (Komlos et al., 2004) and the role of education (Nayga, 2001).

However, little empirical evidence has been gathered on the association between obesity and self-image. Individuals' social interactions may well be important in explaining their attitudes towards the development of their own body mass. Indeed, acknowledging the role of self-image implies focusing on the social nature of individual behaviour, and its effects on the production of body mass which might be regarded (to an extent) under individual control. Social interactions may lead to individual pleasures such as 'the pleasure of being seen as having a shifted body' and individuals' desire for distinction inside their social environment may make this a factor when they consume food. Over the years many experts have acknowledged the role of social interaction in explaining human behaviour. Social interactions include the role of demonstration (Duesenberry, 1949) bandwagon and snob influences (Leibenstein, 1950) and more general interactions (Becker, 1974) However, they seem to have played a minor role in the economic analysis of individuals' body mass in spite of the fact that people's behaviour often aims to emulate that of others.

This paper presents an empirical evaluation of the determinants of obesity in Spain by examining the condition jointly with individuals' self-image. Social interactions are significant though endogenous determinants of obesity in modern societies. Such as obesity, social interactions might capture some of the influencing part effect of the socio-economic determinants of obesity. The importance of social interactions is grounded on theoretical models of individual interactions (Becker, 1974). An empirical model is developed in which the determinants of obesity with individuals' concern with their self-image are corrected. The results suggest that self-image is a significant predictor of individuals' body mass and also of obesity and overweight.

II. SOCIAL INTERACTIONS AND INDIVIDUAL BODY MASS

The conceptual model

As social animals, human beings interact in their daily lives in the pursuit of common social goals, which, it is hypothesized, are to drive their physical appearance and ultimately, their social interactions. Everyone in the population is assigned a specific role guided by gender, education and lifestyle. According to Ackerloff and Kranton (2000), behavioural prescriptions ('social norms') affirm one's self-image within the social environment. If this self-image is violated, the result is anxiety and unease. Individuals choose who they want to be and adapt their behaviour accordingly. Therefore, social interactions determine individuals' preferences, and ultimately their behaviour at various levels, such as feeding, doing sport and dressing. Therefore, individuals' decisions regarding their social identity preclude to an extent their specific body mass. Although individual's weight is in part an endowment determined by genetics and specific human biology it is largely recognized to influence food intake. Therefore, putting on weight might be the result of an individual's decision (e.g., chosen lifestyle) which determines calorie intake and results in body mass generation. However, it may well be that individuals might have to face conflicting goals between satisfying their tastes – and thus consuming food at their full appetence – or refraining from following their appetence to allow their body shift in line with their desired identity. That is, some share of individuals in their daily decision making trade-off their own desired identity and their consumer preferences based on tastes. That is, food intake decisions are driven by individuals' willingness to adapt their body to a specific desired physical constitution.

Although the production of fat and the rise in the individuals' body mass are heavily dependent on individual biological constitution and lifestyle (e.g., the rate at which an individual burns calories), social interactions at certain ages may to an extent determine individuals' physical constitution. Some economists find explanations for obesity in the expanding food supply resulting from technological change (Philipson, 2001). However, looking at individuals in developed societies one might well argue that social interactions, as determining the role each person plays at each point of the life cycle, are likely to preclude an uncontrolled development of body mass and obesity. In a recent paper Wansink (2004) argues that the eating environment determines food intake. By food environment is meant the ambient factors associated with the eating of food, but that are independent of food. However, social interactions should be distinguished from the food environment or the factors that directly relate to the way food is provided or presented. Indeed, determining how much to eat or drink relies on consumption norms determining an acceptable quantity to eat. In addition, prior research finds that as the number of eating companions increases, the average variability of how much is eaten may actually decrease (Clendennen *et al.*, 1994). However, this refers not to social interactions but to the fact that certain food environments might lead to increase the food intake. In fact what is suggested in this paper is that people who exhibit a more intense social life would be those that might hypothetically care about their self-image.

Individuals are assumed to choose an identity so that each person has a conception of his/her own categories and that of other people. $s*(.)$ refers to desired social self-image resulting from their social interactions which fit in some specific identity. Individual self-image leads to a desired body mass $h*(.)$; both enter the utility function. Both self-image (S) and individual's body mass (B) are determined by individual's income (Y), variables proxying human capital such as education, experience and environmental variables (E) and other variables (Z). At any time, households allocate both time and economic resources to the production of commodities such as health and social interactions – both leading to a certain self-image and desired health. Thus, individuals maximize a joint utility function subject to technology

and income constraints. That is, the individual j maximizes its utility function:

$$U_j = U(h^*, s^*, Z_j)$$

$$h^* = h(B_j, Y_j, E_j) \qquad (1)$$

$$s^* = s(S_j, Y_j, E_j) \qquad (2)$$

$$s.t \quad p^s S_j + B_j \leq Y_j$$

where P^s refers to the price of social interactions and the price of a unit of body mass taken as a numeraire. Therefore, the individual's body mass (B) and social interactions (S) will be:

$$B_j = b(E_j, Y_j, S_j, Z_{1j}) \qquad (3)$$

$$S_j = s(E_j, Y_j, B_j, Z_{2j}) \qquad (4)$$

That is, social interactions and the individual's body mass are inversely associated in so far as they both compete for the allocation of income and time. One potential issue for the simple model is that it does not take into account the time dimension, as far as one is concentrating in the contemporaneous consequences of obesity. Therefore, the study does not examine the fact that obese people will live shorter lives but concentrates on what determined the onset of obesity rather than the potential effects on mortality.

The empirical specification

According to the conceptual framework, both individual body mass and individuals' concern with their self-image are potentially endogenous variables which might be subjected to significant interactions in both ways. Thus, in analysing the determinants of obesity one of the not yet well understood issues refers to the role of potential endogenous variables, mostly from individuals' decisions regarding their own lifestyle and nutrition variables. Therefore, individuals may self-select their own body mass by investing in the pursuit of their desired self-image. To examine this issue we will estimate the determinants individuals body mass, obesity and overweight using a sample selection procedure proposed by Heckman (1979). Heckman's sample selection model is based on the following two latent variable models:

$$B = \beta' X + u_1 \quad \text{if } (S = 1)$$

$$S = \delta' Z + u_2 \qquad (5)$$

where X is a k-vector of regressors, Z is an m-vector of regressors and the error terms u_1 and u_2 are jointly normally distributed, independently of X and Z, with zero expectations. B refers to body mass – as well as obesity or overweight – and S refers to social interactions. Furthermore, the latent variable S itself is not observable – only its sign. Therefore, a positive value is observed if social interactions take place and zero otherwise. The same applies to obesity and over (under) weight. In the remaining case, instead of an OLS model to estimate B, a two stage probit model is used, estimated using maximum likelihood (Van der Ven and Van der Praag, 1981).

III. DATA AND VARIABLES

The data

The database used in this study is the European Community Household Panel (ECHP), wave 5, survey year 1998, for Spain. This is a specific, longitudinal EU survey designed by Eurostat to supply information on household and individual income. The ECHP contains rich information on several sources of income (including social transfers), and also on labour market variables, housing, health and other socio-economic indicators concerning the living conditions of private households and persons. After deleting some missing values the sample comprised 12 591 individuals aged 16 to 89 years old, of whom 6143 (48.8%) are men and 6448 (51.2%) women.

To assess the prevalence of overweight and obesity in the data we use the widely accepted Body Mass Index (BMI) indicator, which is defined as weight in kilograms divided by the square of height in metres (kg/m^2). According to the World Health Organization classification, a BMI over $25\,kg/m^2$ is defined as overweight, and a BMI of over $30\,kg/m^2$ as obese; BMI below $18.5\,kg/m^2$ is considered underweight. However, within the obese category a value below 35 is considered as moderate, between 35–40 is classified as severe and over 40 as extreme. Table 2 provides a description of the data labels and descriptive means.

Central to the investigation are individual social interactions. Given the difficulties to measure empirically this variable it was decided to proxy it through the use of the question of how often respondents meet friends or relatives not living with them. Social interaction refers to the intensity of an individual's social life. A positive association is assumed between the ability of an individual to meet people and their self-image. This variable has five categories ranging from a score of one if individuals answer 'on most days' to five if the answer is 'never'.[4]

Another key variable in the regressions is the natural logarithm of individual income which is constructed from information on the total net household income declared by each interviewee. Specifically, per adult equivalent income

is derived by deflating net household income by the OECD equivalence scale, which allows for differences in size and demographic composition of the household.[5] Educational level of respondents was calculated using information on the highest level of general or higher education completed. This is a dummy variable with a code of 1 for those who finished higher education, a code of 2 for the second stage of secondary education and a code of 3 for individuals who completed the first stage of secondary education (or less).

This investigation also analyses the existence of geographical variations in the prevalence of obesity. However, the survey provides too aggregate information since the question on the location of the household is measured in NUTS aggregates. For Spain seven regions are considered: Region 1, Galicia, Asturias and Cantabria; Region 2, the Basque Country, Navarre, La Rioja and Aragon; Region 3, the Community of Madrid; Region 4, Castile and Leon, Castile and La-Mancha; Region 5, Catalonia, Valencia and Balearic Islands; Region 6, Andalusia and Murcia and Region 7, the Canary Islands. Other independent variables investigated are gender, age, marital status, household size and the cross relations between them.

3.2 Preliminary evidence

Table 2 displays the means and standard deviation as well as the definition of the variables used in this study. These preliminary data show that 12.6% of total respondents are obese, 34.4% are overweight while the remaining 50% of respondents are within their recommended weight range. These figures suggest that, as pointed out in the introduction, Spain is part of the obesity epidemic but is not a country in which obesity is highly prevalent. In addition, obesity is associated to specific characteristics as age and gender. Interestingly, while obesity displayed no significant gender difference, approximately 42% of men are overweight and this figure is just 27.3% in the case of women. Almost 5% of women are under their normal weight; this feature is negligible in men, below 1%. It is also worth noting that age raises the prevalence of obesity: the percentage of obese younger than 30 years old is around 7.4%, but around 43% for those at age 60 and older.[6] In other words, in the 50–79 year age group obesity ranges from 19.7% to 22.3%, well above the average of the entire dataset (12.6%), and the prevalence of overweight averages 46%, higher than the sample average, 34.4%.

---

[4] This variable was recorded since a value of 1 means that the individual responds 'on most days' or 'once or twice a week' and 0 otherwise ('once or twice a month', 'less often than once a month' or 'never').

[5] This equivalence scale adopts a value of one for the head of the household, 0.7 for other adults and 0.5 for those younger than 14 years old.

[6] Similarly, 14.6% of the overweight are below 30; this figure is 35% for the over-60s.

Table 2. *Variable description and means*

Variable	Description	Mean ($N = 12\,591$)	Std. Dev. ($N = 12\,591$)
Dependent variables			
Log of BMI[a]	Log of body mass index	3.21	0.163
Obese	1 if individual is obese, 0 otherwise	0.126	0.332
Overweight	1 if individual is overweight, 0 otherwise	0.344	0.475
Self-image	1 if indiv. meets friends or relatives not living with him/her very/quite often; 0 otherwise	0.9249	0.263
Independent variables			
Gender	1 if men; 0 if women	0.488	0.499
Age	Age in years	44.99	19.27
Age_square	Square of age in years	2395.36	1901.21
Log of Income[b]	Log of total net equivalent income	13.67	0.886
Square of Log of Inc.	Square of log of total net equiv. income	187.73	21.01
Married	1 if married; 0 otherwise	0.5883	0.492
Sep./Div./Widowed	1 if separated, divorced or widowed; 0 otherwise	0.1056	0.307
Single	1 if never married; 0 otherwise	0.3061	0.461
NutsReg_1	1 if indiv. lives in Nuts 1 (Galicia, Asturias and Cantabria); 0 otherwise	0.1282	0.334
NutsReg_2	1 if indiv. lives in Nuts 2 (Basque Co, Navarre, La Rioja and Aragon); 0 otherwise	0.1471	0.354
NutsReg_3	1 if indiv. lives in Nuts 3 (Comm. of Madrid); 0 otherwise	0.0943	0.292
NutsReg_4	1 if indiv. lives in Nuts 4 (Castie-Leon, Castile-La Mancha and Extremadura); 0 otherwise	0.1587	0.365
NutsReg_5	1 if indiv. lives in Nuts 5 (Catalonia, Valencia, I. Baleares); 0 otherwise	0.2154	0.411
NutsReg_6	1 if ind. lives in Nuts 6 (Andalucia and Murcia); 0 otherwise	0.1900	0.392
NutsReg_7	1 if indiv. lives in Nuts 7 (Canarias); 0 otherwise.	0.064	0.392
Education_1	1 if indiv. completed 3rd. level of education, 0 otherwise	0.1749	0.379
Education_2	1 if indiv. completed the second stage of secondary education; 0 otherwise	0.1901	0.392
Education_3	1 if indiv. completed less than the second of secondary education; 0 otherwise	0.6343	0.482
Household size	Size of the household	3.625	1.536
Age*Gender	Age multiplied by variable gender	21.404	25.538
Age*Income	Age multiplied by variable income	616.558	268.902
Age*Married	Age multiplied by variable married	29.302	27.189
Age*(Sep./Div./Wi)	Age multiplied by variable separated, divorced and widowed		

[a] BMI variable is measured as weight in kilograms divided by the square of height in metres (kg/m^2).
[b] Equivalent income is measured as household income divided by the OECD equivalence scale.

Socio-economic variables are also relevant explanatory factors. For instance, among the unemployed (9% of the total sample) the share of both obese and overweight (34%) was significantly below the average (47%). At the same time, the prevalence of recommended weight (a BMI between 18.5 and $25\,kg/m^2$) was 61.4%, well above the average value of 50%. However, in the category 'working more than 15 hours per week' (41.4% of sample) and the 'economically inactive' group (47.8%) the proportion of obese and overweight was equivalent to that of the total sample. This suggests that individuals' demand for leisure may be associated to the probability of obesity. The longer the leisure time, the more likely individuals are to care

for and be aware of their own body. In addition, the unemployed are effectively seeking to attract the attention of potential employers and as a result may take more of their physical appearance.

Marital status and education also have a notable effect on body mass. In general, there is a casual association between being married and weight gain, possibly though its relation with child bearing. Our data seem to confirm this, given that the proportion of married obese (15.2%) and overweight (40.7%) categories are again higher than in the average sample. Similarly, among obese individuals (overweight) close to 71% (70%) are married, a figure that is much higher than that of married individuals in the sample (59%). On the other hand, the data indicate that obesity is negatively related to education. The share of obesity in respondents who completed higher education is just 5.7% and the rate for those who finished secondary education is 7%, well below the average.

Finally, an interesting regional pattern also emerges for obesity in the dataset.[7] Surprisingly, the prevalence of obesity is relatively high in the south (Andalusia and Murcia) and the Canary Islands (15.4%), compared with a prevalence of just 8.2% in the Autonomous Community of Madrid.

IV. RESULTS

The empirical strategy of this study is to estimate the predictor of individuals' social interactions along with the production of body mass, obesity and overweight. In addition to the variables in Table 2, interaction effects are included in the model to capture the possible non-linearities that some variables might exhibit in determining both individuals' weight and social interactions. Table 3 examines the determinants of the body mass index accounting for the selectivity of social interactions. Table 4 examines a sample selection model for obesity and Table 5 for overweight. In all models, Log Likelihood tests for the independence of the two processes rejected the null hypothesis of independence as the Mills Lambda was significant at a level of 5%. In addition, the correlation coefficient of the error terms of the processes is negative, suggesting that social interaction might make individuals 'fitter', and thus less obese and overweight.

As expected, males had higher body mass, though when the interaction effect was included it was more affluent middle-aged men who presented the highest body mass. Interestingly, both age and income displayed a quadratic effect, suggesting in the first case that people may be presumably induced to lose weight when older and that richer individuals are more likely to invest on their self-image so that they adapt their body mass better to the one that is desired. Education and regional dummies are used as observation variables. Those that have been married at some point – divorced, widowed or separated – and those currently married are more likely to display a higher body mass than those who have never married; this is especially the case of married males. The results were robust regardless of the specification.

Social interactions are explained by age; older individuals are more likely to devote time to social interactions, especially if married (Table 3). Interestingly, gender is never an explanatory variable for social interactions while education is positively associated with social interactions,

and this is especially the case of married low educated individuals who are predicted to be less likely to be involved with others. Household size is inversely associated with social interactions. A possible explanation might be that the larger the household the less likely individuals are to meet others outside the household. Similarly, in explaining social interactions, individuals in southern and Mediterranean regions are more likely to interact with others. The high significance of the variable household size and the non-linear effect with age suggest that social life declines due to fertility, which in turn has an effect on obesity. These effects coexist with human capital effects, in so far as low educated individuals who are married are more likely to be obese.

Looking at specific determinants of obesity in Table 4 we find that men, consistently with the results in Table 3, are more likely to be obese than women. Again, income has a non-linear effect: middle-income individuals tend to have a higher body mass. The same non-linear effect applies to age: individuals' age increases obesity, but at a certain age it starts to decrease. This is consistent with the assumption of time preference as determining individuals' body mass (Komlos et al., 2004). The separated, divorced and widowed are more likely to be obese than married subjects. Introducing interaction terms we find that being married male are more likely to be obese. On the other hand, younger women have a lower body mass and that more affluent men are likely to have a higher body mass. Sedentary lifestyle was no longer significant when interaction terms were included.

Table 5 displays the two-stage sample selection model for overweight. It is worth noting that compared to obesity and body mass estimates, age has a quadratic effect on overweight, and income is not a significant predictor. However, marital status remains an important determinant of overweight, which interacts with age and gender. Relatively richer men as well as older women are more likely to be overweight. This result suggests that social determinants of overweight, among them income, may be less explanatory in determining whether an individual's weight is above the ideal. Again it is age that shifts individuals' weight down. If age slows down time preference then we would expect older individuals to experience higher 'preference for the future'.

V. CONCLUSIONS

This paper has sought to examine the determinants of individuals' body mass, obesity and overweight in connection with individual social interactions. Results from

---

[7] Unfortunately, the ECHP only offers information at a regional aggregate basis (NUTS1 aggregates).

Table 3. *Regression model with sample selection (two step estimation) for log of BMI*

	Log of BMI ($N = 12{,}526$)		Log of BMI ($N = 12{,}526$)	
	Coefficient	Std. Error	Coefficient	Std. Error
Intercept	2.7600**	0.0525	2.6561**	0.0818
Gender	0.0674**	0.0033	−0.0541	0.0442
Age	0.0117**	0.0006	0.0122**	0.0017
Age Square	−9.0E-05**	5.74E-06	−9.0E-05**	5.83E-06
Log of Income	0.0302**	0.0084	0.0394**	0.0098
Sq. of Log of Income	−0.0016**	0.0004	−0.0020**	0.0004
Married	0.0224**	0.0049	0.1761*	0.0596
Sediwi	0.0434**	0.0074	0.0914	0.1019
NutsReg_2	−0.0045	0.0072	0.0084	0.0060
NutsReg_3	−0.0068	0.0074	−0.0100	0.0063
NutsReg_4	−0.0107	0.0075	−0.0073	0.0062
NutsReg_5	−0.0142*	0.0067	−0.0117*	0.0055
NutsReg_6	0.0015	0.0075	0.0054	0.0061
NutsReg_7	−0.0093	0.0097	−0.0048	0.0079
Age*Gender			−0.0026**	0.0002
Age*Income			2.88E-05	1.0E-05
Age*Married			0.0002	0.0003
Age*Sediwi			0.0004	0.0004
Gender*Income			0.0164**	0.0032
Married*Income			−0.0118*	0.0043
Sediwi*Income			−0.0063	0.0074
Gender*Married			0.0162*	0.0076
Gender*Sediwi			0.0124	0.0134
	Social-interactions		Social-interactions	
Intercept	2.2738**	0.1487	2.3375**	0.1762
Gender	−0.0377	0.0347	−0.1186	0.0995
Age	−0.0222**	0.0060	−0.0251**	0.0070
Age Square	0.0001*	5.61E-05	0.0001	7.03E-05
Education_1	−0.1006*	0.0479	−0.0093	0.1428
Education_2	0.0002	0.0506	0.1446	0.1363
Married	0.0148	0.0533	−0.1089	0.1631
Sediwi	−0.1085	0.0735	−0.0151	0.3175
Household size	−0.0495**	0.0115	−0.0531**	0.0117
NutsReg_2	−0.1947**	0.0580	−0.2025**	0.0583
NutsReg_3	−0.1403*	0.0660	−0.1416*	0.0644
NutsReg_4	0.2472**	0.0640	0.2418**	0.0644
NutsReg_5	0.1762*	0.0584	0.1672*	0.0588
NutsReg_6	0.2780**	0.0620	0.2741**	0.0623
NutsReg_7	0.3533**	0.0903	0.3465**	0.0907
Age*Gender			0.0033	0.0022
Age*Married			0.0069*	0.0029
Age*Sediwi			0.0028	0.0048
Gender*Married			−0.1166	0.0925
Gender*Sediwi			−0.0287	0.1563
Education_1*Age			0.0022	0.0038
Education_2*Age			−0.0008	0.0040
Education_1*Married			−0.2742*	0.1187
Education_2*Married			−0.1560	0.1277
Education_1*Sediwi			0.2065	0.3058
Education_2*Sediwi			−0.2948	0.2258
Mills Lambda	−0.1756**	0.0436	−0.1129*	0.0527
	Wald Chi2 (24) = 2,185.61		Wald Chi2 (38) = 3,067.67	

* Statistically significant at the 0.05 level; ** Statistically significant at the 0.01 level.

Table 4. *Selectivity corrected probit models*

	Obese (N = 12,526)		Obese (N = 12,526)	
	Coefficient	Std. Error	Coefficient	Std. Error
Intercept	−3.2218**	0.4003	−4.2382**	0.9091
Gender	0.1081**	0.0277	0.1221	0.4168
Age	0.0586**	0.0054	0.0668**	0.0152
Age Square	−0.00004**	5.0E-05	−0.0005**	6.51E-06
Log of Income	0.1783*	0.0612	0.2495*	0.0963
Sq. of Log of Income	−0.0097**	0.0027	−0.0112**	0.0031
Married	0.0557	0.0439	0.9382	0.6104
Sediwi	0.2033**	0.0593	0.7695	0.9183
NutsReg_2	0.0366	0.0521	0.0341	0.0544
NutsReg_3	−0.0104	0.0609	−0.0253	0.0637
NutsReg_4	−0.1088*	0.0515	−0.1041*	0.0533
NutsReg_5	−0.0387	0.0482	−0.0344	0.0500
NutsReg_6	0.0170	0.0504	0.0245	0.0536
NutsReg_7	−0.0153	0.0662	−0.0028	0.0693
Age*Gender			−0.0118**	0.0020
Age*Income			3.66E-05	0.0011
Age*Married			0.0009	0.0025
Age*Sediwi			0.0016	0.0038
Gender*Income			0.0322	0.0300
Married*Income			−0.0721	0.0444
Sediwi*Income			−0.0545	0.0659
Gender*Married			0.1731*	0.0799
Gender*Sediwi			0.1036	0.1260
	Social-interactions		Social-interactions	
Intercept	2.2722**	0.1414	2.4272**	0.1718
Gender	−0.0174	0.0349	−0.1471	0.0993
Age	−0.0235**	0.0059	−0.0296**	0.0069
Age Square	0.0001*	5.61E-05	0.0001*	7.03E-05
Education_1	−0.2115**	0.0397	−0.1844	0.1244
Education_2	−0.0886*	0.0428	0.0121	0.1220
Married	−0.0072	0.0529	−0.1026	0.1552
Sediwi	−0.1069	0.0727	−0.1136	0.3055
Household size	−0.0290*	0.0096	−0.0337**	0.0104
NutsReg_2	−0.1855*	0.0576	−0.1894**	0.0579
NutsReg_3	−0.1111	0.0660	−0.1156	0.0664
NutsReg_4	0.2412**	0.0640	0.2394**	0.0641
NutsReg_5	0.1837*	0.0581	0.1768*	0.0584
NutsReg_6	0.2645**	0.0619	0.2638**	0.0623
NutsReg_7	0.3546**	0.0900	0.3547**	0.0903
Age*Gender			0.0038	0.0022
Age*Married			0.0061*	0.0029
Age*Sediwi			0.0007	0.0047
Gender*Married			−0.0981	0.0915
Gender*Sediwi			−0.0186	0.1573
Education_1*Age			0.0041	0.0032
Education_2*Age			−0.0002	0.0033
Education_1*Married			−0.2850*	0.1018
Education_2*Married			−0.0980	0.1088
Education_1*Sediwi			0.0108	0.2806
Education_2*Sediwi			−0.2892	0.1907
ρ	−0.9484**	0.0367	−0.9304	0.0584
	Wald Chi2 (13) = 427.82		Wald Chi2 (22) = 401.63	
LL ratio	−7,261.135		−7,219.809	

* Statistically significant at the 0.05 level; ** Statistically significant at the 0.01 level.

Table 5. *Selectivity corrected probit models*

	Overweight ($N = 12{,}526$)		Overweight ($N = 12{,}526$)	
	Coefficient	Std. Error	Coefficient	Std. Error
Intercept	−1.8082**	0.3926	−0.9873	0.7118
Gender	0.4067**	0.0240	−1.0622*	0.3806
Age	0.0509**	0.0041	0.0437*	0.0142
Age Square	−0.00004**	3.97E-05	−0.0004**	4.95E-05
Log of Income	−0.0285	0.0623	−0.0940	0.0824
Sq. of Log of Income	0.0011	0.0027	−0.0007	0.0030
Married	0.1572**	0.0360	0.7226	0.5218
Sediwi	0.1541*	0.0521	−0.0475	0.8842
NutsReg_2	0.0167	0.0441	0.0087	0.0464
NutsReg_3	0.0551	0.0500	0.0561	0.0515
NutsReg_4	−0.0435	0.0436	−0.0312	0.0455
NutsReg_5	−0.0878*	0.0410	−0.0774	0.0423
NutsReg_6	−0.0390	0.0421	−0.0264	0.0441
NutsReg_7	−0.1055	0.5664	−0.0899	0.0585
Age*Gender			−0.0110**	0.0016
Age*Income			0.0013	0.0010
Age*Married			−0.0079**	0.0021
Age*Sediwi			−0.0020	0.0034
Gender*Income			0.1397**	0.0282
Married*Income			−0.0215	0.0380
Sediwi*Income			0.0052	0.0639
Gender*Married			0.1270	0.0671
Gender*Sediwi			0.0510	0.1119
	Social-interactions		Social-interactions	
Intercept	2.2430**	0.1435	2.3785**	0.1718
Gender	−0.0253	0.0347	−0.1330	0.0995
Age	−0.0219**	0.0058	−0.0264**	0.0069
Age Square	0.0001*	5.53E-05	0.0001*	7.03E-05
Education_1	−0.1537**	0.0442	−0.0732	0.1348
Education_2	−0.0428	0.0469	0.0784	0.1302
Married	0.0009	0.0515	−0.1273	0.1601
Sediwi	−0.1177	0.0725	−0.0330	0.3135
Household size	−0.0404**	0.0105	−0.0476**	0.0115
NutsReg_2	−0.1953*	0.0575	−0.2015*	0.0581
NutsReg_3	−0.1462*	0.0656	−0.1406*	0.0663
NutsReg_4	0.2358**	0.0638	0.2357**	0.0643
NutsReg_5	0.1703*	0.0582	0.1664*	0.0587
NutsReg_6	0.2692**	0.0616	0.2692**	0.0622
NutsReg_7	0.3633**	0.0896	0.3571**	0.0909
Age*Gender			0.0034	0.0022
Age*Married			0.0071*	0.0029
Age*Sediwi			0.0030	0.0048
Gender*Married			−0.0974	0.0925
Gender*Sediwi			−0.0153	0.1563
Education_1*Age			0.0032	0.0036
Education_2*Age			−0.0005	0.0037
Education_1*Married			−0.3055*	0.1124
Education_2*Married			−0.1240	0.1214
Education_1*Sediwi			0.1373	0.3006
Education_2*Sediwi			−0.1933	0.2138
ρ	−0.9637**	0.0554	−0.8148	0.1400
	Wald Chi2 (13) = 1,094.00		Wald Chi2 (22) = 840.71	
LL ratio	−10,132.94		−10,028.98	

* Statistically significant at the 0.05 level; ** Statistically significant at the 0.01 level.

several sample selection models suggest that social interactions enable individuals to compare themselves with each other, and encourage behaviours that might prevent obesity and overweight. Interestingly, the results highlight the significance of regional variables and marital status as well as household size. Therefore, in the light of the findings it can be suggested that social interactions, which are found to determine social image, may also explain the differences in obesity among European countries, which is an issue that to date remains relatively unexplored. The results may be considered as surprising in suggesting that obesity might be a social phenomenon connected to individuals' social life and that by promoting social interactions, individuals may change their own self-image, or in the terms of Akerloff and Kranton (2000), their desired identity. However, it should be noted that due to data limitations the study does not include relevant variables connected with individual's lifestyles such as food intake, smoking and drinking habits along with sport practice.

In agreement with these findings, it is observed that income and age display a non-linear effect in determining obesity. Arguably, these effects suggest that obesity is concentrated in middle income individuals, which suggests that it is not the lower social position that determines obesity or, at least, that other factors are also at work. Interestingly, the estimates suggest that obesity is more likely in married men and less likely in young women. Overweight is more likely in high income men and less likely in younger women, as well as relatively older individuals who declare as being married. One may cast some doubts on the relationship between obesity and income resulting from possible labour market discrimination. However, if this is the case, because unemployed in Spain receive a public subsidy, one should find that obesity is determined by low income groups which is not the case. This doesn't imply that there might still be labour discrimination in the Spanish labour market.

The results should be interpreted with some caution since certain relevant individual variables are not included explicitly in the model such as interactions between health and time preference. Other caveats refer to the way social interactions are measured. The survey only contained a variable for individuals' social life and may overlook other social interactions. An important caveat that should be noted is the fact that one does not look at the long run effects of obesity, and thus the model does not maximize utility over the lifetime. This means one does not consider the fact that obese people will live shorter lives. Therefore, one might argue that one of the consequences of obesity is that the onset of some illnesses happens before the non-obese population, being that the reason for an association between social interactions and obesity. However, a similar causal relationship is found for those overweight which provide some evidence that the pattern identified is not exclusively a specific influence of obesity related health effects. On the other hand, some other concern might rely in the interpretation of the causality of the results. For instance, one might argue that obese people may find it more difficult to find friends, which implies that Equation 2 might need to be reinterpreted as the feasible self-image rather than the one individual's desire. Finally, it should acknowledge the existence of significant unobserved heterogeneity in the sort of data examined. This might place some effects on the relationship between obesity and social interactions. For instance, although it is found that the relationship is guided by some sort of substitution, it might well be that for some individuals both are complements. However, the latter would mainly refer to the environmental determinants of food intake while the former would refer to the social interactions as influencing body shape.

ACKNOWLEDGEMENTS

We acknowledge the comments from John Komlos although any remaining errors are our own. In addition, we are grateful to financial help received from CICYT under the project SEC2002-00019.

REFERENCES

Ackerloff, G. A. and Kranton, R. E. (2000) Economics and identity, *Quarterly Journal of Economics*, **115**(3), 715–53.

Becker, G. (1974) A theory of social interactions, *Journal of Political Economy*, **82**(6), 1063–93.

Cahnman, W. J. (1968) The stigma of obesity, *Sociological Quarterly*, **9**(2), 283–99.

Clendennen, V., Herman, C. P. and Polivy, J. (1994) Social facilitation of eating among friends and strangers, *Appetite*, **23**(1), 1–13.

Duesenberry, J. S. (1949) *Income, Savings and the Theory of Consumer Behaviour*, Harvard University Press, Cambridge, MA.

Heckman, J. (1979) Sample selection bias as a specification error, *Econometrica*, **47**(1), 153–61.

IOTF (International Obesity Task Force) (2002) *Obesity in Europe. The Case for Action*, European Association for the Study of Obesity (www.iotf.org).

IOTF (International Obesity Task Force) (2003) *Obesity in Europe-2. Waiting for a Green Light for Health?: Europe at the Crossroads for Diet and Disease*, European Association for the Study of Obesity (www.iotf.org).

Komlos, J., Smith, P. and Bogin, B. (2004) Obesity and the rate of time preference: is there a connection?, *Journal of Biosocial Science*, **36**(2), 209–19.

Leibenstein, H. (1950) Bandwagon, snob and Veblen effects in the theory of consumer demand, *Quarterly Journal of Economics*, **64**(2), 183–207.

Nayga, R. (2001) Effect of schooling on obesity: is health knowledge a moderating factor?, *Education Economics*, **2**(2), 129–37.

Philipson, T. (2001) The world-wide growth in obesity: an economic research agenda, *Health Economics*, **10**(1), 1–7.

Spanish Ministry of Health (2003) Instituto de Informacion Sanitania, Estadísticas Sanitarias España.

Sundquist, J. and Johansson, S. E. (1998) The influence of socio-economic status, ethnicity and lifestyle on body mass index in a longitudinal study, *International Journal of Epidemiology*, **27**, 57–63.

Van der Ven, W. and Van der Praag, B. (1981) The demand for deductibles in health insurance, *Journal of Econometrics*, **17**(2), 229–52.

Wang, Y., Monteiro, C. and Popkin, B. M. (2002) Trends of obesity and underweight in older children and adolescents in the United States, Brazil, China and Russia, *American Journal of Clinical Nutrition*, **75**(3), 971–7.

Wansink, B. (2004) Environmental factors that unknowingly increase a consumer's food intake and consumption volume, *Annual Review of Nutrition*, **24**(1), 455–79.

WHO (World Health Organization) (1998) *Obesity: Preventing and Managing the Global Epidemic*, World Health Organization, Geneva.

WHO (2003a) *The Global Strategy on Diet, Physical Activity and Health*, World Health Organization, Geneva.

WHO (2003b) *Diet, Nutrition and the Prevention of Chronic Diseases*, Who Technical Report Series 916, World Health Organization, Geneva.

Zhang, Q. and Wang, Y. (2004) Socio-economic inequality of obesity in the United States: do gender, age and ethnicity matter?, *Social Science and Medicine*, **58**(6), 1171–80.

Low carbohydrate information, consumer health preferences and market demand of fruits in the United States

Laxmi Paudel[a], Murali Adhikari[b], Jack Houston[c] and Krishna P. Paudel[d]

[a]*Citi Corporation, Irving, USA*
[b]*Global Future Institute, Baton Rouge, USA*
[c]*Department of Agricultural and Applied Economics, University of Georgia, Athens, USA*
[d]*Department of Agricultural Economics and Agribusiness, Louisiana State University, 70803, Baton Rouge, USA*

We assessed the impacts of low carbohydrate information on the market demand of US fruits using almost ideal demand system, Rotterdam and double-log models. Results indicated significant positive impacts of low carbohydrate information on the market demand of grape and lemon. However, a significant negative effect exists on market demand of apples and bananas. Majority of the estimated elasticities are consistent in terms of expected sign and magnitude across all models.

I. Introduction

Concerns about the carbohydrate level in foods have increased substantially in the United States (US) in recent years mostly due to the growing problems of overweight and obesity. A number of medical research studies have suggested that overweight, obesity and obesity related medical conditions can be successfully controlled by reducing the carbohydrate in-take in the diets or by adopting low carbohydrate diets (Astrup *et al.*, 2004). Our article focuses on the impacts of low carbohydrate information and its impact on market demand of fruits. The secondary objective of this study is to explore the robustness of the estimated parameters and consistency of the empirical results, when the same data are used in estimating some of the popular demand models.

The article is organized as follows. In Section II, we give a synopsis of three demand models used in the article. Following to that section, we describe the data used in the study. Results and Discussions are presented in Section IV. Conclusions from the study are drawn in Section V.

II. Model

Almost ideal demand system model

We estimate the linear approximate almost ideal demand system (AIDS) (LA/AIDS) as (Deaton and Muellbauer, 1980):

$$s_i = \alpha_i + \sum_j \gamma_{ij} \ln p_j + \beta_i \ln \frac{Y}{P^*} + \theta \ln \text{CI}, \quad i = 1, \ldots, n$$

$$(1)$$

where

$$P^* = \alpha_0 + \sum_i \alpha_i \ln p_i + \frac{1}{2} \sum_i \sum_j \gamma_{ij}^* \ln(p_i) \ln(p_j) \quad (2)$$

where n is the number of included fruits, p_j is the price of fruit j, Y is the total expenditure on the included fruits, CI is carbohydrate index, s_i is the budget share in the ith equation ($s_i = p_i q_i / Y$, where q_i is the respective quantity) and P is the weighted price based on Stone's price index and defined as:

$$\log(P^*) = \sum_{i=1}^n w_i \log(p_i) \quad (3)$$

the γ_{ij} in Equation 2 shows the change in the ith fruit's budget share with respect to change in the jth price with real fruit expenditure (Y/P), holding remaining prices constant. The β_i shows a change in the ith fruit's budget share with respect to a change in real expenditure on the fruits, holding prices constant. Share equations are estimated using theoretical restrictions of symmetry, adding up and homogeneity.

Rotterdam model

We specify the Rotterdam model as (Barten, 1969).

$$\varpi_i \mathrm{d} \ln q_i = \alpha_i + \beta_i \mathrm{d} \ln Q + \sum_j^5 \pi_{ij} \mathrm{d} \ln p_j + \phi_i \mathrm{d} \ln \mathrm{CI} + v_i$$

$$(4)$$

where i indexes the equation ($i = 1$, 2, 3, 4, 5 for apples, bananas, pears, grapes and lemons, respectively) and $\mathrm{dln}\, Q = \sum_i w_i \mathrm{d} \ln q_j$ is the Divisia volume index, a third-order approximation to real expenditure on the fruits.

In the above model,

$$\varpi_i = \frac{1}{2}(\omega_{li} + \omega_{il-1}) \quad (5)$$

and ω_i is the expenditure share of fruit i in the time period t, dln (.) represents the first difference of ln (.), P_j is the nominal price of fruit j in time period t, CI represents the carbohydrate information variable. An intercept captures the trend related changes in tastes and preferences that affect the demand of US fruits.

Double-log model

A popular *ad-hoc* model in empirical demand analysis, the double-log model is easy to estimate and generally provides a good fit to the data. The estimated coefficients are directly interpreted as elasticities. The price and expenditure elasticities

are constant over time. In our analysis, price, expenditure and carbohydrate information variables are specified in the logarithmic form as:

$$\ln q_i = \alpha_i + \beta_i \ln\left(\frac{y}{p^*}\right) + \sum_j^5 \pi_{ij} \ln p_j + \theta_i \ln \mathrm{CI} + v_i$$

$$(6)$$

where y represents the expenditure on the included fruits, $\ln p^*$ is the stone price index and p_j is the price of jth fruits. The theoretical restrictions of price homogeneity and price symmetry are imposed in estimating the model.

III. Data

Annual data for the period of 1980 to 2003 were used for the analysis purposes. Price and quantity data of apple, banana, grape, pears and lemon were collected from the fruit and nut yearbook, USDA (2004). A carbohydrate information index was constructed following Kinnucan *et al.* (1997) and Adhikari *et al.* (2007). The carbohydrate information index was created by scanning 1170 abstracts, which appeared when searched using two keyword phrases 'low carbohydrate diets and weight loss' and 'low carbohydrate diets and obesity.' Search also included restrictions on keywords, language, date and category in the PubMed database – a service of the National Library of Medicine (NLM), which includes over 15 million citations for biomedical articles back to the 1950s.

Mathematically, the carbohydrate information index (CI) was specified:

$$\mathrm{WCII}_t = \tau_t \mathrm{FAV}_t \quad (7)$$

where WCII_t is the net positive publicity of low carbohydrate diets on weight loss, obesity and obesity related medical conditions. The FAV_t is the sum of favourable articles supporting low carbohydrate diets and τ_t, a weighting factor, is a relative proportion of all favourable and unfavourable articles in period 't'. That is, $\tau_t = \mathrm{FAV}_t/(\mathrm{FAV}_t + \mathrm{UNFAV}_t)$ where UNFAV_t is the cumulative sum of unfavourable articles on low carbohydrate diets.

IV. Results and Discussion

Autocorrelation is frequently a serious problem in demand studies using time-series data. The Durbin–Watson statistic showed no evidence of serial

103

correlation in the unrestricted equations. As majority of exogenous variables yielded expected signs and significant results, we ignored the issue of multicollinearity. The Wald test rejected the hypothesis that the carbohydrate information variable is insignificant in the US fruit demand at the 5% level of significance suggesting the low carbohydrate information variable be included in the model.

The parameters for the LA/AIDS, Rotterdam and double-log models with price homogeneity and symmetry imposed are estimated. In our analysis, the LA/AIDS model yielded R^2 values of 0.82 for bananas, 0.83 for pears, 0.86 for apples and 0.86 for lemons suggesting a good fit of the model to the given data. The Rotterdam and double-log models also showed a good fit of the model, with the R^2 values ranging from 0.80 to 0.92. The estimated own-price and cross-price elasticities of corresponding models are presented in Table 1.

Own-price effects

Own-price elasticities were found to have negative signs in all three models consistent with demand theory and *a priori* expectations (Table 1). Those with insignificant price elasticity include banana in the LA/AIDS model, apple and pears in the Rotterdam model and grape and lemon in the double-log model.

Expenditure effects

In general, the expected signs were consistent with *a priori* expectations for expenditure for all three models (Table 1). In the LA/AIDS model, the study results showed the significant, positive impacts of expenditure on the market demand of apples, lemons and grapes. The estimated expenditure elasticity of 1.38 for grape and 1.04 for banana (insignificant) indicate that these two fruits may be luxury goods. With the expenditure elasticity of less than unity, lemons and apples are necessity goods. In the Rotterdam demand system, expenditure elasticity was found to be positive and significant except for lemon. In the double-log model, expenditure shows significant positive impacts on the market demand except for pear. The estimated expenditure elasticities of apple compared favourably between double-log and Rotterdam models.

Carbohydrate information effects

The low carbohydrate information impacts were consistent across all demand model specifications (Table 2). In the Rotterdam model, except for banana, the study results confirm the significant influence of low

carbohydrate information on the market demand of apple, grape, lemon and pears. Results suggest a significant negative influence of low carbohydrate information on apples and pears. Though negative, impacts of low carbohydrate information was not significant for bananas. In Rotterdam model, results suggest that grapes and lemons benefited from the flow of the low carbohydrate information largely at the expense of apple and pears.

Estimated low carbohydrate information effects were strong across all fruits types in the LA/AIDS Model. Study results suggest a positive, significant impact of low carbohydrate information on the demand of grapes and lemons. Analysis, however, suggests significant, negative effects of low carbohydrate information on the demand of apples, bananas and pears.

The analysis using double-log model reveals the significant negative impacts of low carbohydrate information on the demand of apples and bananas. In double-log model, except pears, the expected sign and carbohydrate information elasticities were statistically significant across all fruit types. However, low carbohydrate information emerges as a significant, positive determinant of grapes and lemon consumption demand. In our analysis, the estimated low carbohydrate information elasticities of double-log model compared favourably with LA/AIDS model for banana, apple and lemon. Similarly, magnitude of estimated low carbohydrate information elasticities of Rotterdam and AIDS model are very similar for banana, pears and apple.

V. Conclusions

The major focus of this study was to examine the impacts of low carbohydrate information on the market demand of apples, bananas, grapes, lemons and pears in the US. In our analysis, irrespective of demand model specifications, the major conclusions and findings were mostly similar among the selected models. Of course, some inconsistencies in terms of expected signs, magnitude of estimated elasticities of own price and expenditure did exist. But, the estimated price and expenditure elasticities appeared to be relatively insensitive to demand system approaches. The robustness and consistency of estimated elasticities were more apparent in the carbohydrate information, where the majority of estimated low carbohydrate information elasticities of LA/AIDS, Rotterdam and double-log models compared favourably in terms of expected signs and magnitudes.

Even though fruits are generally considered a favourable substitute of the high carbohydrate foods,

Table 1. Estimated price and expenditure elasticities for US fresh fruits (year 1980–2003) evaluated at sample mean

| | Prices of | | | | | | | | | | | | | | | Expenditure elasticity | | |
| | Apple | | | Banana | | | Grapes | | | Lemon | | | Pears | | | | | |
Quantity	M1	M2	M3	M1	M2	M3	M1	M2	M3	M1	M2	M3	M1	M2	M3	M1	M2	M3
Apple	−0.77*	−0.05	−0.21*	0.22*	0.12	−0.33*	−0.18*	−0.03*	−0.18*	−0.01*	−0.04*	−0.23*	0.03*	−0.10*	−0.37*	0.73*	1.05*	1.25*
Banana	−0.26*	0.16	−0.33*	−0.84	−0.25*	−0.58*	0.18*	0.11*	−0.01	−0.01*	−0.01	−0.08	−0.11*	−0.01*	0.28*	1.04	0.64*	0.73*
Grapes	−0.51*	−0.04*	−0.18	0.11*	−0.008*	−0.01*	−0.89*	−0.17*	−0.87	−0.07	−0.083	0.16	−0.01	0.012	−0.38	1.38*	1.77*	1.23*
Lemon	−0.15*	−0.25	−0.23*	0.91*	−0.05	−0.08	−1.44	0.29	0.16	−0.18*	−0.16*	−0.15	C.07	0.17*	−0.07*	0.91*	0.09	0.22*
Pears	−0.76*	−0.62*	−0.37*	−0.50*	−0.04*	0.28*	0.07	0.04	−0.38*	0.14	0.18*	−0.07*	−0.19*	−0.50	−0.28*	0.94	0.57*	0.26

Notes: M1 stands for Rotterdam model, M2 stands for AIDS model and M3 stands for double-log model.
*Indicates coefficients are significant at a 10% level.

Table 2. Estimated carbohydrate information elasticity (CI) of US fresh fruits demand evaluated at sample mean

Model	Banana	Pears	Grapes	Apple	Lemon
M1	−0.03	−0.05*	0.03*	−0.02*	0.02*
M2	−0.03*	−0.04*	0.07*	−0.04*	0.14*
M3	−0.05*	0.09	0.19*	−0.05*	0.12*

Notes: M1 stands for Rotterdam model, M2 stands for AIDS model and M3 stands for double-log model. CI represents the carbohydrate information index.
*Indicates the coefficients are significant at a 10% level.

apples and bananas are still not recommended fruits substitutes in high carbohydrate diets. This might justify the presence of negative impacts of the low carbohydrate information on the aggregate demand of apples and bananas. Low magnitudes of carbohydrate information elasticities are of interest, given the ongoing carbohydrate craze in the US. In our analysis, the carbohydrate information elasticities ranged from −0.02 to 0.05. These estimated elasticities of carbohydrate information are consistent with other health information studies from cholesterol studies (Kinnucan *et al.*, 1997).

References

Adhikari, M., Paudel, L., Paudel, K., Houston, J. and Bukenya, J. (2007) Impact of low carbohydrate information on vegetable demands in the United States, *Applied Economics Letters*, **14**, 939–44.

Astrup, A., Larsen, T. and Harper, A. (2004) Atkins and other low-carbohydrate diets: hoax or an effective tool for weight loss?, *Lancet*, **364**, 897–99.

Barten, A. P. (1969) Maximum likelihood estimation of a complete system of demand equations, *European Economic Review*, **1**, 7–73.

Deaton, A. S. and Muellbauer, J. (1980) An almost ideal demand system, *American Economic Review*, **70**, 312–26.

Kinnucan, H. W., Xiao, H., Hsia, C. J. and Jackson, J. D. (1997) Effects of health information and generic advertising on US meat demand, *American Journal of Agricultural Economics*, **79**, 13–23.

US Department of Agriculture (USDA) (2004) *Fruits and Nuts Yearbook*, Economic Research Service, Washington, DC.

Demand for carbonated soft drinks: implications for obesity policy

Rigoberto A. Lopez[a] and Kristen L. Fantuzzi[b]

[a]*Department of Agricultural and Resource Economics, University of Connecticut, Storrs, CT 06269-4021, USA*
[b]*Keystone Community Living, South Plainfield, NJ 07080, USA*

This article examines consumer choices of Carbonated Soft Drinks (CSDs) and their implications for obesity policy. Demand in relation to product and consumer heterogeneity is estimated via a random coefficients logit model (Berry *et al.*, 1995) applied to quarterly scanner data for 26 brands in 20 US cities, involving 40 000 consumers. Counterfactual experiments show that caloric taxes could be effective in decreasing caloric CSD consumption though having little impact on obesity incidence.

I. Introduction

Obesity, the leading public health crisis in the US, continues to increase at an alarming rate with an estimated social cost of over $140 billion a year and growing. The main culprits are the increase in the consumption of high-calorie foods and beverages and decrease in exercise (Kuhn, 2002). Paralleling the increase in obesity is the increase in consumption of Carbonated Soft Drinks (CSDs; DiMeglio and Mattes, 2000; Center for Science in the Public Interest, 2005).[1]

Concerns about the adverse effects of excessive consumption of CSDs has generated a healthy volume of studies on the link between soda consumption, obesity and taxes, particularly from the medical and health economics literature. With 33 states having sales taxes on soft drinks (with a mean tax of about 5%), there are proposals in a few states (Maine, New York, Washington State) to significantly increase such taxes to curb consumption, and hence obesity (Brownell and Frieden, 2009). Although the empirical evidence on the effect of increased taxes on soda consumption is mixed, depending on the magnitude of the price elasticities of demand (Chouinard *et al.*, 2007; Sturm *et al.*, 2010), the preponderant empirical evidence point to sales taxes, having an insignificant effect on the obesity incidence (Ebbeling *et al.*, 2006; Fletcher *et al.*, 2010; Marlow and Shiers, 2010).

This article examines US consumer CSD choices and their implications for obesity policy. Unlike previous studies, it incorporates product and consumer heterogeneity in consumer CSD choices using a random coefficients logit model (Berry *et al.*, 1995; Berry–Levinsohn–Pakes, hereafter BLP) to estimate

---

[1] Carbonated soft drinks (CSDs) are a very large part of the American diet. These well-liked drinks account for approximately 30% of all beverages (alcoholic and nonalcoholic) consumed in the US (US Department of Agriculture, Economic Research Service, 2008). In 2000, Americans spent $61 billion on CSDs (National Soft Drink Association, 2003) with more than 15 billion gallons sold in the US, which equals every American consuming at least one 12-ounce can per day, or an average of 53 gallons per year (Squires, 2001).

demand at the brand and consumer levels with particular reference to price and calorie content responses. The estimated parameters are then used to assess the effectiveness of a tax levied on caloric CSDs through counterfactual experiments. Empirical results point out that higher income consumers have significantly lower price elasticity of demand, therefore their CSD choices are less sensitive to price (and hence, taxes). Furthermore, lower income consumers have a preference for caloric CSDs. Combined, a tax on caloric CSDs will have a more significant impact on low-income consumers. Empirical results also indicate that younger and male consumers have a stronger preference for caloric CSDs, further indicating that these groups among the most affected. Although CSD choices exhibit a strong degree of brand loyalty (relatively low cross-price elasticities), a 10% *ad valorem* tax on caloric drinks would have a significant effect on consumption (between 2 and 10% drop for caloric drinks and 3–5% increase for diet drinks, depending on the brand). However, the direct effect on the Body Mass Index (BMI)[2] is negligible.

II. The Model

Following the BLP model, the consumer, in choosing one unit of a CSD brand among competing products, maximizes utility, driven by the brand characteristics as well as his/her own characteristics. The indirect utility of consumer i from buying a unit of brand j is

$$U_{ij} = \underbrace{\beta x_j + \alpha p_j}_{\delta_j} + \underbrace{\phi D_i x_j + \lambda D_i p_j + \sigma_i x_j + \gamma v_i p_j + \varepsilon_{ij}}_{\mu_{ij}} \tag{1}$$

which can be expressed in two components: (1) the mean utility term δ_j, determined solely by brand characteristics, and (2) the deviation from the mean, μ_{ij}, capturing the interactions between consumer and brand characteristics.

In Equation 1, x_j is a vector of observed product characteristics of brand j; p_j the price of brand j; D_i represents observed consumer characteristics (such as demographics) with a probability density function $h(D)$; v_i the unobserved consumer characteristics with a probability density function $g(v)$, which is assumed to be normally distributed $N(0, 1)$; α, β, δ, and σ are fixed parameters; and ε_{ij} an error term, which has a

probability density function $f(\varepsilon)$. Note that in this framework individual taste parameters with respect to price and brand characteristics are given by $\alpha_i = \alpha + \lambda D_i + \gamma v_i$ and $\beta_i = \beta + \phi D_i + \sigma v_i$, respectively.

In order to define the market and market shares, an outside good is introduced. Let $k = 0$ denote the outside good, which gives the consumer the option not to buy any of the J brands included in the choice set as well as excluded CSD brands and substitute beverages. The utility of the outside good is normalized to be constant over time and to equal zero. In this model, consumers choose one unit of a brand in the choice set that is assumed to yield the highest utility or the outside good. Aggregating over consumers, the market share for the jth brand equals the probability that the jth brand is chosen, given by

$$s_j(p, x, \theta) = \int I\{(D_i, v_i, \varepsilon_{ij}) : U_{ij} \geq U_{ik} \, \forall k = 0, \ldots, N\}$$
$$\times \, dH(D) dG(v) dF(\varepsilon) \tag{2}$$

where $H(D)$, $G(v)$ and $F(\varepsilon)$ are cumulative density functions for the indicated variables, assumed to be independent of each other, and $\theta = (\alpha, \beta, \lambda, \phi, \gamma, \sigma)$ a vector of parameters.

The price elasticities of the market shares for individual brands are

$$\eta_{ijk} = (\partial s_j / \partial p_k)(p_k / s_j)$$
$$= \begin{cases} p_j / s_j \int \alpha_i s_{ij}(1 - s_{ij}) \, dH(D) \, dG(v), & \text{for } j = k \\ -p_k / s_j \int \alpha_i s_{ij} s_{ik} \, dH(D) \, dG(v), & \text{otherwise} \end{cases} \tag{3}$$

where each consumer has a different price elasticity for each individual brand.

Given the interest in policy, the taste parameters for calories and price from the BLP model are used in a counterfactual experiment of the impact of *ad valorem* taxes levied on caloric CSDs on consumption and BMI.

III. Data and Estimation

To estimate the BLP model, we used sales data on 26 brands of CSDs in 20 cities across the US, over 20 quarters (1988 to 1992), resulting in 10 400 total

[2] The National Institute of Health adopted BMI as the common public health measure (US Department of Health and Human Services, 2001). The BMI is the most convenient measure available in assessing overweightness and obesity, taking into account a person's weight and height to gauge total body fat. A BMI under 18.5 is considered underweight, a BMI of 18.5 to 24.9 is considered a healthy weight, a BMI of 25 to 29.9 is considered overweight, and a BMI of 30 and higher is considered obese.

product brand observations.[3] The sales data, from the Information Resources, Inc. (IRI) Infoscan database provided by the Food Marketing Policy Center at the University of Connecticut, consist of dollar sales, volume sold (in 288 ounces/case units), and the percent volume sold with any display promotion. The retail prices (p_j) were computed by dividing the dollar sales of each brand by the number of 12-ounce servings sold. The market size was assumed to be the per capita per day consumption of all CSDs, water, and fruit juices. Other definitions of market size (e.g. including fluid milk) neither significantly altered nor improved the results. Market shares were computed by dividing the number of servings sold by the market size. The outside good market share was defined as the residual between one and the sum of the observed market shares for the J brands in the choice set. The nutritional brand characteristics (x_j) were collected by examining the labels on each CSD brand for caffeine, calorie and sodium content per 12-ounce serving.

The observable consumer characteristics (D) consisted of age, income and a male dummy. They were obtained by 100 random draws per market from the Behavioral Risk Surveillance System (BRFSS).[4] For estimation purposes, a market was defined as each city and quarter combination, resulting in 400 markets (20 cities × 20 quarters). Another 100 random draws per market were obtained from a normal distribution with zero mean and unitary variance. Thus, this sample includes 40 000 consumer observations. All interactions of price and nutritional characteristics with consumer characteristics were considered in the model.

Instrumental variables were used to control for potential endogeneity of prices due to their correlation with brand characteristics. Different sets of instrumental variables (176 in total) were interacted with error terms in the last part of the BLP estimation procedure. The first set of instruments involved 130 interactions between brand dummy variables and input prices, as in Villas-Boas (2007). Input prices included electricity prices (US Department of Energy, Energy Information Administration, 2007), wages for the different cities (US Department of Labor, 2007), the cost of sugar (US Department of Agriculture; USDA, Economic Research Service, 2007), the cost of materials (National Bureau of Economic Research, 2007) and the federal funds effective rate

(Federal Reserve Board, 2007). The next set of instrumental variables used the housing price index (National City Corporation, 2007) for each city interacted with brand dummy variables. The last set of instruments consisted of 20 city dummy variables (one for each city in the sample) to capture the differences with regard to pricing of the CSD brands among the 20 cities. Finally, this article follows Berry (1994), relying on formation of a generalized method of moments estimator for estimating a proxy of the integral in Equation 2.

The BLP model was estimated using Matlab and the tax simulations were done using Excel. The econometric and policy simulation results are presented in the following section.

IV. Empirical Results

Table 1 presents the estimated taste parameters of the demand for CSDs. The parameter estimate of the mean utility for price is statistically significant at the 5% level, indicating that for the average consumer, the CSD price creates disutility, as one would expect. The other mean utility estimates for promotion, calories, caffeine and sodium are not statistically discernable from zero. However, the distribution of the parameters for these product characteristics and price are significantly associated with consumer heterogeneity, resulting in a distribution of parameters rather than just a single point estimate.

As shown in the results of Table 1, the parameters for the taste of price indicate that although the mean utility is negative, as expected, older and wealthier male consumers are less sensitive to price. The implication for tax policies is that these groups would be affected less by a general price increase in CSDs. On the other hand, calories are particularly negative valued by older wealthier and older female consumers. Thus, a caloric tax on CSDs would affect these groups less than other groups based on their calorie preference alone. Perhaps not surprisingly, the results for caffeine and sodium preferences follow a similar pattern to those for calories, which may reflect some health concerns.

Since a large number of cross-price elasticities were computed, Table 2 presents only a sample of cross-price elasticities, averaged over the 20 cities in

---

[3] Atlanta, Baltimore, Chicago, Cincinnati, Hartford, Houston, Indianapolis, Kansas City, Los Angeles, Louisville, Miami, Milwaukee, Minneapolis, Nashville, New York, Omaha, Phoenix, Raleigh, Salt Lake City, Seattle.
[4] The BRFSS is a yearly telephone health survey consisting of more than 350 000 observations per year. The survey is conducted by each of the 50 state health departments with support from the Centers for Disease Control and Prevention. The BRFSS survey has been successfully used in economic analysis of obesity (Chou et al., 2004; Burke and Heiland, 2007).

Table 1. Estimates of the BLP discrete choice model

Variable	Mean utility	Deviations			
		Age	Income	Male	Unobservables
Constant	2.078	−1.807	−1.483	1.472	2.203**
	(5.361)	(16.473)	(5.089)	(8.388)	(0.265)
Price	−8.086**	2.718	3.787**	1.326	1.975**
	(1.080)	(4.090)	(1.394)	(2.333)	(0.106)
Promotion	0.345				
	(0.411)				
Calories	−0.003	−1.494**	−1.445**	0.885**	−0.751**
	(0.588)	(0.180)	(0.122)	(0.162)	(0.044)
Caffeine	0.159	−1.956**	−1.192**	1.679**	−1.373**
	(0.708)	(0.884)	(0.283)	(0.967)	(0.135)
Sodium	−0.886	1.740	−2.206**	1.584	−0.907**
	(3.102)	(1.361)	(0.337)	(0.987)	(0.072)

Notes: SEs are given in parentheses.
** Denotes test statistic significance at the 5% level.

the sample. The cross-price elasticities are all positive, as expected, implying that the brands are substitutes. Note that the cross-price elasticities are quite low when compared to the own-price elasticities. This confirms that although consumers are sensitive to CSD prices with respect to their chosen brands, they have brand loyalty and will substitute to the outside good rather than choosing another brand of CSD. Given the estimated price elasticities and the assumption of a full tax transmission rate, the effect of a 10% *ad valorem* calorie tax on CSDs was estimated at the product brand level.[5] These results are presented in Table 3.

The magnitude of the own-price elasticities in Table 2 is in the range of previously estimated elasticities using brand-level demand with scanner data on CSDs. For example, Chan (2006) reports larger own-price elasticities that range between −5 and −11 for CSDS using household-level data on CSD purchases. On the other hand, Dhar *et al.* (2005) report lower own-price elasticities for broader CSD product definitions, ranging between −2.7 and −4.4.

The own-price elasticities reported in Table 2 and brand-level elasticities from previous studies are much larger than the elasticities reported for aggregate CSD or soft drink categories in previous studies. For example, Andreyeba *et al.* (2010) report the price elasticity from 14 previous studies for the aggregate soft drink category to have a mean of −0.79 and to range between −0.8 and −1.0 (95% confidence interval). Two factors might explain much of the differences in the magnitude: (1) the much lower of aggregation used in this study, namely at the brand

(and city) level of CSDs rather than an aggregate soft drink category which includes CSDs and other products (e.g. fruit juices); (2) Table 2 reports partial own-price elasticities, i.e. elasticity of only changing the price of a brand leaving the other prices constant. In terms of the scope of this study, we are interested in changing the price of all caloric CSDs not only changing the price of one brand assuming all other CSD prices constant.

Since there is no analytical expression to aggregate our elasticity results to a national soft drink category, we compute the net elasticity assuming all CSD prices in the sample increase by 1% and also the ones driven by a tax policy only targeting caloric CSDs. Given the foregoing, it would be appropriate to compare instead the net elasticity of response; that is, the elasticity if all brands experience the same price increase. To partially address this, the results in Table 3 show the quantity response for a 10% price increase only for *all* caloric CSDs due to a 10% *ad valorem* tax (resulting in a 10% increase in price under full transmission, the price of diet CSDs remaining constant). These results suggest an average of −0.58 net price elasticity of demand for caloric CSDs (17 brands) and −0.42 for diet CSDs (which, of course, will show an increase due to substitution as they would not be subject to the tax). These net elasticities with respect to an increase in the price of caloric CSDs are lower than the aggregate elasticities reported by Andreyeba *et al.* (2010) for all soft drinks indicating a lower consumption response to taxes than their price elasticities would suggest.

[5] Simulated calorie tax reductions are based on per capita annual CSD consumption in ounces and calories (US Department of Agriculture, Economic Research Service, 2007) using 3500 calories per pound of body weight (American Diabetic Association, 2003).

Table 2. Sample of own- and cross-price elasticities

Brands	7 UP	A&W	Canada Dry	Cherry 7 UP	Cherry Coke	Coke	Coke Classic	Diet 7 UP	Diet Cherry 7 UP	Diet Coke	Diet Dr Pepper	Diet Pepsi
7 UP	-10.119	1.124	0.127	0.108	0.082	0.204	1.586	0.057	0.019	0.061	0.005	0.061
A&W	0.392	-6.377	0.129	0.117	0.081	0.202	1.487	0.017	0.013	0.005	0.000	0.003
Canada Dry	0.183	0.056	-3.747	0.574	0.066	0.181	0.156	0.101	0.030	0.476	0.014	0.409
Cherry 7 UP	0.408	1.157	0.129	-7.405	0.081	0.221	1.670	0.063	0.021	0.052	0.004	0.060
Cherry Coke	0.466	1.198	0.191	0.827	-9.101	0.911	0.665	0.008	0.002	0.137	0.006	0.044
Coke	0.349	0.715	1.870	0.706	0.276	-10.119	0.902	0.005	0.001	0.289	0.054	0.047
Coke Classic	0.347	0.773	1.977	0.708	0.276	1.309	-10.058	0.007	0.003	0.368	0.057	0.058
Diet 7 UP	0.106	0.011	0.047	0.021	0.003	0.004	0.067	-3.886	0.403	0.448	0.082	0.526
Diet Cherry 7 UP	0.119	0.013	0.056	0.023	0.003	0.005	0.085	1.751	-3.182	0.396	0.083	0.463
Diet Coke	0.020	0.000	0.030	0.003	0.007	0.054	0.051	0.014	0.022	-4.850	0.259	1.339
Diet DR Pepper	0.043	0.001	0.022	0.006	0.007	0.022	0.016	0.500	0.097	0.569	-4.098	1.335
Diet Pepsi	0.050	0.001	0.057	0.007	0.005	0.025	0.023	0.033	0.059	3.053	0.151	-3.109

Table 3. CSD consumption and BMI changes from a 10% *ad valorem* calorie tax

Brand	Percentage change in quantity	Change in ounces consumed (per capita yearly)	Change in calories consumed (per capita yearly)	Change in body weight (pounds) (per capita yearly)	Change in average consumer BMI
7 UP	−9.936	−568.51	−7106.32	−2.030	−0.322
A&W	−5.611	−321.03	−4761.88	−1.361	−0.216
Canada Dry	−2.683	−153.49	−1790.70	−0.512	−0.081
Cherry 7 UP	−1.450	−82.96	−1036.95	−0.296	−0.047
Cherry Coke	−9.405	−538.12	−6995.53	−1.999	−0.317
Coke	−9.775	−559.27	−6804.42	−1.944	−0.308
Coke Classic	−8.063	−461.36	−5613.22	−1.604	−0.254
DR Pepper	−4.517	−258.44	−3230.55	−0.923	−0.146
Minute Maid	−7.663	−438.44	−6028.49	−1.722	−0.273
Mountain Dew	−1.740	−99.56	−1410.39	−0.403	−0.064
Pepsi	−4.819	−275.73	−3492.58	−0.998	−0.158
Pepsi Free	−2.942	−168.32	−2103.97	−0.601	−0.095
RC	−4.567	−261.33	−3484.44	−0.996	−0.158
Schweppes	−7.782	−445.26	−4452.55	−1.272	−0.202
Slice	−5.418	−309.99	−5114.77	−1.461	−0.232
Sprite	−6.668	−381.51	−4514.49	−1.290	−0.204
Sunkist	−5.677	−324.81	−5142.84	−1.469	−0.233
Diet 7 UP	4.176	238.91	0	0	0
Diet Cherry 7 UP	5.084	290.87	0	0	0
Diet Coke	4.694	268.57	0	0	0
Diet DR Pepper	4.811	275.27	0	0	0
Diet Pepsi	3.260	186.53	0	0	0
Diet Pepsi Free	3.699	211.65	0	0	0
Diet Rite	3.727	213.26	0	0	0
Diet Slice	4.185	239.44	0	0	0
Diet Sprite	4.277	244.73	0	0	0

Such a tax would have the effect of reducing the quantity of caloric CSDs consumed and increase the consumption of noncaloric (diet) CSDs. However, the substitution is imperfect and consumers would also switch to the outside good (water, fruit juices and residual CSDs). Assuming brand loyalty and that consumers reduce their consumption of caloric CSDs by switching to noncaloric soft drinks, the reductions in caloric CSDs would translate to less than a pound of weight loss for the average consumer, or approximately one tenth of their BMIs. This is an upper bound as consumers could also switch to caloric alternatives that are not taxed (e.g. fruit juices), especially among those who are price sensitive such as low-income consumers.

The results for the impact of a 10% *ad valorem* tax on changes in BMIs or obesity rates indicate that such a tax would have a very weak effect on reversing the obesity epidemic, as Kuchler *et al.* (2005) also found. In addition, such a tax, like other nutrition regulation policies, is likely to face stiff political opposition from a well-organized industry lobby (Nestle, 2002). Finally, a 10% tax is greater than most state sales tax rates, which may be interpreted as excessive, given the ongoing food price inflation.

In addition, given the choices of low-income consumers, this tax would be regressive with respect to income, since low-income consumers spend a larger portion of their income on food. Therefore, any policy that increases the price of food will have the greatest impact on lower income consumers.

In sum, this article adds to the mounting empirical evidence that point that taxes on caloric CSDs are not an effective policy tool to curb obesity, although they are effective in generating revenue. If the policy objective is the former, then alternative programmes (e.g. educational campaigns advertising policy), perhaps funded by a soda tax, are probably more effective than using taxes as a stand-alone policy instrument. As demonstrated by their preferences, these policies can be more effective when targeting younger, low-income consumers.

V. Concluding Remarks

This article examined consumer choices of CSDs using a random coefficients logit demand model (BLP, 1995) and scanner data, and then examined the impact of a tax policy to address the obesity epidemic.

Empirical demand results indicate that consumer choices of CSDs are driven by both product and consumer characteristics. More specifically, lower income and younger consumers, as well as male consumers, tend to have a more positive valuation of calories, suggesting that they are less concerned about obesity consequences. Furthermore, higher income and older consumers as well as male consumers are less sensitive to price changes, suggesting they care less about higher prices. By the same token, younger, low-income consumers who are male have relative preference for caloric CSDs. A counterfactual experiment shows that an *ad valorem* tax on caloric CSDs would be effective in decreasing consumption of CSDs but would have a hardly discernable effect on the incidence of obesity. Thus, a more comprehensive programme is needed rather than a stand-alone tax policy on caloric drinks.

References

American Diebetic Association (2003) A simple 100 calories a day can be the difference in weight maintenance versus gain or loss. Available at http://www.eatright.org/Public/NutritionInformation/index_17622.cfm (accessed 23 August 2006).

Andreyeba, T., Long, M. and Brownell, K. (2010) The impact of food prices on consumption: a systematic review of research on the price elasticity of demand for food, *American Journal of Public Health*, **100**, 216–22.

Berry, S. (1994) Estimating discrete choice models of product differentiation, *RAND Journal of Economics*, **25**, 242–62.

Berry, S., Levinsohn, J. and Pakes, A. (BLP) (1995) Automobile prices in market equilibrium, *Econometrica*, **63**, 841–89.

Brownell, K. and Frieden, T. (2009) Ounces of prevention: the public policy case for taxes on sugared beverages, *New England Journal of Medicine, Perspective*, **30**, 1–4.

Burke, M. and Heiland, F. (2007) Social dynamics of obesity, *Economic Inquiry*, **45**, 571–91.

Center for Science in the Public Interest (2005) Soft drinks by the numbers. Available at http://www.saveharry.com/bythe numbers (accessed 2 June 2007).

Chan, T. (2006) Estimating a continuous hedonic-choice model with an application to demand for soft drinks, *RAND Journal of Economics*, **27**, 1–17.

Chou, S., Grossman, M. and Saffer, H. (2004) An economic analysis of adult obesity: results from the behavioral risk factor surveillance system, *Journal of Health Economics*, **23**, 565–87.

Chouinard, H., Davis, D., LaFrance, J. and Perloff, J. (2007) Fat taxes: big money for small change, *Forum for Health Economics and Policy*, **10**, 1–28.

Dhar, T., Chavas, J. P., Cotterill, R. and Gould, B. (2005) An econometric analysis of brand-level strategic pricing between Coca Cola Company and Pepsico, *Journal of Economics and Management Strategy*, **14**, 905–31.

DiMeglio, D. P. and Mattes, R. (2000) Liquid versus solid carbohydrates: effects on food intake and body weight, *International Journal of Obesity*, **24**, 794–800.

Ebbeling, C., Feldman, H., Osganian, S., Chomitz, V., Ellenbogen, S. and Ludwig, D. (2006) Effects of decreasing sugar-sweetened beverage consumption on body weight in adolescents: a randomized, controlled pilot study, *Pediatrics*, **117**, 673–80.

Federal Reserve Board (2007) Selected interest rates. Available at http://www.federalreserve.gov/releases/h15/data.htm (accessed 15 August 2007).

Fletcher, J., Frisvold, D. and Tefft, N. (2010) Can soft drink taxes reduce population weight?, *Contemporary Economic Policy*, **28**, 23–35.

Kuchler, F., Tegene, A. and Harris, J. M. (2005) Taxing snack foods: manipulating diet quality or financing information programs?, *Review of Agricultural Economics*, **27**, 4–20.

Kuhn, B. (2002) Weighing in on obesity, *Food Review*, **25**, 38–49.

Marlow, M. and Shiers, A. (2010) Would soda taxes really yield health benefits?, *Regulation*, **33**, 34–8.

National Bureau of Economic Research (2007) *Manufacturing industry database*. Available at http://www.nber.org/nberces/nbprod96.htm (accessed 5 September 2007).

National City Corporation (2007) Housing valuation analysis. Available at http://nationalcity.com (accessed 15 October 2007).

National Soft Drink Association (2003) About soft drinks. Available at http://www.nsda.org (accessed 16 October 2007).

Nestle, M. (2002) *Food Politics*, University of California Press, Berkeley, CA.

Squires, S. (2001) Soft drinks, hard facts, *Washington Post*, 27 February 2001, Health Section, p. 15.

Sturm, R., Powell, L., Chriqui, J. and Chaloupka, F. (2010) Soda taxes, soft drink consumption, and children's body mass index, *Health Affairs*, **29**, 1–7.

US Department of Agriculture, Economic Research Service (2007) Sugars and sweeteners: data tables. Available at http://www.ers.usda.gov/sugar/data/htm (accessed 15 August 2007).

US Department of Agriculture, Economic Research Service (2008) Beverages: per capita availability. Available at http://www.ers.usda.gov/Data/FoodConsumption/spreadsheets/beverage.xls (accessed 13 August 2008).

US Department of Energy, Energy Information Administration (2007) Energy prices and trends. Available at http://www.eia.doe.gov/emeu/aer/contents.html (accessed 15 August 2008).

US Department of Health and Human Services (2001) *The Surgeon General's Call to Action to Prevent and Decrease Overweight and Obesity*, US Government Printing Office, Washington, DC. Available at http://www.surgeongeneral.gov/topics/obesity (accessed 12 August 2008).

US Department of Labor (2007) Bureau of labor statistics: wages, earnings, and benefits. Available at http://www.bls.gov (accessed 5 September 2007).

Villas-Boas, B. (2007) Vertical contracts between manufacturers and retailers: inference with limited data, *Review of Economic Studies*, **74**, 625–52.

Calories, obesity and health in OECD countries

Mario Mazzocchi[a] and W. Bruce Traill[b]

[a]Department of Statistics, University of Bologna, I-40126 Bologna, Italy
[b]Department of Agricultural and Food Economics, University of Reading, Reading RG6 6AR, UK

Theoretical models suggest that decisions about diet, weight and health status are endogenous within a utility maximization framework. In this article, we model these behavioural relationships in a fixed-effect panel setting using a simultaneous equation system, with a view to determining whether economic variables can explain the trends in calorie consumption, obesity and health in Organization for Economic Cooperation and Development (OECD) countries and the large differences among the countries. The empirical model shows that progress in medical treatment and health expenditure mitigates mortality from diet-related diseases, despite rising obesity rates. While the model accounts for endogeneity and serial correlation, results are affected by data limitations.

I. Introduction

It is well known that there is an obesity 'epidemic' in the Western world, but perhaps less well known that levels of overweight are already reaching similar proportions in Latin America, the Middle East and the European transition states and that the incidence of overweight has overtaken underweight globally, including China, several other Asian countries and even some of the poorest parts of Africa (Traill and Mazzocchi, 2005; World Health Organization (WHO), 2006; Mazzocchi et al., 2009).

Even in the Organization for Economic Cooperation and Development (OECD), many countries did not start collecting obesity data until quite recently, but almost all of those countries recorded sharp increases between 1980, 1990 and the present (Table 1). The USA leads the way with over 30% of the adult population obese, the other Anglo-Saxon countries have reached levels of more than 20% and Greece, Hungary, Luxembourg, Mexico and Slovakia are closing in. A large number of countries have around 10% of their populations obese, but only in Japan and Korea the figure is below 5%.

For overweight (Body Mass Index (BMI) between 25 and 30) and obese combined, the USA and the UK 'lead' the pack with, respectively, 66% and 62% of adults overweight or obese, whereas in Norway, the figure is 43% and in Japan, only 25%. The health consequences of obesity are now widely known: increased risk of heart disease, stroke, type 2 diabetes mellitus and many cancers (WHO/Food and Agriculture Organization (FAO), 2003).

Of course, the linkages between diet and health are not solely through overweight and obesity; smoking has harmful consequences, exercise is beneficial (in its own right as well as through its impact on obesity); and the composition of the diet also matters. Particular attention has been paid to the fat composition of diets and its impact on low- and high-density lipoprotein levels in the bloodstream, fruit and vegetables and their protective roles against certain cancers, and salt as a factor in hypertension (WHO/ FAO, 2003). Individual genetic and perhaps

Table 1. Obesity rates in OECD countries (percentage of population with BMI > 30)

	1980	1990	2003
Australia	8.3	10.8[c]	21.7[i]
Austria		8.5[d]	9.1[i]
Belgium			11.7[j]
Canada			14.3
Czech Republic		11.2[e]	14.8[k]
Denmark		5.5[f]	9.5[l]
Finland	7.4	8.4	12.8
France		5.8	9.4[k]
Germany			12.9
Greece			21.9
Hungary			18.8
Iceland			12.4[k]
Ireland			13.0[k]
Italy		7.5[g]	8.5[k]
Japan	2	2.3	3.2
Republic of Korea			3.2[j]
Luxembourg			18.4
Mexico			24.2[l]
The Netherlands	5.1[a]	6.1	10.0[k]
New Zealand		11.1[c]	20.9
Norway			8.3[k]
Poland			11.4[m]
Portugal			12.8[i]
Slovakia			22.4[k]
Spain		6.8[f]	13.1
Sweden		5.5[c]	9.7
Switzerland		5.4[h]	7.7[k]
Turkey			12.0
UK	7	13.0[d]	23.0
USA	15[b]	23.3[d]	30.6[k]

Source: OECD health statistics (2002).
Notes: Body Mass Index (BMI) defined as weight in kg, divided by height in metres squared.
[a]1981; [b]1978; [c]1989; [d]1991; [e]1993; [f]1987; [g]1994; [h]1992; [i]1999; [j]2001; [k]2002; [l]2000; [m]1996.

phenotypic factors are important for obesity and health (Schmidhuber and Shetty, 2005).

The wide cross-country differences in obesity and its health consequences are matters of interest and importance but remain largely unexplained. If the wide disparities in obesity and diet-related Noncommunicable Diseases (NCDs) can be better understood, emerging economies will be better able to recognize the likely scale and timing of the problem in their countries and act accordingly with appropriate policies introduced in a timely fashion. Louriero and Nayga (2005) have modelled obesity in a single equation cross-country relationship with the dependent variable the proportion of the population obese[1] and calorie consumption exogenous. Statistically significant independent variables were: per capita

calories consumed, percentage of population living in rural areas, percentage of individuals older than 65 years, percentage of female labour market participation, per capita Gross Domestic Product (GDP), percentage of GDP dedicated to education, per capita kilometres driven by private vehicles, percentage of smokers, share of value of agricultural output per worker and agricultural transfers from consumers. Huffman *et al.* (2006) estimated the supply and demand functions for health in a selection of OECD countries, but did not model obesity.

In this article, we expand these two analyses in an attempt to explain calorie intake rather than assume it to be exogenously determined, to model obesity as well as its health consequences, and to employ panel data for all of the OECD countries. To do so, we employ a structural set of relationships rather than the quasi-reduced form equation of Loureiro and Nayga (2005); our model is well founded in economic theory and biology. Because our interest is in trends and developments over time and across countries, we have included a longer than usual discussion of some of the data and their limitations.

Several other authors have exploited aggregate country- or state-level data to look into the relationship between economic determinants, lifestyle factors and health outcomes. For example, Thornton and Rice (2008) estimate a regression model on US state-level aggregate data to explain differences in state health care expenditure through a set of explanatory variables which include the percentage of obese individuals, exercise rates, smoking, an ageing index and per capita income. Based on the World Bank data for a cross-section of developing countries, Webber (2002) explores the impact of (under-)nutrition and education on economic growth and suggests that the latter has a stronger influence. Panel data models include the cointegration approach adopted by Freeman (2003) on US state-level data to estimate the income elasticity of health care expenditure. Based on a balanced data set for 75 countries on the World Bank data, Erdil and Yetkiner (2009) exploit panel Vector Autoregression (VAR) modelling to look into bidirectional (Granger-) causality between per capita GDP and health care expenditure. Panel data on OECD countries were used in the above-cited study by Louriero and Nayga (2005) and in Caliskan (2009) to look into the relationship between country-level pharmaceutical expenditure and health outcomes (life expectancy), also accounting for heterogeneity in fruit and vegetable intakes.

More often, applied models of the complex relationship between nutrition and economic factors have

[1] Proportion overweight in another version.

been based on microdata. Examples include research on the weight–health relationship accounting for socio-economic differences (Lin, 2008); labour market studies as in Bastida and Soydemir (2009) and Shimokawa (2008); the effects of information, food prices and income on calorie and nutrient intakes (Leung and Miklius, 1997; Huang, 1999; Variyam et al., 1999; Adhikari et al., 2007; Paudel et al., 2008); the influence of social interaction on obesity (Costa-Font and Gil, 2004); the impact of diet and health factors on the composition of food demand (Nayga et al., 1999); and the role of socio-economic factors on the awareness of diet–health relationship and weight (Nayga, 1997, 2000).

This article is structured as follows. The next section provides a theoretical framework grounded in household production theory. Section III presents the data set and discusses its limitation. The empirical model is introduced in Section IV and the results are summarized in Section V. We draw some conclusions in the final section.

II. Economic Theory of Obesity

Suppose that individuals derive utility from eating and drinking, smoking (S), consumption of other goods which do not contribute to health (Z), their leisure (L) and their state of health (H), which is partially a behavioural variable as it relates to smoking and weight (Chen et al., 2002; Chou et al., 2002). For the sake of simplicity, assume that the utility from food and drink consumption can be represented by calorie intake (K), a common assumption (Philipson and Posner, 1999; Lakdawalla and Philipson, 2002; Cutler et al., 2003). Leisure may be taken as a free time after working and exercise taken for health reasons.

$$U = U(K, S, L, H, Z) \qquad (1)$$

Health is related to weight (W), other aspects of diet quality (D_Q) (e.g. the intake of saturated fatty acids which may have an impact on health independent of weight), smoking, medical treatment (M), exercise (E), which is taken to provide health benefits independent of its impact on weight, and exogenous factors (Ω_H) which include genetic and socio-demographic factors, the latter including education which may affect an individual's knowledge and ability to combine health inputs to optimize the health function (Chen et al., 2002)

$$H = H(W, S, M, E, D_Q, \Omega_H) \qquad (2)$$

In this construction, we abstract from dynamics which would recognize that the current health also depends on the past levels of weight, diet quality, smoking and exercise. It can be thought of as a long-run equilibrium relationship.

Weight gain occurs when calorie intake exceeds calorie expenditure. The latter depends on activity in the workplace, in travel (on foot or by bicycle) and at home for leisure and nonleisure exercise; on an individual's metabolic rate (hence the genetic component to overweight and obesity); and on weight. Hence, as Cutler et al. (2003) point out that there exists an equilibrium (steady state) weight associated with any level of calorie intake. The achievement of this steady state is not, of course, instantaneous. Within the behavioural framework established here, exercise itself is endogenous in the sense that an individual may choose to achieve any particular weight either by consuming a large number of calories and exercising a lot or by consuming a lower number of calories and exercising less. A reasonable simplifying assumption would be that physical activity at work is exogenous (people do not choose their jobs with a view to weight control). In general terms, one may express this as a long-run equilibrium relationship

$$W = W(K, E, \Omega_W) \qquad (3)$$

where Ω_W represents the exogenous factors such as level of physical activity at work and genetic predisposition.

Formally, the utility function in Equation 1 is maximized subject to the health function (Equation 2), the weight function (Equation 3) and a full income budget constraint in which time may be enjoyed as leisure or transformed into income at the prevailing wage rate or exercise for health purposes (as opposed to leisure purposes). Food, drink, cigarettes, health care and other goods up to the level of income may be purchased at prevailing prices.

$$V + P_W(T - L - E) = P_K K + P D_Q D_Q \\ + P_S S + P_M M + P_Z Z \qquad (4)$$

In Equation 4, V is nonlabour income, T the total time, L and E the leisure and exercise time and P_W the wage rate. Income, leisure and exercise are all endogenous in this framework, as of course are calorie intake, smoking, the level of medical treatment, exercise and health status. Solving the system of equations leads to a set of reduced form equations in which the optimal level of each of the endogenous variables depends on the wage rate (P_W) and the prices of food and drink (P_K), diet quality (PD_Q), smoking (P_S), medical treatment (P_M) and the price of goods unrelated to health (P_Z) as well as the levels of the exogenous variables $(\Omega_H$ and $\Omega_W)$.

It is worth exploring intuitively some implications of such a behavioural approach to the subjects of weight, health and eating. Imagine a technological advance in medical treatment, for example, better screening and medicine for hypertension. A person could increase his/her utility through consuming unchanged levels of other variables in the health function and therefore having improved health or by taking advantage of the opportunity to consume higher levels of health-reducing activities like smoking, eating and drinking so as to achieve the same level of health as before but gain utility from the extra consumption of cigarettes, food and drink (as well as of the health neutral goods, Z) or a combination of these. Thus, an improvement in health technology would likely lead to an increase in utility maximizing weight as people take the opportunity to eat more because the risks of doing so are lower. The same would be true if we consider the level of smoking to be at least partially exogenous – perhaps over time social norms change such that the utility derived from smoking falls. Lower smoking enhances health, again allowing higher levels of other risky activities like putting on weight by eating more (or exercising less). In this framework, there is a behavioural explanation for the often-observed negative correlation between smoking and weight (e.g. Chou et al., 2002; Lye and Hirschberg, 2004; Gruber and Frakes, 2005; Loureiro and Nayga, 2005) though traditional explanations linked to appetite suppression and the impact of smoking on the metabolic rate remain relevant. Both of these examples mirror similar evidence with respect to other risky behaviours, for example, safer cars and the compulsory wearing of seat-belts lead motorists to drive faster.

Remember that the cost of food, as specified in the budget constraint (Equation 4), includes the time cost of shopping and cooking as well as the direct monetary cost. Technological change which reduces the time of food preparation (convenience foods) lowers the overall cost of food, leading to higher levels of consumption. This has been identified as a major explanation for weight gain in the USA since the 1980s (Philipson and Posner, 1999; Lakdawalla and Philipson, 2002; Cutler et al., 2003). If, as claimed by nutritionists, convenience foods (including foods from fast food restaurants) are more calorie dense than home prepared foods (Smil, 2000), there is also an adverse impact on diet quality.

III. Main Data Sources

In the empirical model of Section IV, compromises are necessary. We cannot assume that all of the variables, for example income, are endogenous, nor do data exist for variables like the amount of exercise people take. Using aggregate data for cross-country analysis also inevitably involves compromise between quality, comparability and coverage. What we attempt to do is to estimate a set of relationships based as closely as possible on the structural Equations 2 and 3 above, plus an estimate of the demand for calories, but assuming that prices and income are exogenous to the system, the former is a reasonable assumption given the level of intervention in agricultural markets and given that the small country assumption is reasonable for most countries. As noted, exercise data are unavailable and so are proxied by urbanization (assumed exogenous) in the obesity equation. In the health equations, smoking is assumed exogenous and medical treatment is proxied by health expenditure and a time trend for technological development.

The obesity data are described in Section I. Health and diet data are described in the following sections. Finally, other variables employed in the empirical model are presented briefly.

Health data

Comparable health data are available only for OECD countries; and they refer only to mortality, not prevalence. By far, the highest mortality rate associated with diet-related NCDs is from heart disease; in 2000, the average mortality rate among the reporting OECD countries was a little under 120 per 100 000 population compared to less than 10 per 100 000 population for diabetes; although the prevalence of type II diabetes associated with weight has likely increased (Kleinfield, 2006), not many people die from it. The death rate from heart disease has almost halved in OECD countries from its peak in the late 1960s and the variation among countries has decreased dramatically; in the late 1960s, the mortality rate was above 300 per 100 000 people in Australia, Canada, Finland and the USA but below 100 in France, Japan, Spain and Mexico. By 2000, only the new member countries Hungary and the Slovak Republic reported mortality rates above 200 per 100 000 population and among the old member countries, only Finland and Ireland had mortality rates above 150 per 100 000 (Table 2).

To the extent that these changes are exogenously attributable to the advances in medical treatment and detection, the theoretical model would suggest that

Table 2. Mortality rates from ischaemic heart disease per 100 000 population in OECD countries

	1960	1970	1980	1990	2000
Australia	338	345.8	242.5	179.3	108
Austria	232.8	198.3	147.1	147.3	125.3
Belgium	130.5	158.4	126	83.9	79.0[a]
Canada	351.8	309.4	231.8	154.2	108.4
Czech Republic				297	179.1
Denmark	269.4	276.9	261.2	201.6	106
Finland	330.8	293.8	265.2	229.4	167.7
France	74.4	69.5	73.5	59.5	46.8
Germany	204.3	156.2	162.2	147.4	121
Greece	102.3	66.4	76.3	91.8	82.8
Hungary	259.5	239.4	217	226.5	214.8
Iceland	201.3	262.1	224.5	166.4	116.8
Ireland	319.4	267.3	264.9	228.5	158.7
Italy	232.7	140.1	123.2	90.4	70.2
Japan	91	60	52	36.5	33.4
Republic of Korea				17.3	32
Luxembourg	163	215.1	137.6	103.4	78.7
Mexico		54		92.6	106.0[b]
The Netherlands	215.9	199.5	167.2	125.9	82.8
New Zealand	308.2	303.9	277.2	200.5	129.7
Norway	211.1	230	200.6	180.3	110.9
Poland	81	77	101.5	112.3	133.4
Portugal	136.9	162.1	89.6	79.6	59.9
Slovak Republic					278.5
Spain	93		75.1	70.5	62.3
Sweden	276.9	280.1	276.8	179.2	118
Switzerland	265.1	107.2	115.6	105.6	86.8
Turkey					
UK	302.9	254	247.7	207.1	129.0[c]
USA	374	362	237.1	166.7	139.6

Source: OECD health statistics.
Note: [a]Data for 1997, [b]data for 1995 and [c]data for 2001.

because the risks from being overweight or obese have fallen sharply, informed individuals would rationally choose to be more overweight; though whether people really are informed about this is debatable given the seemingly continuous flow of scare stories about the dangers of obesity. If not of course, they act on their perceptions of risk. In any case, early death is not the only health risk of obesity, diabetes being a particularly unpleasant disease.

Food consumption

The only data that are comparable across countries and over time are FAO food availability data from food balance sheets as reported in FAOSTAT (FAO, 2005). Food availability is derived from a commodity balance, i.e. from production adjusted for trade,

industrial usage, stock changes, feed use, processing and an estimate of post-harvest losses.[2] The data, therefore, represent a national average 'apparent' consumption at the retail level rather than actual consumption at the household or individual level.

These data are far from perfect, their most important shortcoming being that they exclude household and retail waste. This is more important for some product categories than others, notably fruit and vegetable availability exceeds intake recorded in household surveys by around 40% (e.g. in the UK, FAOSTAT show availability in 2002 as 519 g per capita per day, whereas intake from the Food and Expenditure Survey was 324 g in 2003–2004). Likewise, cooking oil is usually discarded after use rather than consumed and fat is often cut from meat and discarded or fed to pets, so the percentage of total energy from fats may be a slight overestimate. An important but unresolved issue relates to the trend in energy availability/intake. Almost always, the trend in availability according to FAOSTAT is upwards, whereas the trend in intake shown in surveys is often stable or even falling – for example in UK, Japan and Korea. This divergent trend is also apparent in some developing countries, notably China. It is probable that there is an increasing proportion of waste as intake and income rise, but unlikely that the marginal propensity to waste food is higher than one – so it is hard to believe that actual consumption falls while availability increases. Survey data could increasingly under-estimate actual intake over time if the level of under-reporting increases among the overweight; as average weight increases so would the level of under-reporting of consumption. Meals eaten outside the home are often excluded from surveys and even if not, it is likely that snacks and meals eaten outside the home are more under-reported than food eaten at home – and the share of food eaten outside the home is increasing everywhere. The gap between energy availability and energy intake from surveys is also much larger than expected, for example, in the UK, availability is 3400 calories per person per day, whereas survey data record an average intake of 2100 calories. The authors have found no explanation for these incompatibilities, particularly the divergent trends. Although survey data are considered by nutritionists to be the gold standard, in addition to the likely under-reporting of alcohol, snack foods and meals outside the home, there is the likelihood of changed behaviour during the survey period. Although

---

[2] Food supply in the FAO food balance sheets is defined as the availability at the retail level. It has been corrected for post-harvest and processing losses, but still includes all forms of 'post-retail' losses, notably household waste, retailing losses and pet food.

Table 3. Nutrient content of diets, 1980 and 2002

	Calories (per capita per day)		Fat (percentage of energy from)		Sugar (percentage of energy from)		Fruit and vegetable (grams per capita per day)	
	1980	2002	1980	2002	1980	2002	1980	2002
Australia	3057	3053	33.6	38.7	17.4	13.9	436	509
Austria	3353	3673	39.5	38.8	12.8	11.5	577	617
Belgium/Luxembourg	3300	3584	38.0	40.1	10.7	14.2	436	526
Canada	2946	3589	37.4	36.7	14.7	15.5	584	686
Czech Republic	n.a.	3171	n.a.	33.5	n.a.	12.6	n.a.	389
Denmark	3127	3439	39.6	36.5	14.5	13.4	316	687
Finland	3124	3100	37.8	35.7	11.8	10.3	340	457
France	3376	3654	39.4	42.1	9.5	10.2	489	652
Germany	3340	3496	36.7	37.7	12.4	12.0	471	565
Greece	3216	3721	34.9	36.9	7.8	8.5	995	1130
Hungary	3494	3483	33.7	38.0	12.5	12.7	448	483
Iceland	3252	3249	38.8	36.2	16.2	15.7	237	460
Ireland	3661	3656	35.8	32.6	12.8	10.7	380	501
Italy	3590	3671	32.3	38.8	9.4	8.1	771	773
Japan	2721	2761	22.7	27.6	11.8	10.0	484	446
Republic of Korea	2971	3058	11.1	22.7	4.9	11.0	595	756
Mexico	3123	3145	22.7	25.0	14.7	15.2	374	467
The Netherlands	3071	3362	38.3	38.6	14.2	14.0	481	626
New Zealand	3123	3219	36.5	32.2	14.0	17.5	490	694
Norway	3350	3484	39.9	37.6	12.5	12.3	402	500
Poland	3597	3375	29.2	30.1	12.2	13.0	390	404
Portugal	2786	3741	27.7	33.6	9.4	8.4	437	859
Slovakia	n.a.	2889	n.a.	34.7	n.a.	10.6	n.a.	341
Spain	3063	3371	33.0	40.3	9.6	9.7	729	729
Sweden	2992	3185	37.2	35.5	14.4	14.1	351	511
Switzerland	3491	3526	41.3	39.9	12.4	15.3	644	518
Turkey	3281	3357	23.0	24.6	7.1	7.2	852	898
UK	3159	3412	39.0	36.6	13.4	11.7	379	519
USA	3155	3774	36.2	37.3	17.4	17.5	580	652

Source: FAOSTAT (FAO, 2005).

FAOSTAT data have their problems, so do the alternatives and FAOSTAT at least has the virtue of employing common methods across countries and over time.

Diet components

Table 3 shows calorie availability and the share of calories from fat and sugar as well as availability of fruit and vegetables in OECD countries. Calorie availability has been stable or rising everywhere, with particularly sharp increases in Canada, Denmark, France, Greece, The Netherlands, Portugal, Spain and the USA. On average, calorie availability has increased over the 20-year-period by around 250 calories from a little under 3200 calories to a little over 3400 calories per capita per day. Only Japan, Korea, Mexico, Poland, Portugal (1980 only) and Turkey have fat intake below the 30% of total energy upper limit recommended by WHO/FAO (2003);

France (1980 only), Greece, Italy, Korea (1980 only), Portugal, Spain and Turkey have sugar consumption below the recommended 10% of total energy. There is no clear upward or downward trend across countries. The trend in fruit and vegetable intake has been more uniformly upwards and by 2002, only Slovakia fell below the recommended intake, but remember that, given high levels of waste, probably at least 600 g availability is needed to register the recommended minimum of 400 g per capita per day of actual intake.

Other data

Smoking prevalence (S) is the proportion of the population who smoke and health expenditure per capita is a proxy for medical treatment, both from OECD Health Data (OECD, 2005), exercise (E) is proxied by the percentage of the population living in urban areas (FAOSTAT) – an imperfect measure, but a recognition that urban employment and transportation generally demand less exercise than rural employment and transport. The real price of food and real per capita income (per capita GDP at purchasing power parity) are derived from OECD data. Other exogenous variables (e.g. genetic or cultural heterogeneity) are represented in all three equations by fixed-effect dummies.

IV. Model and Estimation

The empirical model based on the economic theory discussed in Section II and adjusted to cope with the data availability constraints is the following:

$$
\begin{cases}
CAL_{it} = \mu_{it} + \gamma_1 PRICEF_{it} + \gamma_2 INC_{it} + \gamma_3 FAT_{it} \\
\quad + \gamma_4 SUGAR_{it} + \gamma_5 FRV_{it} + \gamma_6 AGE + u_{it} \\
OBESE_{it} = \delta_{it} + \gamma_7 CAL_{it} + \gamma_8 URB_{it} \\
\quad + \gamma_9 SMOKE_{it} + v_{it} \\
DDIA_{it} = \lambda_{it} + \gamma_{10} OBESE_{it} + \gamma_{11} SATF_{it} \\
\quad + \gamma_{12} URB_{it} + \gamma_{13} HEXP_{it} + \gamma_{14} t + w_{it} \\
DHEART_{it} = \lambda_{it} + \gamma_{15} OBESE_{it} + \gamma_{16} SATF_{it} \\
\quad + \gamma_{17} URB_{it} + \gamma_{18} SMOKE_{it} + \gamma_{19} HEXP_{it} \\
\quad + \gamma_{20} t + z_{it}
\end{cases}
\tag{5}
$$

where CAL is the daily per capita calorie availability; $PRICEF$ is an index of real food prices; INC is the per capita GDP at purchasing power parity; FAT, $SUGAR$, FRV and STF are the shares of energy intake from fats, sugar, fruit and vegetable and saturated fats, respectively; AGE is the ageing index (i.e. the share of population about 65); URB is the urbanization index (the share of population living in urban areas); $SMOKE$ is the prevalence of smokers, $DDIA$ and $DHEART$ are the mortality rates for diabetes and ischaemic heart disease, respectively; $HEXP$ is the real per capita health expenditure; $OBESE$ is the percentage of obese individuals; and t is a time trend used as a proxy of medical progress.

The estimation of a simultaneous equation system as in Equation 5 with pooled data is subject to several assumptions on how to model country heterogeneity. If no heterogeneity is assumed, then a common constant term appears and coefficient estimates obtained by least squares are consistent and efficient. However, this is unlikely to be the case when the model specification does not account for all sources of heterogeneity. In order to account for omitted variables, we chose a fixed-effect linear panel model specification. The country-specific fixed effects

are country-specific intercepts. These are assumed to account for any effect which is not explained by the included exogenous variables. An alternative specification is based on random effects as in Louriero and Nayga (2005). The choice on the specification of country-specific intercepts (unobserved effects) depends on whether these can be assumed to be uncorrelated with the existing explanatory variables or not. If there is correlation, then the most appropriate specification is the fixed-effect approach. If there is no correlation between the individual effects and the included variables, then the random effect approach could be implemented. In the latter case, the individual effect is modelled through a country-specific random element. This latter specification is more parsimonious, but it presumes that the sampled cross-sectional units (i.e. the countries) were drawn from a large population and no correlation exists between the estimated effect and the included variables. This is unlikely to be the case for model (5), especially considering that some variables are proxies for omitted variables, like urbanization for physical activity.

The model in Equation 2 is estimated by weighted two-stage least squares with autoregressive errors to account for serial correlation in the residuals using the procedure described by Fair (1984, p. 210).[3] Weighting takes account of heteroscedasticity, the weights in the second stage given by the inverse residual variance matrix.

V. Empirical Results

Table 4 shows the empirical model estimates. The endogenous variables in the system are calories, obesity, health, health expenditure and the mortality rates from diabetes and heart disease and the functional form is double logarithmic, so that coefficients represent elasticities. Each equation was estimated by Weighted Two Stage Least Squares (W2SLS) using all exogenous variables as instruments. For the obesity and health outcome equations, the (unbalanced) estimation sample goes from 1990 to 2002, while for the calorie equation, the sample can be extended to 1975. One observation for each country is lost to account for serial correlation. There are a limited number of missing data either at the beginning or at the end of the sample for a few countries. Details on the samples are provided in Table 4. Estimates of the fixed effects are shown in the Appendix.

---

[3] This is the procedure adopted by the software Eviews 4®.

Table 4. Structural model estimates

	Calories	Obesity	Diabetes	Heart disease
PRICEF	**−0.065 (−2.319)**			
INC	**0.143 (6.947)**			
FAT	0.011 (0.349)			
SUGAR	**0.036 (2.686)**			
FRV	−0.005 (−0.478)			
AGE	−0.047 (−1.528)			
CAL		*0.196 (1.752)*		
URB		*2.180 (1.681)*	*2.415 (1.949)*	−1.531 (−1.419)
SMOKE		0.010 (0.521)		−0.033 (−1.552)
OBESE			0.077 (1.125)	−0.035 (−1.191)
SATF			0.070 (0.543)	−0.052 (−0.794)
HEXP			**−0.145 (−5.313)**	**−0.100 (−2.462)**
TREND			−0.117 (−0.539)	**−1.327 (−3.981)**
Sample	1975–2002	1990–2002	1990–2002	1990–2002
Obs.	627	321	284	311
R^2	0.83	0.84	0.52	0.92
AR(1)	**0.844 (38.606)**	**0.880 (35.347)**	**0.704 (18.268)**	**0.885 (33.855)**
DW (mean)	2.08	1.52	2.48	2.22

Notes: Student *t*-ratios are in parentheses. Values significant at 0.05 level are reported in bold and values significant at 0.10 level are in italics.

Calories

Calorie intake is explained by per capita income, the real price of food, smoking prevalence, the shares of fats, sugar and fruit and vegetables in total energy intake, ageing of the population and the fixed effects. The diet component shares are included because calorie density (calories per gram) is thought to contribute to overeating. Fats and sugar have high calorie density, whereas fruit and vegetables have low calorie density, thus the first two should have positive coefficients, the latter negative. The price elasticity is relatively low but significant (−0.07), suggesting that a 1% decrease in real prices leads to an increase of 0.07% in calorie intake, while the impact of rising incomes is larger (0.14). The diet components show the expected signs, although only the share of energy from sugar is statistically significant. Ageing of the population, as expected, results in lower calorie intakes.

Considering an individual who consumes about 3000 calories per day and has an income of about $2000 per month, the estimates above suggest that: (a) a 1% increase in the sugar share of energy from the recommended 10% level increases calorie intake by around 11 calories; (b) an increase in income of $100 per month increases calorie intake by around 15 calories per day and (c) a price cut of 10% increases the daily calorie intake by 20 calories.

Obesity

The calories variable is significant at the 10% level with an elasticity of 0.2 implying that at the mean, a 100 calorie increase in daily consumption would raise the proportion of obese people in the population by around 0.7% – which is very close to the 0.8% estimated in Loureiro and Nayga's (2005) model. As expected, urbanization is associated with lifestyle changes which result in less physical activity and more obesity. At the aggregate level, smoking seems to be unrelated to obesity rates.

We should remind the readers that the short time series of available data precludes exploration of the long-run relationship between calorie intake and obesity.

Heart disease and diabetes

Ischaemic heart disease mortality is explained by obesity, smoking, saturated fat share of energy intake (as suggested in WHO/FAO, 2003), per capita health expenditure to account for time and geographic differences in the incidence of health care on mortality, and a trend, which serves as a proxy for medical progress. The trend is negative and strongly significant, reflecting the major advances that have seen mortality rates fall at the same time as obesity has risen sharply in many countries. This is also consistent with the significant effect of health expenditure. Considering the OECD average per capita expenditure of about $1700 and an average (age-standardized) mortality rate of about 170 per 100 000 inhabitants over the sample period, raising health expenditure to $2000 reduces the mortality rate by about three deaths per 100 000 inhabitants. All other variables, including obesity, are nonsignificant and show the wrong sign. This unexpected result is partly explained by the fact that obesity effects on health are not instantaneous. While this would call for the inclusion of lagged variables, lack of a sufficiently long time series data prevents us from testing the lagged effects of obesity. One attempt to evaluate the relevance of the delayed impact of obesity could be based on the correlation between the estimated fixed effects – which are expected to capture unexplained country differences over the sample period 1990–2002 – and the absolute level of obesity in 1990. Correlation is positive and high (0.68) and significant at the 99% level despite being based on only 28 observations, suggesting that the link between obesity and heart disease does exist although its macrodynamics cannot be estimated with precision due to the lack of adequate time series data. According to the above estimate, a 1% difference in the 1990 obesity level leads to a 1.6% difference in the estimated fixed effects (i.e. unexplained mortality rates).

Focusing on the diabetes equation, we also find a strong relationship between mortality and health expenditure, suggesting that countries with a larger per capita health expenditure are more effective in reducing mortality from diabetes. Urbanization (taken as a proxy for decreased physical activity) is also significant at the 10% level. For example, considering Sweden and Norway, there is a difference of about 12% in the urbanization rate (higher in Sweden). *Ceteris paribus*, this would explain a difference of about two deaths per 100 000 inhabitants between the two countries (which is actually the case). For the diabetes equation, all other variables are also nonsignificant, although they show the correct sign and are closer to significance. Repeating the correlation exercise, we find again a positive relationship (0.17) with lagged obesity, but nonsignificant. Here, the data limitations are made worse by the lack of time series on diabetes prevalence rather than mortality, as the former is sharply increasing as a consequence of changing lifestyles, while the latter is decreasing thanks to increased effectiveness of medical treatment as captured by the health expenditure variable (Wild *et al.*, 2004).

VI. Conclusions

Modelling nutrition behaviours, obesity and their health consequences is a complex exercise. While other studies have attempted to model these relationships before, we claim that adequate modelling needs to take into account the endogeneity of the decision process. The application of a panel simultaneous equation system to OECD countries models this endogeneity.

The availability of good quality data at the macro level is far from adequate. Time series of obesity data which are comparable at international level are only available for 15 years at most. Many of the other relevant variables also suffer data limitations. For example, time series data are only available for mortality rates which have fallen but not for prevalence which, at least in the case of diabetes, have almost certainly risen. A more reliable series of disease prevalence would greatly improve the quantification effort. Another key variable which is completely lacking is the amount of physical activity over time and across countries. While urbanization proves to be a relatively satisfactory proxy, a more specific measure is clearly desirable for accurate policy calibration.

Despite these data limitations, there are several advantages in the technique adopted for this study. First, pooling cross-section and time series data increases the number of available observations, although this does not solve the problem of modelling long-term relationship with short spans of time series data. Second, the fixed-effect approach accounts for omitted variable problems, as the country-specific intercepts are expected to capture the amount of heterogeneity not explained by the right-hand side variables. In order to obtain consistent estimates of the behavioural parameter, it is also necessary to account for serial correlation in the residuals, which emerges as highly relevant.

One may then try to relate the time-invariant estimates of country fixed effects to other potential determinants. Since the starting obesity level may contribute to interpreting international differences in calorie intakes and health outcomes, this suggests that the availability of a longer time series for the obesity variable would improve the model by accounting for lagged and cumulated effect.

Acknowledgements

The contents of this article draw on the work of the authors commissioned by the Global Perspective

Studies Unit of FAO. The authors would particularly like to thank Jelle Bruinsma and Josef Schmidhuber for their input and encouragement with the work. The views expressed are the authors' and do not necessarily reflect those of FAO.

References

Adhikari, M., Paudel, L., Paudel, K., Houston, J. and Bukenya, J. (2007) Impact of low carbohydrate information on vegetable demands in the United States, *Applied Economics Letters*, **14**, 939–44.

Bastida, E. and Soydemir, G. A. (2009) Obesity and employment as predictors of diabetes in Mexican Americans: findings from a longitudinal study, *Applied Economics*, **41**, 2533–40.

Caliskan, Z. (2009) The relationship between pharmaceutical expenditure and life expectancy: evidence from 21 OECD countries, *Applied Economics Letters*, **16**, 1651–5.

Chen, S. N., Shogren, J. E., Orazem, P. F. and Crocker, T. D. (2002) Prices and health: identifying the effects of nutrition, exercise and medication choice on blood pressure, *American Journal of Agricultural Economics*, **84**, 990–1002.

Chou, S.-Y., Grossman, M. and Saffer, H. (2002) An economic analysis of adult obesity: results from the behavioral risk factor surveillance system, Working Paper No. 9247, National Bureau of Economic Research, Cambridge, MA, 55 pp. Available at http://www.nber.org/papers/w9247 (accessed 26 March 2010).

Costa-Font, J. and Gil, J. (2004) Social interactions and the contemporaneous determinants of individuals' weight, *Applied Economics*, **36**, 2253–63.

Cutler, D. M., Glaeser, E. L. and Shapiro, J. M. (2003) Why have Americans become more obese?, *Journal of Economic Perspectives*, **17**, 93–118.

Erdil, E. and Yetkiner, I. H. (2009) The Granger-causality between health care expenditure and output: a panel data approach, *Applied Economics*, **41**, 511–18.

Fair, R. C. (1984) *Specification, Estimation, and Analysis of Macroeconometric Models*, Harvard University Press, Cambridge, MA, USA.

Food and Agricultural Organization (FAO) (2005) FAOSTAT database. Available at http://faostat.fao.org/ (accessed 26 March 2010).

Freeman, D. G. (2003) Is health care a necessity or a luxury? Pooled estimates of income elasticity from US state-level data, *Applied Economics*, **35**, 495–502.

Gruber, J. and Frakes, M. (2005) Does falling smoking lead to rising obesity?, Working Paper No. 11483, National Bureau of Economic Research, Cambridge, MA, 28 pp. Available at http://www.nber.org/papers/w11483 (accessed 26 March 2010).

Huang, K. S. (1999) Effects of food prices and consumer income on nutrient availability, *Applied Economics*, **31**, 367–80.

Huffman, W. E., Huffman, S., Tegene, A. and Rickertson, K. (2006) The economics of obesity-related mortality among high income countries, contributed

paper at *The International Association of Agricultural Economics Conference*, Australia, 12–18 August, 16 pp.

Kleinfield, N. R. (2006) Diabetes and its awful toll quietly emerge as a crisis, *New York Times*, 9 January, 10 pp.

Lakdawalla, D. and Philipson, T. (2002) The growth of obesity and technological change: a theoretical and empirical examination, Working Paper No. 8946, National Bureau of Economic Research, Cambridge, MA, USA, 41pp.

Leung, P. S. and Miklius, W. (1997) Demand for nutrition versus demand for tastes, *Applied Economics Letters*, **4**, 291–5.

Lin, S. J. (2008) An analysis of lifestyles and health in Taiwan, *Applied Economics Letters*, **15**, 399–404.

Loureiro, M. L. and Nayga, R. M. (2005) International dimensions of obesity and overweight related problems: an economics perspective, *American Journal of Agricultural Economics*, **87**, 1147–53.

Lye, J. N. and Hirschberg, J. (2004) Alcohol consumption, smoking and wages, *Applied Economics*, **36**, 1807–17.

Mazzocchi, M., Traill, W. B. and Shogren, J. S. (2009) *Fat Economics: Nutrition, Health, and Economic Policy*, Oxford University Press, Oxford, UK.

Nayga, R. M. (1997) Obesity and heart disease awareness: a note on the impact of consumer characteristics using qualitative choice analysis, *Applied Economics Letters*, **4**, 229–31.

Nayga, R. M. (2000) Schooling, health knowledge and obesity, *Applied Economics*, **32**, 815–22.

Nayga, R. M., Tepper, B. J. and Rosenzweig, L. (1999) Assessing the importance of health and nutrition related factors on food demand: a variable preference investigation, *Applied Economics*, **31**, 1541–9.

Organization for Economic Co-operation and Development (OECD) (2005) Health data. Available at www.oecd.org (accessed 26 March 2010).

Paudel, L., Adhikari, M., Houston, J. and Paudel, K. P. (2008) Low carbohydrate information, consumer health preferences and market demand of fruits in the United States, *Applied Economics Letters*, **14**, 939–44.

Philipson, T. J. and Posner, R. A. (1999) The long-run growth in obesity as a function of technological change, Working Paper No. 7423, National Bureau of Economic Research, Cambridge, MA, USA, 35 pp.

Schmidhuber, J. and Shetty, P. (2005) The nutrition transition to 2030. Why developing countries are likely to bear the major burden, *Food Economics*, **2**, 150–66.

Shimokawa, S. (2008) The labour market impact of body weight in China: a semiparametric analysis, *Applied Economics*, **40**, 949–68.

Smil, V. (2000) *Feeding the World – A Challenge for the Twenty-first Century*, The MIT Press, Cambridge, MA and London.

Thornton, J. and Rice, J. (2008) Determinants of healthcare spending: a state level analysis, *Applied Economics*, **40**, 2873–89.

Traill, W. B. and Mazzocchi, M. (2005) The economics and policy of diet and health, *Food Economics*, **2**, 113–16.

Variyam, J. N., Blaylock, J. and Smallwood, D. (1999) Information, endogeneity, and consumer health behaviour: application to dietary intakes, *Applied Economics*, **31**, 217–26.

Webber, D. J. (2002) Policies to stimulate growth: should we invest in health or education?, *Applied Economics*, **34**, 1633–43.

World Health Organization (WHO) (2006) Press release, 3 September 2006. Available at http://mdn.mainichi-msn.co.jp/international/news/20060903p2g00m0in006000c.html (accessed 26 March 2010).

WHO/FAO (2003) Diet, nutrition and the prevention of chronic diseases, Report of a Joint WHO/FAO Expert Consultation, WHO Technical Report 916, Geneva.

Wild, S. H., Roglic, G., Green, A., Sicree, R. and King, H. (2004) Global prevalence of diabetes: estimates for the year 2000 and projections for 2030, *Diabetes Care*, **27**, 1047–53.

Appendix: Fixed-effect Estimates

Country	Fixed-effect estimates			
	Calories	Obesity	Diabetes	Ischaemic heart disease
Australia	6.90 (25.76)	−7.51 (5.46)	−7.16 (4.96)	17.66 (4.23)
Austria	7.05 (26.13)	−7.76 (5.03)	−6.35 (4.58)	17.38 (3.86)
Belgium	7.05 (26.24)	−8.66 (5.48)	−7.54 (5.06)	17.48 (4.28)
Canada	6.95 (25.73)	−7.88 (5.26)	−6.53 (4.81)	17.42 (4.07)
Czech Republic	7.01 (26.12)	−7.71 (5.16)	−7.17 (4.73)	17.61 (3.98)
Denmark	6.96 (25.88)	−8.27 (5.35)	−6.85 (4.91)	17.39 (4.14)
Finland	6.91 (25.72)	−7.53 (4.94)	−6.74 (4.49)	17.40 (3.78)
France	7.06 (26.36)	−8.06 (5.22)	−7.04 (4.75)	16.56 (4.02)
Germany	7.03 (26.20)	−7.84 (5.39)	−6.79 (4.93)	17.82 (4.17)
Greece	7.13 (27.17)	−7.83 (4.92)	−7.03 (4.47)	16.76 (3.78)
Hungary	7.12 (27.28)	−7.29 (4.99)	−6.26 (4.55)	17.80 (3.85)
Ireland	7.08 (26.80)	−7.74 (4.90)	−6.35 (4.44)	17.35 (3.77)
Italy	7.08 (26.56)	−8.10 (5.05)	−6.09 (4.61)	16.74 (3.89)
Japan	6.81 (26.04)	−9.35 (5.03)	−6.89 (4.58)	15.97 (3.87)
Republic of Korea	6.90 (26.74)	−9.87 (5.28)	−5.86 (4.84)	16.37 (4.11)
Mexico	7.01 (28.03)	−7.49 (5.17)	−4.92 (4.74)	17.46 (4.01)
The Netherlands	6.94 (25.66)	−7.93 (5.02)	−6.05 (4.54)	16.81 (3.87)
Norway	6.95 (26.27)	−7.97 (5.34)	−6.80 (4.90)	17.86 (4.15)
New Zealand	6.95 (25.70)	−8.15 (5.24)	−7.06 (4.75)	17.32 (4.04)
Poland	7.08 (27.92)	−7.52 (4.95)	−6.46 (4.50)	17.31 (3.81)
Portugal	7.09 (27.19)	−7.14 (4.82)	−5.23 (4.31)	16.32 (3.70)
Slovak Republic	6.95 (25.84)	−7.04 (4.84)	−6.05 (4.40)	17.95 (3.71)
Spain	7.01 (26.11)	−7.95 (5.20)	−6.66 (4.76)	16.85 (4.02)
Sweden	6.91 (25.65)	−8.32 (5.32)	−7.13 (4.87)	17.54 (4.11)
Switzerland	6.97 (25.55)	−8.51 (5.04)	−6.27 (4.62)	17.05 (3.89)
Turkey	7.17 (29.48)	−7.68 (5.03)	−7.13 (4.55)	16.51 (3.90)
UK	6.98 (26.04)	−7.69 (5.39)	−7.71 (4.95)	17.79 (4.18)
USA	7.00 (25.77)	−7.28 (5.26)	−6.31 (4.80)	17.83 (4.08)

Note: Student *t*-ratios are in parentheses.

The relationship between fast food and obesity

Michael L. Marlow and Alden F. Shiers

Department of Economics, California Polytechnic State University, San Luis Obispo, CA 93407, USA

Public debate regarding the role of government in lowering obesity often focuses on the fact that rising obesity prevalence is evident in all states. This article focuses on the hypothesized link between obesity and fast food employment by examining data on all states over 2001–2009 and controlling for other factors that may influence obesity prevalence. Our examination indicates no support for the view that fast food is a significant causal factor behind the substantial weight gain exhibited by the US population.

I. Introduction

Rising prevalence of obesity is often referred to as a public health epidemic because it is associated with so many health problems (Dixon, 2010). Obesity is defined as a Body Mass Index (BMI) of 30 or higher. In 2007–2008, the prevalence of obesity was 32.2% among adult men and 35.5% among adult women (Flegal *et al.*, 2010). Many causes for excessive weight gain have been hypothesized that include increased consumption of sugar-sweetened beverages (Vartanian *et al.*, 2007; Bleich *et al.*, 2009), falling food prices (Courtamanche and Carden, 2008), urban sprawl (Zhao and Kaestner, 2010), food engineering that encourages food addiction (Ruhm, 2010), more sedentary lifestyles fostered by technology (Philipson and Posner, 2003; Lakdawalla and Philipson, 2009), increased availability of restaurants (Chou *et al.*, 2004; Larson *et al.*, 2009), fewer grocery stores selling healthy foods (Larson *et al.*, 2009) and agricultural policies that encourage the production of 'unhealthy' foods (Wallinga, 2010).

This article focuses on the hypothesized link between obesity and fast food by examining data on all states over 2001–2009. Public debate regarding the role of government in lowering obesity prevalence often focuses on the fact that rising obesity prevalence is evident in all states. While prevalence has increased significantly in all states, there is wide variation in this pattern across states. Prevalence of the population considered 'overweight' as defined by BMI between 25.0 and 29.9 is also considered separately since it appears reasonable to also question whether fast food causes individuals to become overweight, though not obese.

Previous literature

Maddock (2004) collected data on fast food outlets through examining phone books for the two largest fast food hamburger-based chains and then dividing state land area by the number of restaurants. A positive correlation was found between fast food restaurant density and state-level obesity prevalence in 2002. Jeffery *et al.* (2006) examined a telephone survey that assessed body height and weight, frequency of eating at restaurants and work and home addresses. Proximity of fast food restaurants to home or work was not associated with eating at fast food restaurants or with BMI. Thornton *et al.* (2009) analysed the frequency of fast food purchases from five major fast food chains in Melbourne, Australia, and found that density and proximity of restaurants were not significant predictors of purchases.

Chou *et al.* (2004) concluded that per capita number of fast food and full service restaurants were positively correlated with excessive weight over 1982–2000. But, the authors suggest that the growth of restaurants is likely to be a response to the increasing scarcity and increasing value of household or nonmarket time. They suggested that a fuller model that treated restaurant availability as endogenous might yield different conclusions. Rashad *et al.* (2006) concluded that per capita number of all restaurants exerted a positive and significant effect on BMI and obesity over 1972–1997. The authors discussed the possibility that restaurant density may also be caused by obesity prevalence leading them to experiment with various instrumental variables to control for endogeneity. However, no suitable instruments for restaurant availability were uncovered.

Anderson and Matsa (2011) found that the causal link between the consumption of restaurant foods and obesity is minimal at best. Restaurant access, as measured by distance to the nearest restaurant, and consumption of restaurant food exerted no significant effects on obesity. The endogeneity issue was addressed by using distance from freeways as an instrument for fast food availability. Analyses of food intake data revealed that, although restaurant meals were associated with greater caloric intake, additional calories were mostly offset by reductions in eating throughout the rest of the day. They also found that individuals that frequented restaurants also ate more while at home and that, when eating at home, obese individuals consumed roughly 30% of their calories from 'junk food' such as ice cream, processed cheese, bacon, baked sweets, fries, candies, soft drinks and beer. They concluded that efforts to reduce fast food may lead heavy consumers to substitute into other foods or eat more at home.

In summary, it remains unclear whether fast food causes weight gain, whether overeating causes fast food restaurant availability or some combination of the two. Few studies control for the possible endogeneity problem thus making any positive correlation between fast food restaurants and overeating suggestive at best.

II. Modelling Effects of Fast Food

Percentages of the population that are overweight and obese are two measures of body weight. The total sample size is 449 observations and represents all states except the 2004 value for Hawaii that was not contained within the Centers for Disease Control and Prevention (CDC) Behavioral Risk Factor Surveillance System (BRFSS) survey (http://www.cdc.gov/brfss/technical_infodata/surveydata.htm). The following relationships are estimated:

$$\text{Weight}_{it} = f \begin{pmatrix} \text{Density}_{it}, \text{Black}_{it}, \text{Hispanic}_{it}, \text{Under18}_{it}, \\ \text{Over64}_{it}, \text{Male}_{it}, \text{Income}_{it}, \text{Fruit}_{it}, \\ \text{Exercise}_{it}, \text{College}_{it}, \text{FastFood}_{it} \end{pmatrix}$$

(1)

where i refers to the 50 states and t refers to years 2001–2009. Weight_{it} is defined by two separate measures obtained from BRFSS: overweight prevalence identifies the percentage of the population with BMI between 25 and 29.9 and obesity prevalence identifies the percentage of the population with BMI of 30 or above. In 2001, obesity prevalence averaged 21.1% and ranged from 14.9% (Colorado) to 26.5% (Mississippi). In 2009, it averaged 27.4% and ranged from 19.0% (Colorado) to 35.4% (Mississippi).

Density_{it} measures state population (http://www.census.gov/popest) divided by land area in square miles given the expectation that urban sprawl raises obesity prevalence (Zhao and Kaestner, 2010). College_{it} measures the percentage of respondents with at least a college education, obtained from BRFSS, since studies indicate a negative association between education and being overweight (Webbink *et al.*, 2010). Income_{it} measures the real ($2009) median household income and is obtained from US Census data (http://www.census.gov/hhes). Poverty is often considered a causal factor behind obesity, but it is typically not the poor who have experienced the largest gains in obesity (Chang and Lauderdale, 2005).

Variations in race, age and gender are controlled through data obtained from BRFSS. Black_{it} and Hispanic_{it} measure percentages of population that are of African American and Hispanic heritage. Under18_{it} and Over64_{it} measure, respectively, percentages of population that are aged 18 and under and over age 64. Male_{it} controls for the percentages of population that are male following evidence that obesity is more prevalent in females (Flegal *et al.*, 2010).

BRFSS data on fruit consumption and exercise control for expectations that high values are inversely related to body weight. Fruit_{it} measures the percentage of adults that consume fruits and vegetables five or more times a day. Exercise_{it} measures the percentage of respondents who had participated in physical activities during the previous month. Missing data for 2001, 2004 and 2008 were measured by averaging values of two adjacent years for both variables.

Table 1. Summary statistics

	Mean	SD
Overweight$_{it}$ = percentage of population overweight	36.70	1.23
Obesity$_{it}$ = percentage of population obese	24.30	3.60
Popdensity$_{it}$ = population divided by square miles	189.29	255.54
Black$_{it}$ = Black percentage of population	7.85	8.46
Hispanic$_{it}$ = Hispanic share of population	7.92	8.77
Under18$_{it}$ = under age 18 percentage of population	24.70	1.80
Over64$_{it}$ = over age 64 share of population	12.71	1.74
Male$_{it}$ = male percentage of population	49.32	0.75
Income$_{it}$ = median household ($2009) income	50 824	7719
Fruit$_{it}$ = percentage of adults consuming fruits and vegetables five or more times per day	23.30	3.50
Exercise$_{it}$ = percentage of adults participating in physical activities in the last month	76.08	4.12
College$_{it}$ = percentage of population with college degree or higher	31.38	5.60
FastFood$_{it}$ = fast food employees per capita	0.01	0.002
MW$_{it}$ = 1 if state adopted minimum wage law above federal minimum and = 0 otherwise	0.35	0.48

FastFood$_{it}$ measures the fast food employment per capita in the fast food industry obtained from the Quarterly Census of Employment and Wages for North American Industry Classification System (NAICS) 722211 limited-service restaurants (http://www.bls.gov/cew/data.htm). Employment is expected to be highly correlated with fast food consumption. In 2001, fast food employment per capita averaged 0.0111 and ranged from a high of 0.0144 (Kentucky) to a low of 0.0055 (New Jersey). In 2009, it averaged 0.0115 and ranged from a high of 0.0150 (Hawaii) to a low of 0.0066 (Connecticut).

While states with many fast food employees may also exhibit relatively many overweight citizens, this connection may simply follow from the possibility that fast food employees per capita are more frequently located in areas that exhibit more overweight consumers demanding fast food. In effect, if there is a positive association between obesity and fast food, it might simply stem from heavier people enjoying fast food more than their slimmer counterparts. Our examination sorts out this endogeneity issue by comparing Ordinary Least Squares (OLS) estimation with Two-Stage Least Squares (TSLS) estimation. Briefly, TSLS utilizes an instrumental variable that is correlated with fast food employment but by itself is not correlated with obesity prevalence. An instrumental variable needs to satisfy two properties: it affects fast food employment and it is uncorrelated with other determinants of weight. We develop a dichotomous variable MW$_{it}$ to instrument fast food employment that takes the value of 1 when the state has adopted a minimum wage above the federal minimum and equals 0 otherwise. While all states are subject to the federal minimum wage, states may voluntarily adopt minimums that exceed the federal minimum. As of 2011, 18 states had enacted minimums above the federal (http://www.dol.gov/whd/minwage/america.

htm#Consolidated). The below discussion indicates MW$_{it}$ meets the usual criteria for a good instrument.

The summary statistics are displayed in Table 1.

III. Effects of Fast Food Employment

Table 2 displays OLS regressions. Three control variables exert significant positive influence on overweight prevalence: population density, over age 65 percentage of population and male percentage of population. Control variables that exert significant influence on obesity prevalence are population density (negative), percentage of Black citizens (positive), percentage of Hispanic citizens (negative), male percentage of population (negative), income (positive), fruit consumption (negative), exercise (negative) and college education (negative). Fast food employment exerts a significant negative effect on overweight prevalence, but no significant effect on obesity prevalence. Thus, OLS estimation indicates no support for claims that fast food is an important determinant of obesity.

Table 3 displays TSLS regressions. Column 1 exhibits the first-stage estimation of the fast food employment instrument and indicates fast food employment is significantly influenced by population density (negative), Black percentage of population (positive), male percentage of population (positive), income (positive), fruit consumption (negative), college education (negative) and whether states adopt a minimum wage above the federal law (negative). As a check for whether MW$_{it}$ is a weak instrument, a simple rule of thumb suggested by Stock and Watson (2003) is to demonstrate that the first-stage F-statistic exceeds 10 when testing the hypothesis that coefficients on all instruments are all 0. In this case, an F-statistic value of 38.85 indicates MW$_{it}$ is not a weak instrument.

Table 2. Ordinary Least Squares (OLS) regressions of overweight and obese prevalence with fast food employment

	Dependent variables	
	Overweight	Obese prevalence
$Popdensity_{it}$	0.00094 (2.50)**	−0.00273 (5.54)***
$Black_{it}$	−0.01723 (−1.64)	0.07673 (5.59)***
$Hispanic_{it}$	−0.00919 (1.22)	−0.04183 (4.25)
$Under18_{it}$	−0.02226 (0.39)	−0.03338 (0.45)
$Over64_{it}$	0.11387 (1.82)*	−0.15863 (1.94)*
$Male_{it}$	0.69202 (4.97)***	−1.03575 (5.69)***
$Income_{it}$	−0.00002 (1.06)	0.00007 (3.65)***
$Fruit_{it}$	−0.061942 (2.42)	−0.13334 (3.98)***
$Exercise_{it}$	−0.04474 (1.82)	−0.16549 (5.15)***
$College_{it}$	0.03140 (1.41)	−0.24395 (8.39)***
$FastFood_{it}$	−125.6624 (3.33)***	−15.28822 (0.31)
Constant	8.40808 (1.11)	94.30959 (9.55)***
Adjusted R^2	0.19	0.84
SE of regression	1.1068	1.4452
Mean depth variation	36.70	24.31
F-statistic	6.41	123.54
Observations	449	449

Notes: All regressions include year dummies. Absolute values of t-ratios are reported in parentheses.
*, ** and ***Significant at the 10%, 5% and 1% levels, respectively.

Table 3. TSLS regressions of overweight and obese prevalence with fast food employment

	First stage	TSLS	TSLS
	Fast food	Overweight	Obese prevalence
$Popdensity_{it}$	-2.76×10^{-6} (6.06)***	0.00159 (2.39)**	−0.00313 (8.18)***
$Black_{it}$	5.80×10^{-5} (4.53)***	−0.03028 (1.97)**	0.08444 (4.34)***
$Hispanic_{it}$	1.40×10^{-5} (1.48)	−0.01106 (1.39)	−0.04072 (4.03)***
$Under18_{it}$	-5.90×10^{-5} (0.80)	−0.02815 (.047)	−0.02991 (0.40)
$Over64_{it}$	-4.05×10^{-5} (0.51)	0.10955 (1.69)*	−0.15608 (1.90)*
$Male_{it}$	−0.00030 (1.73)*	0.75631 (4.93)***	−1.07371 (5.50)***
$Income_{it}$	4.54×10^{-8} (2.62)***	-2.51×10^{-5} (1.50)	7.29×10^{-5} (3.42)
$Fruit_{it}$	−0.000254 (8.62)***	−0.00699 (0.13)	−0.16578 (2.47)**
$Exercise_{it}$	4.19×10^{-5} (1.35)	−0.04852 (1.89)*	−0.16326 (5.00)***
$College_{it}$	−0.000105 (3.85)***	0.05261 (1.82)*	−0.25647 (6.96)***
MW_{it}	−0.000864 (4.77)***		
$FastFood_{it}$		78.57526 (0.45)	−135.8870 (0.61)
Constant	0.03149 (3.38)***	2.07785 (0.22)	98.0475 (8.18)***
Adjusted R^2	0.62	0.11	0.84
SE of regression	0.0013	1.144	1.455
Mean depth variation	0.011	36.70	24.31
F-statistic	38.85	5.69	123.64
Observations	449	449	449

Notes: All regressions include year dummies. Absolute values of t-ratios are reported in parentheses. TSLS, Two-Stage Least Squares.
*, ** and ***Significant at the 10%, 5% and 1% levels, respectively.

TSLS results mostly mirror OLS results. However, while OLS estimation indicated fast food employment exerted a significant, but negative, effect on overweight prevalence, TSLS estimation reveals no significant influence on either overweight or obesity prevalence.

IV. Conclusions

Our examination indicates no support for the view that fast food is a significant causal factor behind prevalence of overweight and obese citizens over 2001–2009 and across states. Our research is limited by the assumption that fast food employment is a good proxy for fast food consumption. Future research that examines whether this assumption is valid would be useful. Examination that distinguishes between 'health' and 'unhealthy' fast food is another issue for future research, since fast food does not necessarily mean 'unhealthy' food.

References

Anderson, M. L. and Matsa, D. A. (2011) Are restaurants really supersizing America?, *American Economic Journal: Applied Economics*, **3**, 152–88.

Bleich, S. N., Wang, Y. C., Wang, Y. and Gormaker, S. L. (2009) Increasing consumption of sugar-sweetened beverages among US adults: 1988–1994 to 1999–2004, *The American Journal of Clinical Nutrition*, **89**, 372–81.

Chang, V. W. and Lauderdale, D. S. (2005) Income disparities in body mass index and obesity in the United States, 1971–2002, *Archives of Internal Medicine*, **165**, 2122–8.

Chou, S.-Yi., Grossman, M. and Saffer, H. (2004) An economic analysis of adult obesity: results from the Behavioral Risk Factor Surveillance System, *Journal of Health Economics*, **23**, 565–87.

Courtamanche, C. and Carden, A. (2008) The skinny on big box retailing: wal-mart, warehouse clubs, and obesity, Manuscript, MPRA Paper No. 25326, University Library of Munich, Germany.

Dixon, J. B. (2010) The effect of obesity on health outcomes, *Molecular and Cellular Endocrinology*, **316**, 104–8.

Flegal, K. M., Carroll, M. D., Ogen, C. L. and Curtain, L. R. (2010) Prevalence and trends in obesity among US adults, 1999–2008, *Journal of American Medical Association*, **303**, 235–41.

Jeffery, R. W., Baxter, J., McGuire, M. and Linde, J. (2006) Are fast food restaurants an environmental risk factor for obesity?, *International Journal of Behavioral Nutrition and Physical Activity*, **3**, 2.

Lakdawalla, D. and Philipson, T. (2009) The growth of obesity and technological change, *Economics and Human Biology*, **7**, 283–93.

Larson, N. I., Storey, M. T. and Melisssa, C. N. (2009) Neighborhood environments: disparities in access to healthy foods in the US, *American Journal of Preventive Medicine*, **36**, 74–81.

Maddock, J. (2004) The relationship between obesity and the prevalence of fast food restaurants: state-level analysis, *American Journal of Health Promotion*, **19**, 137–43.

Philipson, T. J. and Posner, R. A. (2003) The long-run growth in obesity as a function of technological change, *Perspectives in Biology and Medicine*, **46**, S87–S107.

Rashad, I., Grossman, M. and Chou, S.-Yi. (2006) The super size of America: an economic estimation of body mass index and obesity in adults, *Eastern Economic Journal*, **32**, 133–48.

Ruhm, C. (2010) Understanding overeating and obesity, National Bureau of Economic Research, Working Paper No. 16149, National Bureau of Economic Research, Cambridge, MA.

Stock, J. H. and Watson, M. W. (2003) *Introduction to Econometrics*, Addison-Wesley, Boston, MA.

Thornton, L. E., Rebecca, J. B. and Anne, M. K. (2009) Fast food purchasing and access to fast food restaurants: a multilevel analysis of VicLANES, *International Journal of Behavioral Nutrition and Physical Activity*, **6**, 28.

Vartanian, L. R., Schartz, M. B. and Brownell, K. D. (2007) Effects of soft drink consumption on nutrition and health: a systematic review and meta-analysis, *American Journal of Public Health*, **97**, 667–75.

Wallinga, D. (2010) Agricultural policy and childhood obesity: a food systems and public health commentary, *Health Affairs*, **29**, 405–10.

Webbink, D., Martin, N. G. and Visscher, P. M. (2010) Does education reduce the probability of being overweight?, *Journal of Health Economics*, **29**, 29–38.

Zhao, Z. and Kaestner, R. (2010) Effects of urban sprawl on obesity, *Journal of Health Economics*, **29**, 779–87.

Index

Note:
Page numbers in **bold** type refer to figures
Page numbers in *italic* type refer to tables
Page numbers followed by 'n' refer to notes

ROUTLEDGE

Related titles from Routledge

The Applied Economics of Transport

Edited by Mark P. Taylor

This book provides an introduction and overview to nine applied financial studies on the theme of transport. The studies cover a wide range of topics, from value based trading of real assets in shipping, to the determinants of efficiency and productivity in European railways, to the market for used cars. The studies employ a variety of applied techniques across a range of countries, analysing a range of different modes of transport.

This book was originally published as a special issue of *Applied Economics*.

December 2011: 276 x 219: 152pp
Hb: 978-0-415-69307-3
£80 / $125

The Applied Economics of Labour

Edited by Mark P. Taylor

This book provides an introduction and overview to seven applied financial studies on the theme of labour. The studies cover a wide range of topics, from the individual effects of becoming disabled on key aspects of labour market outcomes in Germany, to testing whether there is evidence of compression of morbidity using Health and Retirement Study (HRS) data and analysing the effects of this on the labour supply of older people. The studies employ a variety of applied techniques across a range of countries.

This book was originally published as a special issue of *Applied Economics*.

December 2011: 216 x 138: 160pp
Hb: 978-0-415-69306-6
£80 / $125

9 781138 377806